The Hidden Dimension of Illness:
Human Suffering

The Hidden Dimension
of Illness:
Human Suffering

Patricia L. Starck
and
John P. McGovern, Editors

National League for Nursing Press • New York
Pub. No. 15-2462

ISBN 0-88737-544-8

The views expressed in this publication represent the
views of the authors and do not necessarily reflect the
official views of the National League for Nursing Press.

This book was set in Garamond and Goudy by
Pageworks. The editor was Rachel Schaperow; the de-
signer was Allan Graubard. Northeastern Press was the
printer and binder. The cover was designed by Lillian
Welsh.

Printed in the United States of America

Contents

Contributors   vii

Foreword   xi

1. The Nature of Suffering: Physical, Psychological,
    Social, and Spiritual Aspects   1
    Eric J. Cassell

2. The Social Construct of Suffering   11
    Irving Kenneth Zola

3. The Meaning of Suffering   25
    Patricia L. Starck and John P. McGovern

4. Technological Environments as Causes
    of Suffering: The Ethical Context   43
    Stanley J. Reiser

v

5. Is Our Society Insensitive to Suffering?   53
    Roger J. Bulger

6. Suffering as Contrasted to Pain, Loss,
    Grief, Despair, and Loneliness   69
    C. Stratton Hill, Jr.

7. The Influence of Values and Culture
    in Responses to Suffering   81
    Elizabeth Heitman

8. The Responses of Caregivers to the
    Experience of Suffering   105
    Gwen Sherwood

9. Therapeutic Interventions for Suffering:
    Professional and Institutional Perspectives   115
    Jan van Eys

10. The Management of Suffering in a
    Nursing Home: An Ethnographic Study   127
    Patricia L. Starck

11. Suffering in Addiction: Alcoholism and
    Drug Dependence   155
    Robert L. DuPont and John P. McGovern

12. The Suffering of Terminal Illness: Cancer   203
    Lynn W. Brallier

13. The Suffering of Shame and Humiliation in Illness   227
    Aaron Lazare

14. The Suffering of Suicide: The Victim
    and Family Considered   245
    James A. Knight

15. Suffering in Silence and the Fear of Social
    Stigma: Survivors of Violence   269
    Blair Justice

16. A Theoretical and Empirical Review of
    the Concept of Suffering   291
    Mary E. Duffy

Contributors

Lynn W. Brallier, MSN, PhD
Director
Stress/Health Management Center of Metropolitan Washington
Washington, DC

Roger J. Bulger, MD
President
Association of Academic Health Centers
Washington, DC

Eric J. Cassell, MD
Clinical Professor of Public Health
Cornell University Medical College
New York, New York

Mary E. Duffy, PhD, RN
Professor and Division Head
Division of Research, Statistics, and Theoretical Foundations
The University of Texas Health Science Center at Houston
School of Nursing
Houston, Texas

Robert L. DuPont, MD
President
Institute for Behavior and Health, Inc.
Rockville, Maryland
Clinical Professor of Psychiatry
Georgetown University School of Medicine
Washington, DC

Elizabeth Heitman, PhD
Assistant Professor
Program on Humanities and Technology in Health Care
The University of Texas Health Science Center at Houston
Houston, Texas

C. Stratton Hill, Jr., MD
Director, Pain Service
Department of Neuro-Oncology
Professor of Medicine
The University of Texas
M.D. Anderson Cancer Center
Houston, Texas

Aaron Lazare, MD
Chancellor and Dean
University of Massachusetts
Medical Center
Worcester, Massachusetts

Blair Justice, PhD
Professor of Psychology
The University of Texas Health Science Center at Houston
School of Public Health
Houston, Texas

James A. Knight, MD, MPH
Professor of Psychiatry and Medical Ethics
Texas A&M University College of Medicine
College Station, Texas

John P. McGovern, MD, ScD, LLD
Clinical Professor of Pediatrics (Allergy) and Microbiology
Baylor College of Medicine
Houston, Texas

Clinical Professor of Medicine (Allergy)
The University of Texas Medical School at Houston
Houston, Texas

Adjunct Professor of the History and Philosophy of Medicine
Institute for the Medical Humanities
The University of Texas Medical Branch at Galveston
Galveston, Texas

Stanley J. Reiser, MD, PhD
Griff T. Ross Professor of Humanities and Technology in Health Care
Director
Program on Humanities and Technology in Health Care
The University of Texas Health Science Center at Houston
Houston, Texas

Gwen Sherwood, PhD, RN
Associate Professor and Assistant Dean for Educational Outreach
The University of Texas Health Science Center at Houston
School of Nursing
Houston, Texas

Patricia L. Starck, DSN, RN
Professor and Dean
The University of Texas Health Science Center at Houston
School of Nursing
Houston, Texas

Jan van Eys, PhD, MD
Professor and Chairman
Department of Pediatrics
Medical School
The University of Texas Health Science Center at Houston
Houston, Texas

Irving Kenneth Zola, PhD
Mortimer Grymish Professor of Human Relations
Department of Sociology
Brandeis University
Waltham, Massachusetts

Foreword

Human suffering has many faces. Often it cannot be seen on the surface because we humans hide our suffering as we attempt to disguise our vulnerability. After all we live in a society that does not encourage weakness or the admission of weakness, one that prefers that the ugliness of suffering remain invisible. Health professionals, whose lives are centered in the many facets of human suffering, nonetheless strive to understand it, to clarify it, and to be successful in its relief. Therefore, we hope that this book will be helpful especially to the practicing health care professional and the student preparing for a profession in the health care field.

The purpose of this book is to bring the phenomenon of suffering to light, to examine it from many perspectives, to analyze its meanings, to seek answers to the ultimate purpose of suffering in human life. Such a comprehensive attempt requires multidisciplinary knowledge as well as perspectives from theoreticians, clinicians, and researchers. Thus, the editors requested experts in various fields to write chapters, then brought them together in Houston, Texas, in April of 1990 for each to present his or her particular insight. After hearing the critique of fellow chapter contributors at the conference, each chapter author then submitted a final version.

The conference was blessed by one whose very name brings to mind a special dimension of human suffering, Mother Theresa, who prayed for its success for the glory of God and the relief of suffering people everywhere.

This book analyzes the nature of the suffering experience, including its physical, psychological, sociological, and spiritual aspects. Suffering is subjective and, therefore, unique to each of us. It varies in intensity and duration, but it may constitute an unforgettable experience. Suffering often is confused with other related concepts—pain, loss, grief, loneliness, despair—but each of those is a building block in the total suffering phenomenon. It is described by one chapter author as the "perception of undeserved adversity."

As a concept, suffering is a social construction. It is suffering because we have permitted society to shape our values and views to make it so. The suffering of the disabled has been structured by society, a society that until recently made no provisions of its own for this minority to participate fully in living. Suffering is a concept made worse by society's insensitivity; visible suffering is taboo. It is shaped by societal attitudes of individuality, autonomy, and self-sufficiency. Seemingly antithetical to the age-old paradigms of the pursuit of happiness, it does not fit with the challenge of eternal optimism; it is seen rather as a deprivation of joy. Suffering also has been constructed as an adult concept, perhaps too rich for the vocabulary of children. Finally, it is constructed to embrace shame and humiliation. Its exposure is offensive to society. Suffering frequently is silent, although the violence that often causes it is not.

Who can deny the pervasiveness of suffering? There is no greater sense of frustration in the health professions than the inability to alleviate suffering. Though it is our raison d'être, we are taught so little about it. It faces us daily; we confront it with yet more tools of technology and so often we miss the mark.

This book describes the phenomenon of suffering in an age spectrum from the suffering child to the elderly person suffering from a litany of losses. It explores the suffering of addiction, which does not end when the chemical dependency ends. It examines the suffering brought on by cancer, which draws together the suffering of a broken body and broken trusts, and is described from the perspective of the terminally ill and their caregivers. It probes the suffering of those preoccupied with thoughts of suicide—the feeling of being trapped and unable to utter even a weak cry for help except in the self-destructive act. It discusses suffering as growing out of punishment or curse, resulting in self-blame, despair, and hopelessness.

From this morass of horror tales, resilient sufferers emerge. They make it because of, or sometimes in spite of, caring professionals. What empowers them to survive? What are their characteristics? What can be learned from them? Suffering tests the meaning and purpose of life, for the sufferers as well as the caretakers. Humans have choices; if not about their fate, then about their reactions and attitudes toward a fate that cannot be changed. Humans have the capacity to transcend self-centered suffering and find lessons that enrich and enlarge life. Looking for what suffering may teach is the quest for meaning, and this book provides some guidelines for that search.

Still we are left with many questions only partially answered. Is illness synonymous with suffering? Is suffering a single or multiple entity? How is it recognized? How is suffering, the most fundamental problem of religion, affected by cultural archetypes and interpretations of values? How does the world view of suffering differ in the Shamanistic system, in Hinduism, Buddhism, Confucianism, Taoism, Judaism, Christianity, Islam, or the secular and technological culture? How will such ethical challenges as euthanasia be met? What is the compassionate response toward the suffering one? How can we remain open to learning?

This book adds to the knowledge base of suffering, and it will serve the student and novice practitioner as well as the seasoned professional. The book not only has definite implications for practice; it also points us to the need for research, identifying the types and addressing the issues of methodology.

Finally, this book belongs to us all, because nothing is so close to us as the opportunity to suffer. In the uncertainty of the next heartbeat, we may be included among the sufferers.

Patricia L. Starck, DSN, RN
John P. McGovern, MD, ScD, LLD

The Nature of Suffering: Physical, Psychological, Social, and Spiritual Aspects

Eric J. Cassell

My work on suffering had its genesis in the project on suffering of the Hastings Center, an organization dedicated to research and teaching about ethical issues raised by biomedical advance. From its origins, the Hastings Center had done research on ethical issues related to death and dying. As the years passed, the problems of the dying became the increasing concern of many individuals and groups in the United States and Europe. Dr. Elizabeth Kübler-Ross taught, and it had become received wisdom, that many of the problems of the dying arose from the denial of death that was widespread in the culture. If that was the case, one had to wonder why the subject of "death and dying" had become so popular throughout the United States. Courses on death and dying sprang up in schools of all levels, from grammar school to college. Newspapers and magazines ran articles, popular books were written, and even a death-and-dying jargon developed. It seemed a strange kind of denial. This seemed to be, rather, a pornography of death—the thing without the appropriate human emotions. The changed attitude toward death that all this publicity suggested appeared not to have changed the dimensions of personal loss and pain that my colleagues and I observed among our dying patients and their families.

We at the Hasting's Center wondered whether the popularity of the subject of death and dying was in itself a denial of something more painful than death itself—suffering. The project on suffering was born of those conjectures. The search for an understanding of suffering led to an exploration of the plays of classical Greece, Russian literature, suffering in other cultures, and the place of suffering in various theologies (suffering is one of the central problems with which all theologies must deal).

The dominant icon of Western civilization is the suffering figure of Christ who is at the same time a symbol of brutality, of suffering, and of love. For Judaism, the Book of Job makes clear that suffering may not only be inexplicable in human terms but is also not a matter of justice. Rabbi Jack Bemporad has pointed out that the experience of the prophets suggests that not only may the best suffer, but they appear to suffer for their goodness (Bemporad, 1986).

In the face of the fact that suffering has been with humankind since the beginning of time, we must ask why medicine and the other caring professions have become interested at this time. The first answer is that the interest is not new. In every culture the alleviation of suffering is the warrant of medicine. The totemic picture of Florence Nightingale—the lady with the lamp—represents the tireless effort of nurses to relieve suffering. What is new is the discovery that we know so little about suffering, its origins, defining characteristics, and nature. It is a word constantly and carelessly used as are the words hope, health, or happiness. It is frequently confused with its sources as in the phrase "pain and suffering." To be present, as we shall see, suffering requires more than pain or terrible distress. The depth of our ignorance is suggested by raising the possibility that the prophets and the saints, despite their terrible privations—or even because of them, did *not* suffer. That Christ, despite the brutality of the crucifixion, did not suffer except in the awful moment when he cries, "My God, My God, why have you forsaken Me? (Matthew 27:45)"

The answer to the question of why suffering has become a topic for study at this time may lie in the fact that suffering is a personal matter, arising from the nature of the suffering person, and because of this is always in part *private*. (Thus, two persons may undergo identical pain, but only one of them suffers; or all persons subject to a certain pain might suffer but in each of them the suffering will be somewhat different because each of them is a different person.) The personal and the private have only begun in these last decades to emerge into public view. This is partly

ality, also vital to our self-definition, is a child of the 18th century, and
the intensely personal individuality that we know so well has only come
about in these past few generations. I have written extensively on the
nature of the person elsewhere (Cassell, 1991). The list of characteristics
below provides merely a topography of person, but serves to make it clear
that persons are not merely boundaried objects, but rather exist as a
trajectory through time, or, as Alfred North Whitehead might say, as an
historic route of a society of elements. Persons always have character and
personality; they have a lived past and an anticipated future; they have
families and their families always have a past which is part of their past;
they have relationships; they live in a society and they always have a
culture; persons always have a work, something they do and by which they
construct their world, with which they are identified and which identifies
them to others; persons have day-to-day behaviors, habitual things they
do in their daily lives; they have a private (secret) life; they have bodies
and a relationship with the body; they have an unconscious—meanings
and memories that influence their behavior but which are not immediately accessible to awareness; persons also always have a transcendent or
spiritual dimension.

To say that suffering may occur because of any aspect of a person means
that if the source of suffering threatens one of the factors noted above so
severely that personal cohesiveness cannot be maintained, then suffering
follows. This is obvious in relationship to the body. As an example of a
different kind of injury, a person's past may be so radically put in doubt by
some event that the past can no longer be trusted. When that occurs the
person's present is shattered, as is the person, because the present is always
interpreted in terms of the past. The same is true when longstanding
relationships are betrayed or a life's work is destroyed. As a consequence
of its relationship to the parts of a person, suffering is ineluctably individual. As noted earlier, if two persons suffer because of the same pain or
disease their suffering will be different because they are different and
unique. Because of the particularity of suffering, while we may know that
another suffers and even what is the external source of the suffering, we
can *never* fully know from what or where within the individual the suffering arises.

SUFFERING INVOLVES THE FUTURE

Another fact of suffering that helps us know that it is a characteristic
of persons rather than bodies is that for suffering to occur there must be

because the very definition of person has become more personal and interiorized. As these aspects of person have emerged into view, the afflictions of the private person have increasingly become the concern of medicine.

The other fundamental reason we know so little about suffering is that the reductive methods of science, so useful in comprehending nature, inevitably lead *away* from an understanding of suffering. The title of my paper suggests that the problem of suffering can be divided into these pieces, but if we do so, its nature will disappear in front of our eyes. On the other hand, we have all become so accustomed to the language of scientific exploration that if all these aspects are put back together again, we have difficulty talking about the subject.

SUFFERING IS DISTINCT FROM PAIN

Elsewhere I have discussed in detail how suffering is distinct from pain or other physical symptoms (Cassell, 1991). Let me briefly recapitulate. Suffering may be caused by pain that is severe, but from the same kind of pain, some people will suffer while others will not. Suffering may arise from pain that is perceived as never ending or of dire cause although the pain itself is not severe. Suffering may often be relieved by merely demonstrating that the causative pain can be alleviated, even though the pain may continue. Suffering may be present when there is no pain, as in the anticipation of its return. Suffering may be present in the absence of any symptoms, as in the suffering caused by helplessly watching the terrible pain of a loved one.

These and other observations suggest that suffering is the state of distress induced by the threat of the loss of intactness or the disintegration of a person from whatever cause. Suffering is a consequence of personhood—bodies do not suffer, persons do.

SUFFERING IS PERSONAL

Suffering may occur in relation to any aspect of a person. The word "person" is difficult to define with precision although most people know what they mean when they say, "I am a person." The definitional problem arises because in different epochs what is included in the word "person" has varied. For example, our understanding of the word entails the notion of individuality. That idea, in the sense of uniqueness, did not arise until about the 12th or 13th century in the Western world. Political individua concept of the future. Remember, suffering comes into being because the person's intactness is experienced as threatened or disintegrating. At the moment of the threat, however, the person *is* intact. In acute illness the person may say, "If this pain keeps up, I won't be able to tolerate it." At that moment, however, the pain is being tolerated. In chronic illness, where suffering may arise because of public humiliation, the person's suffering starts because of the dread of future humiliation. The future onto which suffering is projected must also contain an idea of the person's identity. That identity must have arisen in the past and be cohesive from the past through the present and into the future. This is merely another way of stating that, unlike ideal objects of science which are free of the influence of space and time, the person is like droplets of space-time along the route of life—unavoidably unique because of this traversal.

In thinking about suffering, then, we should consider that the person, made up of the diverse features listed earlier, is a whole, thinks as a whole, and functions as a cohesive whole to the extent that something which drastically threatens a part, threatens the whole.

THE LOSS OF CENTRAL PURPOSE

No moment of life is without purpose. Most purposes can be seen as small moments of activity. This door is opened, that step taken, this can emptied, this word typed, and so on endlessly. Each of these little purposeful actions make up larger purposes. The door is opened to go outside to the store. This step is taken to walk into the next room to the computer where this word is typed as part of a manuscript being written. All of these composite actions and behaviors ultimately contribute to the central purpose we all have of being ourselves. I am not implying that all purposes are known or planned, or even that most people have a coherent idea of their own central purpose—of who the "I" is that they are each constructing moment by moment by moment. Within awareness or otherwise, purpose informs human living and central purpose gathers within itself myriads of lesser goals.

David Bakan has observed that in serious illness, there is a decentralization of purpose (Bakan, 1968). It is understandable that ill persons focus their purposes on the removal of the source of suffering. That, however, remains a central purpose. It can happen that attention to the source of suffering can so decentralize purpose that the whole organism becomes threatened not only by the disease or distress, but by the loss of central purpose. The image of the apathetic person in pain who can do nothing but talk of the pain, who does not eat, resume usual daily activities, or display interest in anything else is well known to physicians and nurses. It is an image of suffering. These patients are often frustrating to caregivers who wonder why they do nothing to help themselves. Without the help of caregivers, they cannot help themselves because suffering has destroyed the central guiding purpose that is implied in the words "helping themselves."

SOCIAL DIMENSIONS OF SUFFERING

Just as the sufferer is unique and individual, suffering is unavoidably social. Suffering, as noted earlier, is engendered not only because of the pain or insult of this moment alone, but because of its projected future. It is not the severity of the pain or insult that is crucial to suffering, but rather what is believed it represents or will become. Another way to say this is to point out that it is the *meaning* to the sufferer of the insult that leads to suffering. In general, we do not act or react because of events but because of their meaning. Meaning has always at least two aspects: *significace*—what the thing implies, as in the pain signifies the return of cancer, and *importance*—the value or importance ascribed by the person to the thing. Importance is always a personal matter. Both dimensions of meaning, however, are always, at least in part, social. We know what things signify not only from our own experience, but from what we read or learn from others. Similarly, the values we attach to things are not only unique but also shared. If significance and importance did not have social dimensions, there could be no communication between persons. This is why Susan Sontag (1978), in her book, *Illness as Metaphor*, complained about the metaphors attached to cancer when she developed cancer of the breast. She became aware that what happened to her and what she believed might happen were determined, in part, by the meanings connected to her disease. In other words, the suffering of the individual, despite its idiosyncratic and particular nature, is born from shared meanings. One cannot secede from the group because the group—the community of persons—is part of each of us and to separate would further threaten wholeness.

The social nature of suffering is highlighted by the isolation imposed by suffering. Whether from acute pain or chronic disease, suffering forces the sufferer to focus on the source of suffering and to withdraw from the world of others. This isolation itself further adds to the suffering as it disrupts those aspects of person which require social contact. The concentration on individuality by Western culture for these last centuries (and by ethics on autonomy) has obscured the more basic truth that we live in a sea of others without whom existence is literally unthinkable. Language is often cited in proof of this concept, but we could not think, move, remember, pursue our purposes, or even dream in the absence of others. Otherness is implied by self and many by one.

SELF-CONFLICT IN SUFFERING

The National Archives Building in Washington, D.C., has an inscription that reads, "The ties that bind us as a nation are contained within this building. . . ." The Declaration of Independence and the Constitution bind us as a nation because they provide us with common meanings. The bonds that hold us together are not external but within each of us. It is the same with all the myriad social rules, constraints, permissions, and requirements of life. So it is also with the meanings of the words "doctor, mother, pain, cancer, disabled," and the others which define our behavior from morning to morning and form our dreams as well. The wheelchair is both outside its occupant and inside him or her as well. Morphine is inside the patient doing its work (for good or for bad) even before it has been administered because it has meanings for the patient.

When persons are sick they cannot respond in the same degree to all of the social demands, rules, and obligations that are contained within them. Sickness, however, does not keep them from trying. We have all seen the extremes to which the sick will often go to continue a charade of normalcy—the burdens they endure and the effort required. I do not want to be me sick, I want to be me as I know myself. I want to be regarded as normal, "like everybody else." As this is true of acute illness, it is perhaps more so when illness continues. These desires of the sick person to be normal inevitably set up inner conflicts between the behaviors that are required to be normal and normally social and those that are required because of the facts of the sickness. If the social part of the person wins, we may see the common occurrence of persons with disabilities outdoing themselves to be just like everybody else. Such individuals may pay a terrible price because the harder one tries, the more is the awareness of the inner conflict. If the protective (sick) part of the person wins, then the ill person may become increasingly reclusive—and again pay a high price for the conflict between inner notions of normal behavior and the demands of the illness. The conflict may be simply between the demands of the person and the needs of the body. If these struggles are sufficiently severe, the integrity of the person is threatened with disintegration and suffering will ensue. As long as the conflict remains, the suffering continues and in itself worsens the conflict. Another way of seeing this conflict is as a battle of life purposes where the person must choose to (a) maintain one's original purpose even though it is poorly suited to one's new illness state, (b) develop a new set of life purposes more congruent with a life of chronic illness, or (c) lose central purpose altogether.

The psychology of suffering is a psychology of self-conflict. It is not too much to say that all suffering involves self-conflict, even when the source is acute pain. Suffering does not arise solely because of the pain, but because the integrity of the person is threatened. If the threat did not matter, if living or dying were truly a matter of indifference, then there would be pain—even terrible pain—but not suffering. If the person with chronic illness truly did not care about being an object of staring day after day or losing control of bowels or bladder in public (an almost unimaginable idea to someone who is healthy), then he or she might be unhappy or lonely but would not suffer.

WE ARE OF A PIECE

It is evident that in thinking about suffering it is not possible to divide the problem into physical, psychological, and social aspects without losing our grasp of it. In fact, reflecting on suffering should make it possible to see that there is nothing about the body that is not also psychological and social, nothing social that is not physical and psychological, and nothing psychological that is not physical and social. We are of a piece. What happens to one part of us happens to the whole and what happens to the whole happens to every part.

TRANSCENDENCE

Earlier I said that suffering is necessarily individual. We *cannot* know the origins of suffering within the sufferer. We may know the stimulus— the pain, dyspnea, physical disability, loneliness, or loss—but we cannot know why this particular sufferer suffers. Even the sufferer may not know. Yet the word "compassion" suggests that it is possible to know that another person suffers. How does this knowledge come about? One can ask the sufferer—probably the most underutilized method. Sufferers, however, may conceal their suffering from us (or from themselves). We can be told but ourselves deny the knowledge because we feel helpless in the presence of suffering.

Perhaps we know someone is suffering because we see the manifestations of pain or sickness—facial expressions, bodily motions, and changes in behavior. We may hear the sounds of suffering—whimpering or the repetitive grunting sound so common to suffering caused by pain. Despite the importance of heeding such evidence, it is necessary to caution that pain (or other distress) is not necessarily suffering. Because observers may wrongly believe that someone with these manifestations is suffering, it is common to hold back people who are in pain but who might otherwise rise above their pain because of their involvement in their purposes and goals. Such patients, whose activities prevent their suffering, should be encouraged rather than restrained. Sometimes suffering is not appreciated because the observer does not believe the stimulus severe enough to cause suffering. The suffering is the essential fact, not the severity of the pain. Most suffering, however, probably occurs in silence—unknown to observers and perhaps even to the sufferers, who do not know what their distress is. Acute illness and injury should not be the sole model for understanding suffering, just as they should no longer be the sole model for thinking about medical care. Thus, perhaps most suffering will not betray itself directly to our five senses nor be revealed by direct questioning except as it influences the behavior of the sufferer. It may be described by diagnostic psychological terms such as depression. While depression may be a manifestation of suffering, however, the two are distinct.

We are left to account for genuine compassion. There is one more way by which we can know that others suffer—by directly experiencing within ourselves their feelings of desperation and disintegration, in the same manner that parents frequently experience the emotions of their children and psychiatrists of their patients. Directly experiencing the emotions of others is common, but not common knowledge, not part of our everyday language nor of medical discourse. What this basis for compassion teaches is that transcendence—reaching beyond our physical boundaries—is not confined to religious experience, but is part of the everyday world.

Humans are not simply atomistic individuals whose social existence can be likened to bumper cars at a carnival. We are truly transcendent beings whose boundaries are not at our skins. We live in a common medium: not only of air and gravity but a medium of we-ness that binds us together as effectively as air, gravity, and our common physiologic needs. Suffering occurs and is expressed not only physically, psychologically, and socially, but transcendentally as well. Suffering persons lose their transcendent connection to the group—we feel them (or their absence) but they do not feel us. They are isolated in a medium that in itself and by the group remains unacknowledged, so they are doubly isolated. The importance of the loss of transcendence in suffering is suggested by how suffering may be overcome by transcendent means such as spirituality. It is their identification with or reaching toward God mediated by their physical hardships that *prevents* the suffering of the prophets and the saints. The same end may be achieved, however, by connection with overriding purpose or through patriotism. Realizing the importance of transcendence and the medium of we-ness offers caregivers the opportunity of relieving suffering by reaching out to the sufferers and, if possible, returning them to their places within the community.

CONCLUSION

The nature of suffering and the pursuit of its understanding offer us the opportunity to rethink the very nature of understanding itself. They show us the advantages of going beyond the merely reductive knowledge of science in order to comprehend the human condition. They also provide the opportunity to rethink what we mean by person—physical, psychological, social, and transcendent. While seeking to understand the nature of suffering, the caring professions must remain focused on their timeless goal—the relief of suffering.

REFERENCES

Bakan, D. (1968). *Disease, pain, and sacrifice*. Chicago: The Beacon Press.

Bemporad, J. (1986). Job. In J. Spiegelman, A. Marvin, & A. Jacobson (Eds.), *A modern Jew in search of soul*. Phoenix, Arizona: Falcon Press.

Cassell, E.J. (1991). *The nature of suffering*. New York: Oxford University Press.

Sontag, S. (1978). *Illness as metaphor*. New York: Farrar, Straus and Giroux.

2

The Social Construct of Suffering

Irving K. Zola

Before going directly to the substance of my chapter I need to note an intellectual indebtedness that cannot be described by mere references in a text.

My first acknowledgment is to two medical scientists, Sigmund Freud and Rene Dubos, who through devoting their lives to the study and alleviation of suffering also claimed a certain endemic quality to its existence, especially in such works as Freud's (1930) *Civilization and Its Discontents* and Dubos's (1961) *The Mirage of Health*. My second indebtedness is to Ivan Illich and David Bakan, two analysts who began their lives as men of the cloth and who retained in all their work a respect for the nature of pain and suffering and a need to dissect its social origins. The latter is particularly evident in Illich's (1976) *Medical Nemesis* and Bakan's (1971) *Disease, Pain, and Sacrifice—Toward a Psychology of Suffering*. Finally there is the need to recognize the Women's Movement and

Special thanks to Cheryl Davis, a freelance writer in Palo Alto, California, for her extensive editorial and substantive suggestions.

the Independent Living Movement, both of which have emphasized the
importance of alternative views of suffering. The former is perhaps best
embodied in the work of the Boston Women's Health Book Collective
(1973, 1976, 1979, 1984), *Our Bodies Ourselves*. The Independent Living
Movement (Crewe & Zola, 1983) has many voices, but the one most
central to this paper is found in the writings of Paul Longmore (1985,
1987, 1989), author of the most perceptive works I have read on media
portrayals of disability as well as on the ethical issues concerning the right
to die and assisted suicide. Not only is Longmore an excellent historian,
author of a recently praised biography of George Washington, but as a
result of polio he is a ventilator user.

   This third set of acknowledgments leads directly to my first concern—
the social construction of the voice of suffering.

THE SOCIAL CONSTRUCT OF THE
VOICE OF SUFFERING

   Amongst the Women's and the Independent Living Movements' most
consistent criticisms is that the view of their bodily conditions has been
overmedicalized. The complaint is that the nature of their suffering is
most often articulated and verbalized by someone else (such as experts in
charge of their formal therapeutic care). While recognizing the therapeutic utility of expertise and distance from the experience of "the sufferer," both movements claim that this is not the *only* nor necessarily the
most important view of suffering.

   This point can be illustrated with a reference to my own expertise. My
biographical sketch lists degrees, positions, honors, and publications.
While connoting a scholarly legitimation for my words, it does not credit
my experiential credentials.

   In 1950, at the age of 16, I contracted polio. Four years later I was in
a serious automobile accident. As a result of both incidents, I wear a long
leg brace on my right leg, two short ones on my left, a back support, use
two canes for daily ambulation, and a wheelchair for longer trips. In the
words of the medical world, I have "a number of residuals"; in the eyes of
my older children, I "walk funny." In the clearer perception of my
youngest daughter, I have a disability. As I now am well into my second
half-century, I also have many of the accoutrements of aging in addition
to a problematic genetic heritage. I claim not that personal experience

guarantees a more authentic view of suffering, but that it adds a different perspective. Two personal encounters illustrate.

Recently, my surgeon indicated that I needed to undergo a nerve conduction test (electromyogram). In a flippant tone, he added, "Don't worry. . . . It's an easy test. . . . It doesn't hurt."

"How do you know?" I asked, "Have you ever had it done to you?"

"No," he answered sounding surprised, "but my experience tells me. . . . "

"Well," I interrupted, "*my* experience, from having had it performed twice, is that it is the most physically uncomfortable and psychologically disturbing test I have ever undergone."

A second encounter, longer ago but still remembered with keen feeling, was an orthopedic consult, occasioned by a recurring pain in my right shoulder. After a series of tests, the doctor asked his final question: "Tell me again when you most experience it."

"When I throw a football to my son," I said.

"And how old are you now?"

"Pushing fifty," I replied.

"Time to stop playing football," he nodded conclusively as he rose to leave, leaving me in turn feeling impotent and enraged. He had neither asked about nor observed the importance of this activity for a man with many obvious disabilities, for whom this form of play provided an important bond with his son. In both instances, the viewpoint of "the sufferer" adds (or should add) dimensionality to the understanding necessary to appreciate and cope with suffering.

On the other hand, the statements of people who have disabilities cannot be taken at face value, for even their voices are filtered through a social context. Erving Goffman in his book, *Stigma* (1963), made some very perceptive remarks about this subject. Spokespersons, he noted, assume such a role precisely because they are understandable to the dominant group. They are perceived to be not so different from the mainstream. In fact, to the degree that any outsider wishes to join and be part of the mainstream, this being more like them is part of the process by which he or she will get there. The success of such efforts is summed up in what for many years was considered the ultimate praise an able-bodied person could pay to someone with a disability: "I *never* think of you as handicapped." Ironically enough, the latter's adaptation was often measured by the degree to which he or she adhered to the statement "I *never* think of myself as handicapped." Yet, if either statement is operational, then one should reasonably ask how representative are such spokespersons of the group they purport to represent.

Lest this be regarded as merely an interesting theoretical point, let me concretely illustrate with a case where this spokesperson's inability to communicate the quality of suffering was a significant datum in the controversy over accessibility in airline travel. In my introduction, I described my physical disability and the age of onset, crucial elements in appreciating my reactions to the accommodations of airline travel. Over 30 years ago, when questioned about the physical difficulties of airline travel for someone like me, I asserted they were relatively minor or nonexistent. Twenty years later, when it was no longer necessary to pretend I was just like everyone else, my reactions were quite different.

My ordinary mode of travel was to drive to the airport, park in the most convenient spot, and then limp with my baggage (often strapped to my back) to what often seemed the farthest terminal in the airport.

But by the end of the 1970s and early 1980s, the Independent Living Movement (Scotch, 1984) was in full swing and with it some interesting changes in my self-perception. I no longer had to behave like what is known in the disability rights movement as a "supercrip." Though I was still quite *capable* of walking that long distance, I no longer felt it necessary to do so. So, upon arrival at an airport, after parking the car or being dropped off, I would either get into my own wheelchair or the airline's and roll to that farthest terminal. What was completely unanticipated was the difference in my physical condition at the end of my trip: I now arrived *un*tired and *un*needing of a nap, *un*sore from sweating legs and tight braces, *un*cramped from the general strain of extra walking. My conclusion was straightforward: I had *always* been tired, sore, and cramped, but with no pre-travel, pre-polio, pre-wheelchair experience for comparison, these experiences had been *cognitively inaccessible*. I had thought them part of the physical condition, the inevitable suffering resulting from my disability, part of the cost of traveling, as well as being Irving Kenneth Zola. Only after the Independent Living Movement had arrived and after a change in self-consciousness "allowed" me to use a wheelchair, did I realize how much of my travel "suffering" was inherent not in my disability but rather in the society in which I lived. The suffering was *socially created*.

THE SOCIAL CONSTRUCT OF THE NATURE OF SUFFERING: THE "RIGHT TO DIE"

When the Women's Movement took to the streets, one banner was especially prominent in the marches. It read, "Anatomy is not destiny."

The argument was simple and powerful. While acknowledging that there were physical differences between men and women, women argued that this did not account for all the other differences they experienced— neither their oppressions nor their sufferings. When the Independent Living Movement emerged a decade or more later, people with disabilities saw some of the commonalities they shared with women. In particular, they argued that disability is not a biological given, but like gender is socially constructed from biological reality.

We can see how disability is socially constructed by looking at portrayals of disability in the media, particularly those in which the nature of "suffering" is a cornerstone in the creation of social actions and social policy (Longmore, 1985).

In the middle 1970s, "Whose Life Is It Anyway?" (Clark, 1974) opened to critical praise, box office profits, and plum roles for actors and actresses. The movie released in 1981 enjoyed a similar success. In "Whose Life Is It Anyway?" a spinal-cord injured man (played by actor Richard Dreyfuss who is known for his almost uncontainable energy), requests help of the court in ending his life. He claims that there is nothing left for him to do; he is only half a man and an asexual one at that. His fictional physicians do not seriously attempt to refute this belief nor any other "can't do" myths. In fact, the writers also give him an infection which keeps him isolated from all other patients, including other wheelchair users. He is never given a motorized chair or any other assistive device. In fact, a deliberately slanted picture is drawn in which he will be forever helpless, his life full of struggle, and his future hopeless. In effect, the play was a polemical elaboration of one side of a suicidal argument.

In one particularly telling scene, an orderly remarks that the thousands of dollars spent each month on a disabled character such as him could better be used to feed poor children. This attitude pits the costs in sustaining a "useless" individual against the needs of future generations, a sentiment occasionally echoed by public figures. Former Governor Richard Lamm of Colorado has garnered considerable attention for his outspoken comments regarding medical cost containment measures and the idea of an appropriate time for older people to die. Referring to those who reject life-sustaining treatment, Governor Lamm (1984) said, "You've got a duty to die and get out of the way. Let the other society, our kids, build a reasonable life." Daniel Callahan (1987) of the Hasting Center has opined that such decisions may not continue to be voluntary and in his book, appropriately titled *Setting Limits*, he argues that we may need to create social policies that will enhance if not enforce such decisions. When this argument was first uttered, some expressed fear that such a setting of limits is something that could also be applied to people with interminable, painful, and long-suffering conditions—and in recent years it has.

The social reality of the last decade has paralleled and exceeded the fictional dimensions of "Whose Life Is It Anyway?" The issues of the right to die (or in more behavioral terms, the right to assisted suicide) have moved to the forefront of ethical issues. The case which occupied center stage for much of the middle 1980s was that of Elizabeth Bouvia,[1] who came before the public and the courts as someone "who suffers from degenerative and severely crippling arthritis," is on a morphine drip to relieve pain, and as someone whose "physical handicaps of (cerebral) palsy and quadriplegia have progressed to the point where she is completely bedridden," so that "she lays flat in bed and must do so for the rest of her life . . . requiring constant care." While descriptive of what was presented in her petitions by her lawyers to the courts, this is not the truth, the whole truth, nor even a fraction of the truth (so help me God).

Born with cerebral palsy and functionally quadriplegic, Elizabeth Bouvia spent her early years in the care of her divorced mother. At the age of ten, when her mother remarried, she was placed in an institution for "handicapped children." She stayed in a number of such places until age 18, when she moved outside with the help of a California state program called In-Home Supportive Services. This source of funds enabled her, like other disabled Californians, to hire aides to assist her with housekeeping and personal needs such as bathing, dressing, and eating. With such help for eight years, she was able to live independently in Riverside and then in San Diego. During this time, she began pursuing the educational skills necessary for economic security—first an associate degree at Riverside Community College, then a bachelor's degree at San Diego State University, and finally enrollment in the same school's master's degree program in social work, an essential element of which is a fieldwork experience.

The local hospital where she was placed refused to make the accommodations necessary for her to work there, a refusal that her School of Social Work supported, despite the fact that such a refusal violated federal law. The school offered her an alternative placement where she would

---

[1]Though I have followed the case of Elizabeth Bouvia, much of the chronology presented here is derived from Longmore (1987).

work exclusively with other disabled people, something she thought was unduly restrictive. At this time, a professor apparently told her that *if they had known how disabled she was they would never have admitted her to the program and besides, she was unemployable.* In this evaluation her own attorney concurred, saying, "Quadriplegics cannot work." (This would be news to the many quadriplegics holding full-time jobs in the United States.) Apparently the attorney was also unaware that the program under which she received her initial help—In-Home Supportive Services— existed at the same time that Ed Roberts was Commissioner of Rehabilitation. In the 1950s, Roberts, himself functionally quadriplegic as the result of polio, was rejected by his local state rehabilitation agency as unrehabilitable and unemployable. Bouvia lacked Roberts' familial and social support, so when she met with resistance to her requests, she felt (and was) unsupported, despaired of ever achieving a professional degree and career, and left school.

Her life was full of other losses. A brother died; her baby was miscarried; she and her husband separated. It was also reported that she saw the film "Whose Life Is It Anyway?" and became severely depressed. At this time, she sought admission to the psychiatric unit of Riverside County Hospital and asked for assistance in ending her life. When the hospital refused, she turned to the law. While the first hearing denied her petition for assisted suicide, in 1986 the California Court of Appeals stated that what she "really" wanted was the right to refuse medical treatment, and it granted her request. The appeals judges based their decision on their assessment of the quality of her life, one "diminished to the point of hopelessness, uselessness, unenjoyability, and frustration," an assessment devoid of consultation by anyone with expertise in psychosocial aspects of disability. In the judges' opinion,

> *Although alert, bright, sensitive, perhaps even brave and feisty, she must lie immobile, unable to exist except through the physical acts of others. Her mind and spirit may be free to take great flights, but she herself is imprisoned and must lie physically helpless subject to the ignominy, embarrassment, humiliation, and dehumanizing aspects created by her helplessness.* [Longmore, 1987, p. 158]

If she was truly helpless at this time, it was not entirely of her own doing. In their zeal to win the case, some of the "facts" presented by her attorneys were later learned not to be true. Her attending physician revealed at a bioethics symposium that he was not sure she even had

While arguments vis-à-vis instances of requests for assisted suicide or right to die have been largely reactive, in regard to "damages," they have been quite proactive. Thus since the middle 1980s several disability rights lawyers, together with disability rights activists/social scientists like myself, have devised a legal strategy that takes seriously all the humiliation that a person goes through in such a trial and argues that the life of unmitigated suffering a person faces is *socially created.*

In the Biscoe case, the first in which I was involved, the strategy of disability as a life of suffering *per se* was abandoned. (In fact, somewhat to the chagrin of his attorneys, the plaintiff Dr. Biscoe, now a double amputee and, because of the nature of his particular injury, most likely a wheelchair user for the rest of his life, was popping wheelies in the courtroom.) The only medical-psychiatric evidence presented was to note that his disability was not something he was born with but the result of the accident over which he was suing for "damages." All the rest of the testimony was essentially social.

A succession of planners, architects, and sociologists (myself) documented that the "suffering" and "pain" that he would most likely endure was that inflicted by a society that discriminates and refuses to accommodate people who are physically different. Specifically, we documented the extent to which in his daily life he would no longer be free (or allowed) to do the activities that he previously took for granted. We detailed the additional planning it would take for him to do anything or go anywhere. In addition to the social stigma, and the accompanying negative social psychological traits automatically attributed to anyone with a visible disability (Goffman, 1963; Yuker, 1988), especially someone in a wheelchair, we noted that there is not now, nor will there be in any foreseeable future, free and easy access for people in wheelchairs to private dwellings, institutions, or any public buildings—be they museums, schools, theaters, ballparks, auditoriums, public transportation, housing, or restaurants.

In subsequent cases, the plaintiff was often not so securely employed as Dr. Biscoe (he was a vice-president at the University of Tennessee, on loan to the National Science Foundation), nor with an already established family. In these instances, where the individuals were younger, single, and not securely employed, we documented further societal exclusion in dating, marital possibilities, all forms of socializing, and consistent discrimination in regard to future educational and training opportunities, as well as future employment or advancement. In short, having a disability *regardless* of the individuals' real abilities, potentialities, and wishes continually relegates them to the margins of society.

From the lawyers' point of view, such testimony was extremely effective. We won all the cases brought and with amounts equal to or higher than those in which the nature of the suffering was individualized and attributed to the disability itself. The plaintiffs were able to escape the humiliation ritual and, indeed, were able to feel good about themselves. Not only did they no longer have to sit as victims, silent and passive, but they could be angry, fight back, and win. We assisted then in their empowerment. Sociologically, we were able to alter the prevailing "invalid-victim" strategy by shifting the blame and responsibility to specific social forces and institutions. Moreover, we were able to have political effects.

When suffering is individuated, our interventions are limited to giving individual help, but when the suffering is socially induced, it opens the arena for social remediation. In fact, by taking capitalism quite seriously, this social action hit the defendants where it hurt most—in their pocketbooks. This case has had a ripple effect. In 1989, I testified in a California public accommodations case, where an individual was denied free and easy admittance to a restaurant. Ordinarily, both the fines and enforcement in such instances are minimal. Too often it is felt implicitly (and occasionally explicitly) that people with disabilities should not go to such places. Sometimes people claim that they make other customers feel uncomfortable. Taking the American system seriously, the Disability Rights Education and Defense Fund, a group of public interest lawyers in Berkeley, sued the restaurant, part of a national chain, for damages resulting from the social exclusion and humiliation that their client had undergone. I testified that her inability to fully participate in the age-old American practice of "eating out" was due not to her disability, but to a systemic pattern of prejudice and discrimination, socially created and maintained by a society that allowed it to flourish. The jury agreed and awarded a record amount of punitive damages. More important was the precedent it set. Even before the verdict was upheld on appeal, a number of other cases in litigation were settled. An even larger number of restaurants and previously inaccessible institutions saw the handwriting on the wall and began to comply with the law to make their facilities accessible.

CONCLUSION

I will end this chapter with an anecdote that may put much of what I have said in perspective.

A woman is standing by a swiftly flowing stream and sees someone apparently struggling in the water. She leaps in, swims to him, brings him to shore, and applies artificial respiration. Just as he begins to sputter something, she spots someone else struggling in the water. Back in she leaps, grabs him, brings him back to shore, applies artificial respiration, and just when he begins to speak, she spots another struggler. On and on it goes. In fact, she is so busy in this rescuing process that she does not have the time to learn whether all these strugglers want or need to be rescued and who the hell is upstream pushing them all in.

The overall purpose of this international interdisciplinary conference is to examine the meaning and nature of human suffering and to explore therapeutic interventions to aid "the suffering individual." My cautionary tale is to remind us that, whatever other essential work we do, we must not only listen carefully to the voices and experiences of those we seek to help, but we must always keep an eye cocked upstream toward some of those not easily viewed forces, what this conference aptly calls the invisible dimensions of illness.

REFERENCES

ABC News, Nightline. (1989, December 28). Independent living for the disabled. Transcript pp. 1–7.

Bakan, D. (1971). *Disease, pain, and sacrifice—Toward a psychology of suffering.* Boston: Beacon.

Boston Women's Health Book Collective. (1973, 1976, 1979, 1984). *Our bodies ourselves.* New York: Simon & Schuster.

Callahan, D. (1987). *Setting limits: Medical goals in an aging society.* New York: Simon & Schuster.

Clark, B. (1974). *Whose life is it anyway?* Chicago: Dramatic.

Crewe, N., & Zola, I.K. (Eds.). (1983). *Independent living programs for physically disabled people.* San Francisco: Jossey-Bass.

Dubos, R. (1961). *The mirage of health.* Garden City, NY: Anchor.

Freud, S. (1930). *Civilization and its discontents.* London: Hogarth.

Goffman, E. (1963). *Stigma—Notes on the management of spoiled identity.* Englewood Cliffs, NJ: Prentice-Hall.

Illich, I. (1976). *Medical nemesis.* New York: Random House.

"Lamm stirs new furor by calling on aged ill to die." (1984, March 29). *Los Angeles Times,* p. 16.

Longmore, P.K. (1985). Screening stereotypes: Images of disabled people in television and motion pictures. *Social Policy*, 16, 31–37.

Longmore, P.K. (1987). Elizabeth Bouvia, assisted suicide and social prejudice. *Issues in Law and Medicine*, 3, 141–168.

Longmore, P.K. (1989, July 18). Comment: Disabled need access to life not death. *The Detroit News*, p. 11A.

Scotch, R. (1984). *From goodwill to civil rights: Transforming federal disability policy.* Philadelphia: Temple University.

Yuker, H.E. (Ed.). (1988). *Attitudes towards persons with disabilities.* New York: Springer.

3

The Meaning of Suffering

Patricia L. Starck and John P. McGovern

No human being can escape suffering, for it is a part of the human condition. Since it is common to all, and part of the overall experience of life, suffering offers an opportunity to search for meaning and, at the same time, extrapolate a teleologic view of its occurrence.

All suffering, no matter what kind, on some level touches upon and affects the physical, emotional, mental, spiritual, and social being of a person, as has been pointed out in the first two chapters. Indeed, suffering never affects just one part, but always affects the whole of the being. In addition, this viewpoint is inclusive with respect to any one or all types of causative conditions: self-inflicted, other person inflicted, societally inflicted, and/or by chance happenings in nature.

The tendency in nature always is to make a whole of its constituent parts and what affects the part, always, in some way, affects the whole. Suffering in this sense becomes part of nature's schematic and an element within the laws of life, survival of the self, and survival of the species, which apply to all living organisms from the unicellular amoeba on up the chain to Homo sapiens; it is existential.

suffering. Suffering can affect one or more dimensions of a human life. There can be physical suffering that may be associated with pain; psychic suffering, such as the anguish of a mother caring for her terminally ill child; or spiritual suffering, that is, suffering of the human spirit. In any case, there is interaction among the dimensions, and suffering, no matter how great or small, fills the entire human soul.

Suffering Tests Meaning and Purpose in Life

Suffering of the human spirit can result from confusion about or lack of meaning in one's situation. This, Frankl (1959) termed *existential frustration*. A more severe state, *existential vacuum* is the absence of any sense of meaning in life. Travelbee (1971) concluded that purpose and meaning in life are tested in times of suffering; thus, existential frustration and existential vacuum may be evoked.

MEANING SEEKERS

Those who seek meaning in suffering include both the sufferer and the caregiver. The professional caregiver has the role of facilitating positive outcomes and finding some sense of purpose. Suffering has the potential to transform the sufferer and/or caregiver and offers an opportunity for the sufferer and/or caregiver to experience discovery and growth and to give and/or receive compassion and love. Thus, those who suffer can find new meaning in life, as can those who care for the sufferers. For this growth to happen, the element of love or caring must be present within a symbiotic relationship between patient and caregiver. Van Eys and McGovern (1988) described love as being synonymous with deeply caring. He admonished physicians to be knowledgeable in science, versed in the humanities, and caring at every level of the struggle of the patient.

Choice and Responsibility

Choice and responsibility are available to the sufferer. Frankl (1959) points out that humans are able to choose and make decisions for themselves, and thus, are free. With this freedom, however, comes responsibility. Living meaningfully means being fully aware of the true nature of the human situation and accepting it with courage. When unavoidable suffering is one's fate, one is confronted with enormous challenges, but is still free to choose how to respond. One is either the master or the victim of one's attitudes.

Life Transition Theory

In the case of a traumatic event, such as a complete spinal cord transection, one's reality is suddenly and irrevocably changed. The former values and meanings in life are shattered. The uncertainty about the future, the loss of the integrity and dignity of the self, and the life-style changes forced upon the individual create intense suffering. Slowly, at some point in time, the successful patient begins the process that bridges the old reality to a newly designed and realistic present. This process is described by Selder (1989) on the basis of life transition theory. This process of restructuring is to create new meanings in one's life. According to life transition theory, the expectations held by the patient will determine the newly created reality and influence the meaning found in new experiences.

Suffering as a Challenge to Find Meaning

To say "there is meaning in suffering" suggests that to suffer is a desirable thing so that one might experience meaning. It might also imply that in order to have a truly meaningful existence, one has to suffer. However, this is not the premise of logotherapy. Rather, since no one as a human being can escape suffering, the suffering experience stands as a challenge in which to find meaning. New meaning in life can come through a suffering experience, and exclusively through that experience, as can be seen in the following story.

Mr. J. was a 48-year-old man who had become a paraplegic by a gunshot wound from a killer hired by his business partner whose motivation was to collect insurance money. Long after his physical rehabilitation, Mr. J. remained bitter and despondent. Following intervention aimed at helping him discover new meaning in life through his suffering, Mr. J. changed his attitude toward his fate and was instrumental in the development of a program to assist victims of crime. This program, in the state attorney general's office, helped to support the victim in a judicial system that often seems to favor the perpetrator of the crime. Mr. J. stated that it was only because he had gone through this experience that he was able to make new achievements for the public good.

Attribution Theory: Cause Versus Meaning

In examining the question of meaning in suffering, one must distinguish *cause* from *meaning*. Attribution theory (Bardwell, 1986; Brubaker, 1988; Carroll et al., 1987; Corenblum, 1983; Ducette & Keane, 1984; Karanci, 1986; Peterson, 1984; Rossler & Lackus, 1986; Weiner, 1988) examines cause or blame; it explains how one makes causal explanations. The patient's specific causal attribution is sought by the therapist. According to Peterson (1984), the process of forming causal explanations can be seen in the experience of one who suffers a mental health crisis; reacts with some degree of shock, disbelief, or denial; and then begins to wonder why the crisis happened and struggles to identify a reason, a purpose, a meaning. The therapist's goal is for reorganization that will move toward positive resolution. Attribution of the problem to self rather than totally blaming others is indicative of the realization that the crisis logically followed one's own behavior. One may have learned from the crisis by attributing antecedent events correctly, but this is not the same as having found meaning in a situation. Likewise, one can attribute heavy smoking to the cause of cancer; however, finding meaning in and through the experience of cancer is something quite different.

Iatrogenic Suffering

Iatrogenic suffering, or the suffering caused by treatment as opposed to the disease condition itself, deserves attention. In a high-technology-oriented tertiary care center, there are many tools used in the process of treatment that cause suffering. Even though these treatments may be lifesaving, and thus meaningful or rational, this is not what is meant by finding meaning in suffering.

Finding Meaning in Spite of Suffering

Another semantic variation is "finding meaning in spite of suffering." That is, even though one is suffering, it is still possible to find meaning in life by transcending the suffering. The following story is an example.

Mr. K., a C4 quadriplegic, led a very limited life as far as physical activities were concerned. Yet he found new meaning in life in spite of his handicap. He did volunteer telephone work to benefit cystic fibrosis victims. He kept abreast of academic studies so that he could tutor younger relatives. Mr. K. had been the first member of his family to graduate from high school, and he found meaning in encouraging his cousins and nephews to excel academically.

Cognitive Appraisal of the Suffering Experience

Lazarus and Folkman (1984) have added to the understanding of how one finds meaning or significance in life events by their work on cognitive appraisal as an evaluative process that is not necessarily a conscious process. There are three types of cognitive appraisal: primary, secondary, and reappraisal. In primary appraisal, the event is judged to be either irrelevant, benign-positive, or stressful. There are three types of stressful appraisals: (a) harm/loss, (b) threat or anticipated harm/loss, and (c) challenge or potential for gain. In secondary appraisal, the question is what should or might be done. Reappraisal is a revised appraisal based on new information about the environment or the person. Appraisals are shaped by two characteristics of a person: (a) commitments (choices, values, goals) and (b) beliefs (preexisting notions about reality). In addition to person factors, there are three situation factors: (a) imminence, (b) duration, and (c) temporal uncertainty. Person factors and situation factors are always interdependent.

Coping may be thought of as a subject of adaptation. Coping directed at managing or altering the problem causing the distress is *problem-focused coping* or *damage control*. Coping directed at regulating emotional response to the problem is *emotion-focused coping*.

In secondary appraisal, the person asks, "What can I do?" Lazarus and Folkman (1984) identify major categories of coping resources: (a) health and energy, (b) positive beliefs, (c) problem-solving skills, (d) social skills,

(e) social support, and (f) material resources. Holding positive beliefs that serve as a basis of hope is an important psychological resource for coping. Lazarus and Folkman (1984) also raise important questions: Are there costs to positive thinking? Can people who do not think positively be influenced to? Are those most in need of cultivating this capability the least able to do so?

Choice of Suffering

Finally, there is intentional suffering. If faced with a choice involving suffering or not suffering, one may choose the route that leads to suffering because of one's beliefs. A cause worthy of suffering gives meaning to life. How does one go about finding meaning in suffering? Are some people more likely than others to seek for and find meaning in suffering?

WHERE MEANING IS TO BE FOUND

Self-Transcendence

Frankl (1959) states that meaning is found through self-transcendence, that is, getting outside the self or rising above the self. As in the case of Mr. J., only by rising above his own physical problems and limitations and trying to help others, was he able to find meaning and gratification in his life as a paraplegic.

Domains of Meaning

The three domains of meaning, according to Frankl (1959), are creativity, experience, and attitude.

Meaning can be found in creating something or accomplishing a task. Mr. J.'s contribution to the victims of crime project became a creation that gave meaning to his life. Mr. K.'s task, which focused on tutoring younger relatives, gave meaning to his life.

To experience the true, the good, or the beautiful gives meaning to life. Many dying patients express this phenomenon of enjoying a beautiful sunset or cherishing a meaningful relationship. Listening to beautiful music, for example, can fill one with a sense of meaning greater than the moment.

> Mr. L., a 46-year-old male, was at the office where he was a job counselor when he experienced a dizzy spell, coupled with sudden incoherent speech. The dreaded diagnosis turned out to be a parietal malignant melanoma, which followed a previous lesion six years earlier. He had several good months after surgery, even returning to work, as well as to his volunteer job in the county prison helping prisoners qualify for the G.E.D. (High School Diploma Equivalency). After a while, he reexperienced neurologically disabling symptoms resulting from involvement in the cerebrospinal canal. It seemed that sheer determination brought him back to a semiactive state. He became convinced to take early retirement from his stressful job, and, knowing that his time was limited, to concentrate on doing what he enjoyed. He had for several years indulged his hobby of raising cattle. Now he took more time to be out in the wide open spaces. He enjoyed telling about the "mama cows, the bulls, and the young ones who thought they were bulls." He reflected on the endurance of nature and all its mysteries. He got his city-brother to help him take a load of cattle to market; they were like little boys playing again. Always a family man, he made extraordinary efforts to attend weddings and funerals of relatives to bask in the love of his extended family. He became a house-husband, clipping coupons and studying sales ads in a miraculous conversion from macho to domestic. He admitted he had really enjoyed the experience of life in the last few months. He found meaning through his suffering experience.

Kahn and Steeves (1986) also recount experiences of meaning in hospice patients. Isolated incidents in everyday life occur during which people experience ordinary things differently and, as a result, their suffering seems to be temporarily lifted. These descriptions fit into Frankl's category of experiential meaning. For example, one man dying of prostate cancer had a meaningful experience with music. He tuned in to the big band era and found himself swaying with the music. He felt as if he had become one with the music, a sensation of pleasure powerful enough to allow him to rise above his suffering. It was an experience of meaning, not merely understanding. In the experience, a larger picture came into view, and a transcendence over present problems occurred. The experiences were described as involving mind, body, emotions, and spirit.

The attitude one chooses in reacting to a blow of fate can give meaning to suffering. What health professional has not witnessed dichotomies in attitudes among patients with strikingly similar pathologies? One has a will to live while another is resigned to the role of hopeless victim. Choosing to be courageous, to be joyful, can give meaning to suffering. The way one perceives the suffering experience may be influenced not only by the present suffering experience, but also by the memory of past sufferings—one's own and others'—and by the anticipation of future suffering. An attitude of transcendence is not the same as denying reality or hopeless acceptance. It is not objectifying the illness or distancing oneself from it. Rather, it is making a choice to transcend the tragedy and maintain meaning in each moment.

> *Mr. A. was diagnosed as HIV positive after his lover, Mr. C., died from AIDS. As he lay in the hospital bed with a severe bout of pneumocystic pneumonia, he reflected on the suffering he had recently witnessed so clearly in Mr. C. and knew that the same would eventually be his lot. He had already worked through the anger stage. He reflected on an incident years ago when he was hospitalized following an auto accident and how the competencies of the nurses and doctors, as well as their compassion, had sustained him. This time, the network of his family and friends had grown smaller. He knew he would have to rely more on himself. He determined to remain cheerful and keep a positive attitude toward life. He viewed each new setback as a challenge to remain courageous and to savor each moment he interacted with others.*

The Suffering of the Disabled

Nowhere is there more persistent suffering to be found than in the world of the disabled. Robert Murphy (1987), an anthropologist at Columbia University, portrayed the suffering of the disabled in his book, *The Body Silent*, after he became a quadriplegic as a result of a tumor in the spinal column. He recounted his achievement in enabling himself to "transcend simple physical survival and once again find purpose and joy in living" (p. xi). He found that the "lessons to be learned from paralysis also have profound meaning for our understanding of human culture and the place of the individual in it" (p. 4). He concluded that the "study of paralysis is a splendid arena for viewing this struggle of the individual against society, for the disabled are not a breed apart but a metaphor for the human condition" (p. 5).

He chastised health professionals, "the medical people who have had little curiosity about what I think about my condition" (p. 88). He summarized the suffering of the physically disabled as (1) lowered self-esteem; (2) invasion and occupation of thought by physical deficits; (3) a strong undercurrent of anger; and (4) the acquisition of a new, total, and undesirable identity (p. 108). "The disabled serve as constant, visible reminders to the able-bodied that the society they live in is shot through with inequity and suffering; that they live in a counterfeit paradise; that they too are vulnerable. We represent a fearsome possibility" (p. 117).

He stated, "Paradoxically, my physical deficits have helped me get work done, as I am incapable of doing anything else. All I can do now is read, write, and talk—which is what academics call 'work' " (p. 192).

HELPING THE SUFFERER FIND MEANING: WHAT SUFFERING TEACHES

Coping with Suffering

Finding meaning in unavoidable suffering might be thought of as a type of positive coping. Coping is defined by Lazarus and Folkman (1984, p. 141) as "constantly changing cognitive and behavioral efforts to manage specific external and/or internal demands that are appraised as taxing or exceeding the resources of the person." These authors observed that major stress or crisis sometimes causes people to draw upon adaptive resources they never thought they had.

Qualitative Responses in Suffering

Battenfield (1984) conducted an investigation to define the concept of suffering and to identify a stage of relief for the sufferer. The goal was to design a progressive attitudinal scale with a pinnacle toward which the patient could be counseled. Using Frankl's view of finding meaning in life as the zenith of suffering, a hierarchical framework pyramiding toward Frankl's meaning was drafted. A panel of experts was used, and a design of consensus emerged. It was called "Qualitative Responses Observable in Situations of Suffering." Open-ended interview was used in the field testing of nine adults. Context analysis was used as the methodology of interpretation. Three of the patients exhibited characteristics of finding meaning. In all three, the patients described making a decision about the attitude they would have toward unavoidable suffering. Battenfield suggests that the helper guide the sufferer toward expanding self-awareness, developing unity with nature, strengthening interpersonal values, developing creative activities, or finding joy.

LOGOTHERAPY

Logotherapy, originated by Frankl and expanded by others (Lukas, 1984, 1986; Crumbaugh, 1973; Crumbaugh & Garr, 1979; Starck, 1980), is expressly intended to guide the individual to find meaning and purpose in life. The therapist cannot give meaning to the client, but rather assists the client in finding meaning regardless of the circumstances. Logotherapy's goal is to bring the suffering into connection with a meaning the patient can accept (Lukas, 1986). Frankl (1959) explained logotherapy by stating, "If the psychiatrist is a shrink, the logotherapist is a stretch." The therapist teaches and becomes more involved than in a traditional nondirective approach.

Logotherapy may be used singularly or in combination with other therapies in an eclectic approach. Readiness to work with a logotherapist may be determined by the Purpose in Life (PIL) Test (Crumbaugh & Maholick, 1976) and the Seeking of Noetic Goals (SONG) Test (Crumbaugh, 1977). A low score on the PIL Test, indicating a low sense of meaning and purpose in life, coupled with a high score on the SONG Test, indicating a desire to seek for meaning, suggests a readiness for logotherapy. Each test consists of two parts. The first part has 20 items that the client rates on a seven-point Likert scale. The second part is sentence completion.

Although logotherapy encourages creativity and spontaneity on the part of the therapists, certain techniques have been developed to use in the therapeutic encounter as appropriate. These techniques include paradoxical intention, dereflection, and modifying attitudes.

Paradoxical Intention

Paradoxical intention is a technique in which the therapist encourages the very thing that the client fears or is what Lukas (1984) calls turning a wish upside down. Fears limit one's freedom of spirit and block growth toward meaningful potential. Anticipatory anxiety brings about precisely what one fears. Paradoxical intention is helpful in situations where suffering is caused by feeling trapped in a vicious cycle (Lukas, 1986). The strategy is to embrace the dreaded fear, and thus diffuse it. This can be done literally, such as expressing a wish for what one fears, or it can be done by imaging. This strategy makes use of the human capacity for self-distancing in order to break down the vicious cycle of repetitive harmful behavior (Lukas, 1984). Self-distancing is stepping away from self and viewing the self from outside, perhaps even with humor.

> Mr. C., a C$_4$ quadriplegic, admitted he had not been out of his house in five years, except to the doctor's office or hospital. He seemed content with his hospital bed in the living room where all his extended family could visit. Yet, when asked a question on the Purpose in Life Test, "If you have one wish, what would it be?" he replied, "to buy my own clothes." He did not state a wish to walk again; just to buy his clothes. There was no physical reason that kept him from shopping. He could get out of the house; he could be transported to a shopping mall; he could have someone push his wheelchair anywhere he wanted to go. What was his fear? He was terrified of wetting his pants and not even realizing it. He rejected the idea of having a blanket in his lap—too stereotypical of the wheelchair-bound invalid. The nurse took him through a mental exercise of paradoxical intention—imaging the worst possible situation. "Your catheter becomes disconnected from the leg bag and urine is dripping on the floor as the wetness of your pants creeps upward. You don't feel the wetness and you smile cheerfully at those who stare at you. Next, the leg bag breaks and the whole morning's collection of urine sloshes over the mall floor. People are slipping and sliding, and it is a great disaster. Can you imagine this scene?" By this time, nurse and patient are laughing at the absurdity. This exercise diffused the patient's unfounded fear and, after one failed attempt, he did venture out to shop. His most amazing discovery was that the salespeople invited him back! He enjoyed the day immensely, and this was the first of many social outings.

Dereflection

The second logotherapeutic technique is dereflection, which aims at reducing unnecessary suffering. It counteracts the behavior of hyper-reflection so often seen in troubled individuals. Lukas (1986) uses dereflection to lead clients to see the multitude of values that lie beyond their limited view. Dereflection makes use of the human capacity of self-transcendence and is effective where problems are caused by excessive self-observation. The technique frees the patient from unhealthy self-reflection and therapeutically reorders attention. Such a move widens one's circle of meaning. "The essence of dereflection is substituting something positive for something negative" (Lukas, 1984, p. 10). For example, Lukas (1984) described a young patient 16 years of age who suspected himself to be homosexual after one brief encounter. He was filled with anxiety and withdrew into himself. He became increasingly shy, unsure of himself, and trapped in self-diagnosis. Lukas gave him an assignment—to do something nice for one person every day, regardless of who it was, and to take accurate notes of the reaction of others. At first he resisted, wondering why he should go out of his way to be nice when others were not nice to him and wondering what this had to do with his problem. Eventually, he complied and found that his observation of others was a dereflection of his own self-observation. He deemphasized his own sexual identity and lost his fears. Although not part of the therapist's plan, he did, in fact, in one of his good deeds, meet a young lady and soon thereafter canceled his therapy sessions because he was so busy with his social life.

Modulation of Attitude

The third technique useful in logotherapy is modifying attitudes, which enables clients to see value in an unalterable situation that is causing suffering (Lukas, 1986). One's attitude is not determined by the situation, but by the person. When a spouse dies and one is grieving, it may help to ask what would have happened if it had been the other way around and the spouse was left alone to cope. Usually, the griever expresses a feeling that it would have been more difficult for the deceased spouse to have survived.

Socratic dialogue. The use of Socratic dialogue is a way to modify attitudes. By asking questions of the client, the therapist stimulates new thinking in the client. Clients come to resist and defeat their old attitudes. The therapist leads the client through phases of being unsure and questioning the attitudes that have them in a stuck position. Use of the

"Copernican switch" is also helpful in modifying attitudes. It is not we who should question life, but rather life that asks us questions and awaits our response. When a client is recounting his sufferings, the therapist may ask the following questions:

- How can you choose to respond to the challenges life has given you?
- What have you learned from these experiences?
- If you could be free of this problem, which of your loved ones would you give it to?

Use of parables/fables. Travelbee (1971) suggests several indirect and direct therapeutic techniques for assisting patients to find meaning in suffering. These techniques were developed on the basis of her observations that the ill person's major problem is the inability to accept his or her own humanness, frailty, and vulnerability. Indirect communication techniques include (a) the parable method, (b) the veiled-problem approach, and (c) the personal experience approach. Direct methods are (a) questioning in jest, but with intent and purpose; (b) relating opinions purposefully; and (c) discussing beliefs by great teachers and leaders. She advocates stories such as the parable of the mustard seed in which the mother, seeking a mustard seed from a house where no one had died or suffered in order to cure her own dying son, concludes that no home is exempt (Travelbee, 1971). Parables, fables, and other provocative thoughts have been used with spinal-cord injured clients who have suffered a devastating, permanent disability to invoke motivation to choose a positive attitude (Starck, 1980).

The veiled-problem approach is a thin disguise of the patient's problem that allows the patient to react more impersonally and to be more objective about the problem under discussion. For example, discussing patients who have breast cancer may be a veiled way of facing the fact that "I have breast cancer."

The personal experience approach negates what health professionals are taught (i.e., to never, under any circumstances, talk about themselves). However, as a fresh approach, sharing personal experiences that have an intent and purpose may be therapeutic.

Questioning in jest, a direct method, is used to assist persons to acknowledge their human condition. This technique requires a trusting relationship and skill as to timing and appropriateness. An example given by Travelbee (1971) is asking a stroke patient struggling with physical therapy, "What makes you think you are Superman?".

Explaining as a technique may not be effective since emotions, rather than logical reasoning, may prevail. Giving correct information, however, assists one in sorting out meaning and options.

Discussing beliefs about the nature of human beings, the origins and destiny of humankind, and the ultimate purpose for existing may be helpful for some patients. Teachings of great leaders may be useful.

Various health care professionals report the use of therapeutic metaphors and storytelling as summarized by Larkin, a pain management nurse, and Zahourek, a nurse who works in an out-patient alcoholism treatment clinic (Larkin & Zahourek, 1988). Therapeutic storytelling can include fairy tales, parables, or anecdotes from real life. The therapeutic value lies in two realms: (a) absorption and (b) dissociation. One's personal situation can be reframed in storytelling. Suggestions for a change in attitude and behavior can be given because of the third party nature with its safe emotional distance. Client resistance is less in the nonconfrontive or indirect mode that third person reference provides. Storytelling is a nonthreatening communication technique and the patient is especially receptive if in a hypersuggestible state, highly focused on self, as is often the case with hospitalized patients.

The 12-step program of Alcoholics Anonymous incorporates storytelling by individuals who describe their lives, their disease, and their recovery. In the process, there is benefit to the storyteller and the audience.

Collison and Miller (1987) used imaging of the future in work with dying patients and their families, on the basis of the premise that an inherent developmental task in the course of dying is a search for meaning and purpose in one's existence. The art of imaging future events and living through them visually can increase the likelihood of successful grief resolution in family survivors. An example is to encourage dying patients and their families to discuss the impact of their lives on each other, how they will contribute to future generations, and what their, as yet unborn, great grandchildren might be like.

LOVE AND CARING

One caveat of profound basic and general meaning must be mentioned and stressed here before closing. It is that no matter which therapeutic technique is used, within the context of healing through finding meaning in suffering, it is essential, the *sine qua non* for the process to work, that the health professional in a symbiotic relationship care for the patient, not just take care of the patient. This idea was expressed succinctly by Paracelsus, a great physician from antiquity, who clearly recognized the need for a very special dedication and commitment that characterized the art of healing when he said, "Where there is no love there is no art" (Van Eys and McGovern, 1988, p. 7). Likewise, Florence Nightingale, the founder of modern nursing, emphasized love, duty, and kindness. In modern times, that concept has been implicit in the works of many physicians and nurses. Love, in this context, could best be defined as caring for someone and for that person's welfare in an involved, meaningful way.

Caring then is not complete without assisting the patient in the search for meaning in suffering experiences. Suffering becomes a learning opportunity, a potential for growth toward full humanness.

REFERENCES

Adler, A. (1928). *Understanding human nature*. London: George Allen and Unwin, Ltd.

Bardwell, R. (1986). Attribution theory and behavior change: Ideas for nursing settings. *Journal of Nursing Education, 25*(3), 122–124.

Battenfield, B.L. (1984). Suffering—A conceptual description and content analysis of an operational schema. *Image: The Journal of Nursing Scholarship, 16*(2), 36–41.

Brubaker, B.H. (1988). An attributional analysis of weight outcomes. *Nursing Research, 37*(5), 282–287.

Carroll, J.S., Perkowitz, W.T., Lurigio, A.J., & Weaver, F.M. (1987). Sentencing goals, causal attributions, ideology, and personality. *Journal of Personality and Social Psychology, 52*(1), 107–118.

Cassell, E.J. (1982). The nature of suffering and the goals of medicine. *New England Journal of Medicine, 306*(11), 639–645.

Cassell, E.J. (1983). The relief of suffering. *Archives of Internal Medicine, 149*, 522–523.

Collison, C., & Miller, S. (1987). Using images of the future in grief work. *Image: The Journal of Nursing Scholarship, 19*(1), 9–11.

Corenblum, B. (1983). Reactions to alcohol-related marital violence. Effects of one's own abuse experience and alcohol problems on causal attributions. *Journal of Studies on Alcohol, 44*(4), 665–674.

Crumbaugh, J.C. (1973). *A guide to self-fulfillment through logoanalysis*. Chicago: Nelson-Hall.

Crumbaugh, J.C. (1977). *Manual of instructions for seeking noetic goals test*. Murphreesboro, TN: Psychometric Affiliates.

Crumbaugh, J.C., & Garr, G.L. (1979). Treatment of alcoholics with logotherapy. *The International Journal of Addictions, 14*, 845–851.

Crumbaugh, J.C., & Maholick, L.T. (1976). *Purpose in life test.* Murphreesboro, TN: Psychometric Affiliates.

Ducette, J., & Keane, A. (1984). "Why me?": An attributional analysis of a major illness. *Research in Nursing and Health,* (7), 257–264.

Frankl, V.E. (1959). *Man's search for meaning: An introduction to logotherapy.* New York: Beacon Press.

Kahn, D.L., & Steeves, R.H. (1986). The experience of suffering: Conceptual clarification and theoretical definition. *Journal of Advanced Nursing, 11,* 623–631.

Karanci, N.A. (1986). Causal attributions for psychological illness among Turkish psychiatric in-patients and their relationships with hope. *International Journal of Social Psychiatry, 33*(4), 3–12.

Larkin, D.M., & Zahourek, R.P. (1988). Therapeutic storytelling and metaphors. *Holistic Nurse Practitioner, 2*(3), 45–53.

Lazarus, R., & Folkman, S. (1984). *Stress, appraisal, and coping.* New York: Springer Publishing Co.

Lukas, E. (1984). *Meaningful living.* Cambridge: Schenkman Publishing Company.

Lukas, E. (1986). *Meaning in suffering: Comfort in crisis through logotherapy.* Berkeley: Institute of Logotherapy Press.

Murphy, R.F. (1987). *The body silent.* New York: H. Holt.

Peterson, L.C. (1984). Attribution theory and its application in crisis intervention. *Perspectives in Psychiatric Care, 22*(4), 133–136.

Rossler, W., & Lackus, B. (1986). Cognitive disorders in schizophrenics viewed from the attribution theory. *European Archives of Psychiatry and Neurological Sciences, 235*(6), 382–387.

Selder, F. (1989). Life transition theory: The resolution of uncertainty. *Nursing and Health Care, 10*(8), 437–451.

Starck, P.L. (1980). Maslow's needs and the spinal cord injured patient. *Association of Rehabilitation Nurses' Journal, 5*(5), 17–20.

Travelbee, J. (1971). *Interpersonal aspects of nursing.* Philadelphia: F.A. Davis Company.

Van Eys, J., & McGovern, J.P. (1988). *The doctor as a person.* Springfield, IL: Charles C. Thomas.

Weiner, B. (1988). Attribution theory and attributional therapy: Some theoretical observations and suggestions. *British Journal of Clinical Psychology, 27*(1), 99–104.

4

Technologic Environments as Causes of Suffering: The Ethical Context

Stanley J. Reiser

We meet patients as strangers. Increasingly in modern health care, relationships are formed at the point of illness. Patients entering the domain of health care come to a country divided into sovereign territories. Each territory, or specialty, has particular requirements of illness for the patient to receive the passport of entry. Each territory has a unique spectrum of technologies to offer, which focus only on certain features of illness. Thus the medical domain and its particularized cultures present formidable obstacles to finding health care centered on people, not parts. The first portion of this essay explores the causes and consequences for suffering of a specialized approach to illness.

The origin of modern specialization is a theory of illness. Without it, specialization and its acceptance by patients is not conceivable. This theory is the anatomic construct of illness.

Dissection is its basis, an activity reviled in cultures modern and ancient. Its ascendance thus required significant rationale and justification by those who were its advocates. In the mid-18th century, the study of human anatomy as it was altered by disease received a formulation that began its climb to a dominant view. G. B. Morgagni published in 1761 his masterwork *The Seats and Causes of Diseases Investigated by Anatomy.* In this work, Morgagni set forth case studies divided into three parts. The first recounted the history of the patient's illness, and its culmination in death. The second described structural alterations wrought on the body by the illness, revealed by the dissection scalpel. The final section discussed the relation between the symptoms felt and seen by the patient during life and the anatomic changes found in the body after death.

Morgagni declared that this clinico-pathologic correlation was the key to explaining the causes of diseases. The work demonstrated a disease to be the result of discernible structural change and thus advanced the theoretical idea that diseases had, as the title of the work states, "seats" in the body. The anatomic perspective directs the mind and senses to search the body for structural alterations, to seek places that are defective. This view propagates a question that has become the hallmark of medicine— "Where is the disease?" It fosters the notion that diseases create anatomic changes, which not only produce the symptoms that are illness but which leave fingerprints that skillful medical detectives can discern and identify.

The power of this view to reduce the confusion that the plethora of structural and functional signs of disease creates by formulating a clear relation between them, and stating it in the clear conceptual framework Morgagni provided, rather quickly swept away older disease concepts and became dominant. By the turn of the 19th century, physicians and scientists were thinking increasingly of diseases as locally defined phenomena. The stage was thus set for a technologic revolution that would further hold this theory in place.

This revolution stemmed from the idea that if localized structural change in the body was a gold standard upon which disease would be identified, it followed that the time to find such changes should be before the body was matter for the anatomist's scalpel. This meant that the medical climate of that time fostered noninvasive innovations designed to pierce the opaque shell of the living body to discern the lesions within.

The first, most significant, and prototypic invention to begin this movement was made in 1816, by a young French doctor, Rene Laennec. Like other physicians of his day, Laennec gathered the facts of a patient's illness from the story of a patient's life. The doctor was a biographer, who focused on the events surrounding the onset of illness to glean their meaning. Technology was excluded from the process of diagnosis, since its application—both the physical presence of the tool and the action of physical examination—betokened the status of a laborer, tradesman, or farmer, the quintessential users of tools.

A typical history read as follows:

Alice Hurthwaite, aged 15, was admitted into the Dispensary on the 11th of June 1805, labouring under violent pain in the right side of the abdomen, about the middle of the external oblique muscle, accompanied with great thirst, increased heat, frequent shiverings, a quick pulse, nausea, and vomiting. The account that she gave of herself was, that she was seized suddenly with the pain on the 1st of June, and with difficulty walked a few hundred yards from the place where she was in service to her mother's cottage. Of her own accord she took some opening medicine that produced a good deal of purging, which still continues. She feels most easy when the abdominal muscles are relaxed, the knees being brought towards the chin. She does not recollect having received any injury on the abdomen, and has previously enjoyed good health. She is tall, and rather thin. [Reiser, 1978]

On this historic day in 1816 when the place of biography in medicine would be challenged, Laennec was facing a clinical dilemma. He could not determine from the ordinary forms of examination—mainly the patient's history—the precise nature of the heart condition from which she suffered. He then thought of a method of evaluation he had studied from the Hippocratic literature, where physicians would place their ear on the patient's chest to determine the state of the things within. The mores of the day against physical contact on the patient, however, caused him to suspend this idea. Another thought occurred. He remembered that sound may be augmented when passing through solid objects. His mind fused the two thoughts. He seized a sheath of paper from the table beside the bed, rolled it tightly into a tube, placed one end to his ear and the other end to the patient's chest. When distinct sounds of the heartbeat passed to his ear, Laennec realized that he had discovered a technologic window to a new diagnostic universe.

Armed with this tube, soon converted into a wooden cylinder one foot long and pierced down the center by an opening to enhance the conduction of sound, Laennec went from bed to bed at the Necker Hospital in Paris, carefully exploring the patients' chests for the different sounds created by disorders within. When a patient died, Laennec would follow the body to autopsy to learn which structural changes revealed by the scalpel produced the sounds created in the chest of the living patient. With these clinico-pathologic correlations repetitively made and meticulously described, he produced after three years, in 1819, a work, *On Mediate Auscultation* (1821), in which he described his findings to medicine and touted the instrument that had made it possible—the stethoscope.

In this work, physiological signals take center stage as the physician focuses on the sounds instead of the story of illness. This new orientation was argued for on the basis of evidence. When asked to choose between the two alternatives, evidence gathered by self or evidence gathered by others, and when further this self-gathered evidence was discrete and repetitively heard sounds linked to the gold standard of the anatomic lesion, while that gathered by others (patients) was remembered events and sensations linked with and verifiable by no one or thing, physicians naturally chose themselves.

The distancing of the physician from the life of the patient continued during the 19th century, as an increasing array of diagnostic technology was invented. These technologies essentially aided the doctor's sensory probing of the body's cavity. Most were scopes, which allowed the medical gaze to enter openings in the body to search for illness within, such as the gastroscope, the laryngoscope, and the ophthalmoscope. So skillful had physicians become in detecting the physical signs that denoted structural change that one doctor—Arthur Conan Doyle—fashioned the first great literary detective, Sherlock Holmes, after his instructor in surgery, Sir Joseph Bell. Doyle's detective applied to the process of catching criminals the same deductive reasoning used by doctors to find diseases.

Up to the end of the 19th century, though focused on the patient's physical self, the doctor at least took the whole of the patient into account. The generalist yet reigned. However, the seeds of change had been sowed by the growing sophistication of health care technology, the skill required to apply it well, and the growth of knowledge that science and thus technology were producing. The first decade of the 20th century produced an increasing interest in specialization. It provided an answer to the troubling issue of staying up-to-date as helpful information and techniques proliferated. By 1929, about 22,000 physicians who were listed in the American Medical Association directory described themselves as specialists; if those regarding themselves as part-time specialists are added in, almost a third of all doctors were self-identified as specialists (Stevens,

1971). The specialization physicians pursued was taken up by the other health professions as the century wore on, particularly nursing and allied health. Nursing offers a myriad of specialists at the masters degree level. The allied health professions grew in number so that by the middle 1970s, there were 152 identifiable disciplines. If one totals up all recognized specializations at this point in time, the emerging figure is over 200 (Wilson & Neuhauser, 1982).

The 20th century also produced another view of illness that has had as its effect a distancing of practitioners from the lives of their patients—the technology of the cipher. At the same time that the techniques of physical examination were gaining ascendance over the patient's story, mid-19th-century scientists and physicians were developing tools to monitor the body's physiological changes. The data generated by them were numeric and graphic in form. The earliest of these technologies were chemical analyses of body fluids and machines that measured body functions such as·blood pressure.

During the 20th century, these technologies increased and improved so that they now reside at the pinnacle of diagnostic choice. This is because such cipher-driven technologies have several significant features. First, the evidence is easily passed from person to person without ambiguity, and second, it can be precisely stated. For example, before the blood test that provided hemoglobin content numerically, it was determined by evaluating the color of the nail bed. Descriptions such as pink, rosy pink, and pale pink filled patients' charts in connection with the hemoglobin. Such evidence, however, travels badly. What to one nurse or doctor at the bedside might appear pink, to another might be rosy pink. What was one to think upon reviewing a record containing such comments, when the clinicians could not personally observe the nail bed and reach a judgment. In essence, to rely on adjectives to depict clinical events was to depend on imprecise description—a fault remedied by numerical data.

The qualities of group transmission and precision captivated the attention of clinicians; using such evidence seemed to place health care more in the realm of a science than an art. As these analyses of the physiological and biochemical functions of the body grew, so did our understanding of what was wrong.

This advance came at a price, however. The portrait of illness drawn with numerical and graphic evidence omitted features that came from the subjective life of the patient. Imprecise and subjective, these features became increasingly irrelevant in the construction of diagnoses and in the development of therapies.

Thus, the technology of health care, by fragmenting its delivery among a spectrum of specialists and codifying its view of illness in the form of ciphers and graphs, created as an unintended by-product the patient as stranger. Such detachment of the life from the illness of the patient has as its effect suffering.

Patients unable to gain the attention of health care providers to the facets of an illness that affects the basic self, suffer from this barrier to communication. When we are sick, we are like a traveler on a voyage with an uncertain destination. Each new symptom felt, each new medical opinion voiced, may change our course and take us where we do not wish to go. Medical navigators to explain these diversions in our voyage would do much to relieve the anxiety and fear, which perhaps constitute the main burdens of illness. The diversion away from persons and the stories of their lives to special sites in the body depicted objectively with numbers or images prevents health care personnel from assuaging this dimension of illness.

I wish now to turn to a second kind of problem the growth of technology creates—the dilemma of the lingering patient. Its essence is that as the technology of rescue from physiologic collapse has grown more powerful, we are increasingly able to save lives but not people.

Beginning in the 1950s we began to develop the first technology that had the power to sustain lives threatened by a special insult of illness or injury—the artificial respirator. Before this time, patients whose power to breathe was compromised severely often died in a short time. This new technology permitted the sustaining of this vital function, allowing the body time to heal the damage and recover this function. However, in a number of cases such a healing did not take place and health care providers, patients, and families were faced with an ethical crisis of what to do. In many of these cases, patients had lapsed into coma from which there seemed no hope of recovery. Here then was life without experience, life without consciousness, life without relationships. How was it to be treated and encountered by all concerned?

This problem evoked then, and now, tremendous anguish (Pope Pius XII, 1977), not only the anguish of those who experience it, but also those who fear it in their future. For the latter, instruments have been developed to prevent this problem. Living wills are tools through which we can broadly specify conditions under which we would choose not to be kept alive. These instruments, created in the early 1970s, were the first in which persons specifically restrained health care providers from intervening to save or maintain their lives. The threat of lingering had become sufficient to warrant this prohibition.

We now have an increasingly varied group of ways to sustain life functions. Thus, an enlarging number of people can become trapped in the dilemma of the interminable machine—what is appropriate action to gain release?

This suffering is sometimes felt by the patient, but increasingly also by families of patients who are no longer capable of self-decision or even recognition. These families are trapped in technologic environments, where communication is difficult or impossible, and where heroism and guilt are bound in actions taken and contemplated.

Families and practitioners suffer together in the shadow of uncertainty about what is ethical in the technologic environments we create. How can we treat them? Dialogue is crucial. Too often these intensive care settings render it difficult. Either there is a lack of space, or the machines themselves command the attention of the staff and divert them from important discussions. Once again, just as ciphers direct us away from the patient's story, the technology of intensive care focuses our efforts on the physiologic dimensions of illness.

Alternative means of care also are crucial in resolving some of these dilemmas. Perhaps the worst prospect for clinicians is that of having nothing to offer a patient or family. What then to do when intensive technology fails to alter the underlying mechanisms of illness? In the absence of an alternative we tend to keep the machines going.

At the Hermann Hospital in Houston, an alternative has been developed—the Supportive Care Protocols (Appendix 4-1). With the help of the hospital ethics committee, we have developed a viewpoint that the protocol embodies, that when reversal of illness is no longer possible, relief of suffering remains.

The Supportive Care Protocols specify actions that clinical staff can undertake to relieve suffering and actively treat the patient. When it is no longer appropriate—because it is not beneficial—to treat the patient with life-sustaining technology, we can still relieve pain, provide psychological help, move limbs to prevent stiffening, turn patients regularly to prevent bedsores, give oxygen to improve stamina, provide appropriate nutrition, and so forth.

We have found that when staff are presented with positive, definitive steps they can take to actively treat patients who can no longer benefit from life-supporting therapy, they are enabled to turn their attention to appropriate care. In addition to the patient, staff attention in such situations must be directed also at families. The families should be enabled to face the ending of a life; they should not be allowed to dwell in the realm of false hope, in which life-sustaining measures are requested and fought for. Too often, the love and guilt of family combine to create serious mistakes in clinical decisions about patients. Many families suffer the pangs of regret over past failings in relationships, and deal with them at this time by asking the staff to never stop trying. Rather than accede to what is a request for the wrong therapy, the staff should address the suffering of the family with the appropriate means—ones that properly treat the patient and help the family to let go.

The achievements of technology in health care have been spectacular, and the promise of the future is great. As a by-product of its introduction into health care, technology has influenced how we see illness, and what features of it should command our attention. In this respect, technology has produced problems for us. These are problems with remedies, how-ever, principal among which is to refocus our gaze on the suffering that is the subjective experience of illness.

REFERENCES

Laennec, R.T.H. (1821). *On diseases of the chest* (J. Forbes, Trans.). London: T. & G. Underwood.

Morgagni, G.B. (1960). *The seats and causes of diseases investigated by anatomy* (B. Alexander, Trans.). New York: Macmillan.

Pope Pius XII, "The Prolongation of Life" in S.J. Reiser, A.J. Dyck, & W.J. Curran, *Ethics in medicine: Historical perspectives and contemporary changes*. Cambridge, MA: MIT Press.

Reiser, S.J. (1978). *Medicine and the reign of technology*. New York: Cambridge University Press.

Stevens, R. (1971). *American medicine and the public interest*. New Haven: Yale University Press.

Wilson, F.A., & Neuhauser, D. (Eds.) (1982). *Health services in the United States*, 2nd ed. Cambridge, MA: Ballinger.

APPENDIX 4-1

Supportive Care Protocols
(Hermann Hospital)

1. Purpose

   1.1 To establish guidelines for the implementation of decisions concerning supportive care protocols for terminally ill patients.

2. Policy

   2.1 The hospital's policy is to provide high quality health care, with goals of sustaining life in conformity with medical and ethical standards. However, it must be recognized that patients and their families (or other surrogate decision-makers) may make decisions about health care that include changing, limiting, declining, or discontinuing a particular treatment, whether life-sustaining or otherwise.

   2.2 The hospital's philosophy is to promote and protect patient dignity in the face of impending death by instituting medically appropriate care. Comfort will be maintained at all times through the provisions of analgesics, hygienic care, and other appropriate medical and nursing care to all patients.

   2.3 Total support, including cardiopulmonary resuscitation by a Code Team, will be provided to all patients until formal supportive care orders are written. Supportive care orders written by the attending physician or responsible house officer will be recognized by the nursing staff. If the orders are written by the house officer, they must be countersigned by the attending physician within twenty-four hours.

   2.4 Supportive care orders shall remain in effect until

      a. cancelled by written order; or

      b. the patient is transferred to another patient care unit due to a change in the patient's acuity (i.e., same circumstances that cancel other medical orders).

   2.5 Decisions concerning terminal care orders should consider the "Ethical Guidelines for Withholding or Withdrawing Medical Treatment" (1986) as approved by the Institutional Ethics Committee (IEC), Medical Board, and Board of Trustees. The IEC shall be available for consultation to all practitioners.

2.6 Supportive care orders do not determine the unit in which the
patient is treated. Factors determining place of treatment should
be individualized and should include medical and nursing needs
of the patient as well as bed availability. Supportive care orders do
not automatically dictate transfer off an intensive care unit.

3. Documentation and Definitions

3.1 *Supportive Care Protocol I*. Patients for whom this order is written
are treated vigorously, but only to the point of cardiopulmonary
arrest. In this instance, CPR will not be administered, a Code
Team will not be called. Alternative orders which will be recognized to have the same meaning are "No Code," "DNR," or "Do
Not Resuscitate." Orders for modified codes, slow codes, chemical
codes, etc., are unacceptable and will not be honored.

3.2 *Supportive Care Protocol II*. Patients for whom this order is written
will receive no extraordinary measures. Examples of extraordinary
measures are life support with assisting devices, arrhythmia control, CPR, artificial or mechanical organs, transplantation of
organs or tissues (including blood or blood products), invasive
monitoring, parenteral nutrition, and IV infusion of vasoactive
and antibiotic drugs. These patients will receive specific nursing
care for comfort, hygiene, bowel care, skin care, passive range of
motion and positioning, catheter care, analgesia, suctioning,
intake for comfort (including parenteral hydration when appropriate), oxygen for comfort, and facilitated access of patient and
family to clergy or other appropriate support. Alternative orders
which will be recognized to have the same meaning are "Comfort
Measures Only" and "No Extraordinary Measures."

5

Is Our Society Insensitive to Suffering?

Roger J. Bulger

"Is our society insensitive to suffering?" This ought to be a question which most concerned citizens should be willing to take a crack at answering. On the grounds that an attempt at addressing the question will serve as a stimulant for corporate deliberation, I am willing to play the role of the concerned citizen attempting to formulate an answer. Since it is a part of the human condition to suffer, however one defines it, we ought all to be equally qualified to consider suffering. Health professionals, doctors and nurses in particular, should have a dramatically larger experience with the suffering of those others we call "patients," a word which means "sufferer."

DEFINITIONS

It seems to me that we would do well to accept Eric Cassell's (1982) definition of suffering, a definition that embraces the concept of a threat to the human being's life or the integration of her or his persona, a fear and feeling that goes beyond and is distinct from pain. The linkage of suffering with a fear of death, of separation, of isolation is made by a variety of authors (Osterweis, Solomon, & Green, 1984; Feifel, 1965). Ernest Becker (who at least at one time in his life viewed the human race as a random biologic event occurring between two ice ages), in his last book, *Escape from Evil* (1975), builds his case for the doing of evil by humans upon the fact that people are the only animals in the kingdom who know in advance that they will die. Humans seek immortality because they fear not death so much as meaningless extinction. The attempt to avoid the suffering of meaninglessness, then, for Becker has driven humanity to impose cultural venues for achieving perpetual meaning; it is these efforts which invariably cause additional and unnecessary evil and suffering. Fortunato (1987), in his book on the spiritual dilemma which the AIDS epidemic has forced upon society, underscores the idea of the sufferer being excluded or feeling isolated from society. When death becomes inevitable, societal support systems seem to whither away and the suffering of the individual is, therefore, dramatically heightened. Vieth (1988) also deals with these ideas in terms of their theological implications. Since at least some part of our society is influenced by theological considerations, these too should be a part of our calculus in considering the degree of society's insensitivity to suffering.

In his book *Stories of Sickness* (1987), Howard Brody has refined the definition of suffering somewhat, concluding that it comes with a loss of the patient's self-respect. Therefore, suffering can be minimized if self-respect is maintained, and it can be made infinite if self-respect is totally annihilated. It is noteworthy that Margaret Mead equated suffering with exclusion in a (1970) book written toward the end of her life, which sought to address the new relationships between generations in the postmodern era. She concluded that all the suffering citizens must be included in the fabric of society so as to reduce their suffering as well as to increase the strength of the society, reminding one of William Blake's famous lines:

> *The dog starv'd at his master's gate,*
> *Predicts the ruin of the state.*

Thus, the anthropologist and the poet ennoble us with their perceptions of how society must approach suffering. Philosopher Stanley Hauerwas in his (1985) book *The Suffering Presence* points out that our investment in health care can be seen as the society's corporate reaching out toward its suffering members, seeking to bridge the gap between the fully integrated, healthy majority and the unfortunate minority of the sick and dying. In these terms, we can at last take pride that we spend three times as much of our wealth on health than do our British cousins, and that we are first in the world in the size of our efforts to reach out to the suffering presence.

Obviously, such an interpretation is not quite right. We know that we Americans really are not investing in health just to bridge the chasm between the healthy and the suffering, but rather, in part, to defeat suffering and to deny death. We select as medical students people who have the strongest death-denying instincts of all their peers. An English friend of mine rarely misses an opportunity to chide his American physician colleagues and our whole society by saying, "In America, you think that death is optional!" Those of us who have lived through the past four or five decades of extraordinary medical progress must admit that our thrust has indeed been to defeat disease and death. When we fail to do so, we tend to withdraw and consider ourselves all too often as failures, thus enhancing the sense of separation the patients experience from the rest of us. To the extent that our very technologic achievements heighten this sense of failure when cure is not possible, then Hauerwas's vision of medicine as the societal bridge between the healthy and the diseased is severely compromised. Instead of being caregivers, palpably fallible but committed to seeing the patient through, the medical establishment has become a contractor for success and failure; such contracting leads to litigation and adversariness, the exact antithesis of bridge-building of the sort Hauerwas envisions.

An analysis of the whole society and its relative sensitivity or insensitivity to suffering is beyond my abilities and technical reach, but our hopeless pluralism emboldens me to think that no one can write such a definitive analysis; thus perhaps I can contribute by reflecting on some perspectives on our society as seen by average Americans looking through differing prisms. For clarity of presentation, I will talk about these perspectives as though they were true explanations or true factors in any analysis, but keep in mind the subjectivity of the prisms I have selected, the qualitative nature of the observations, and the fact that I am attempting to interpret things through the eyes of some personally envisioned "average American." It should come as no surprise that some of these perceptions may run counter to one another. My hope in using this technique is that by looking at suffering from the perspective of this variety of particularly American characteristics as they affect the average citizen, we might begin to approach a better answer to the question of societal insensitivity to suffering. I have identified nine societal prisms through which to glimpse a reflection on suffering.

THE JEFFERSON-FRANKLIN PARADOX

The first of these is made up of those most fundamental of American values: life; liberty; the pursuit of happiness, individuality, and self-sufficiency (or what I have come to think of as the Jefferson-Franklin Paradox). It is well for us to remember that most people who came to America came because they were poor, persecuted, or desperately unhappy with their native country's government. We are a nation of people who distrust the collectivity, especially as it is reflected in the federal government. We have had generations of success in getting out of the ghetto, of believing in the benefits of individual efforts to better oneself. Americans have seen everyone's standard of living go up through westward expansion to new frontiers, by technologic innovation through the industrial age and into the postindustrial era, and now we are now paused in some confusion on the brink of the space frontier.

We are a nation of activists. No problem need go unsolved for very long; the worst conundrums can be defeated by our genius and industry. When it comes to disease, we seem to relish the most dramatic of innovations aimed at the saving of even one life. Our commitment to the individual goes for health care organization and expenditure as well. Our cultural expectation is that everyone should have as many years as possible to enjoy life, liberty, and the pursuit of happiness. I will quote briefly from Charles Murray's book, *In Pursuit Of Happiness and Good Government*:

> *Happiness was not Thomas Jefferson's idiosyncratic choice of words, nor was "pursuit of happiness" a rhetorical flourish to round out the clause. For the Founders, "happiness" was the obvious word to use because it was obvious to them that the pursuit of happiness is at the center of man's existence, and that to permit man to pursue happiness is the central justification of government—the "object" of government as James Madison wrote in The Federalist No. 62. . . . John Adams calmly asserted that*

*"Upon this point all speculative politicians will agree, that the happiness
of society is the end of Government, as all divines and moral philosophers
will agree that the happiness of the individual is the end of man. [Murray,
1988]*

The implications for the societal view of suffering are even greater
when one juxtaposes these ideas with the concerns of de Tocqueville
about the possible future implications for the American nation if such
rampant individualism as that which Ben Franklin seemed to epitomize
should gain favor (as compared with the greater sense of community
associated with Thomas Jefferson and John Winthrop). De Tocqueville
saw in us in 1835 the future flowering of splendid individual isolation
germinating from the seeds of Poor Richard's Almanac. The philosophy
embodied in the phrase "God helps those who help themselves!" worried
de Tocqueville, who saw in the middle 19th century a growing cadre of
Americans who believed that with their family and their gun and their
good sense and industry they could handle the world without any other
need for community. Robert Bellah and colleagues (1985), in analyzing
the America of the 1980s, believe de Tocqueville to have been prophetic.
    Considering these forces alone, it should come as no surprise if our busy
new nation has had too much going on to waste any time on death or its
surrogate, suffering; rather, death and suffering were to be forestalled,
delayed, or defeated completely. To focus upon them is almost
unpatriotic, because our very Declaration of Independence tells us to
pursue happiness. After all, the world has other cultures from which to
learn about handling suffering.

THE BUSINESS SCHOOL PERSPECTIVE

The second of our nine societal prisms is the cornerstone of much of
what has characterized American behavior and success in the modern (or
what could be called "the Business School Perspective") era, that is,
efficiency, organization, and linear behavior. We work hard; we move a
lot; we sacrifice much in the name of efficiency, greater productivity, and
greater profits. When death occurs to a family member, one is supposed
to get over it after a day or two and return to work with a minimum of
inconvenience for one's co-workers. Men do not cry and now women are

not supposed to either, all of which creates a context in which prolonged suffering seems an unseemly intrusion on others and often suggests that suicide may be the kindest thing one can do in some situations for one's friends and colleagues.

THE VINCE LOMBARDI PRISM

The third (or "Vince Lombardi") prism is the enshrinement of the "fighting spirit" as the epitome of the American character. We admire fighters, not the least because so many of our forebears literally fought their ways out of poverty and lives of ignorance and hardship to attain better things. So, too, most of us have a sense, at some level or another, not only that God helps those who help themselves but that God loves a fighter. Persons who do not fight their disease, we fear, are losers and usually die more rapidly. Children with cancer are shown films suggesting that their phagocytes must destroy the cancer cells, if the disease is to be conquered, and that the children can facilitate that by getting good and mad at the cancer cells. Insofar as a good fighter should not be afraid, there is a tendency to ignore the difficult issues posed by death and suffering or the fear of personal dissolution.

Further, and perhaps most destructively, when suffering cannot be avoided and death seems unavoidable, the sufferers may tend to feel they have failed in their efforts to ward off the evil being experienced.

THE GRETA GARBO GESTALT

The fourth prism is what I have come to think of as the Greta Garbo ("I want to be alone") Gestalt—the decline of community and the decimation of the sense of belonging to a larger group. Much damage has been done to our social ligatures which are, as Dahrendorf (1979) has shown us, the ties that bind us to church, to nation, to place and hometown, to profession, to club or college, and certainly to family and spouse. We have even bastardized our sense of community in the voting booth, where we have tended toward voting for our own special interests, believing perhaps that we cannot really care for one another, doubting our own capacities to incorporate suffering into our collective social life. If suffering is separation, and relief from suffering is a reincorporation with the group, all this disintegration of societal ligatures of all sorts can only tend to make our culture more and more unresponsive and insensitive to suffering in general and in its many particular forms.

THE AYATOLLAH KHOMEINI– MOTHER THERESA DIPOLE

Fifth is the theological prism, a prism which gives us a God of Authority or, in contrast, possibly One involved with relations, with nurturing, and with process (a contrast I like to refer to as the Ayatollah Khomeini— Mother Theresa Dipole). To the extent that one perceives suffering as evil and evil as the antithesis of good and, therefore, of God, then it becomes obvious in the view of some average Americans that at some level suffering is payment for sin and the sufferer deserves to be shunned and to lose dignity before the rest of society. On the other hand, suffering can be viewed as something which offers challenges to individuals as well as to societies. Just as specific individual sufferers can rise to the occasion and find new ways to integrate their lives and to become self-fulfilling again, so, too, the whole society can raise the level of its performance. An example of this rising up is the extraordinary investment our country has made in creating more effective venues for the transportation of the handicapped, and all at great expense to many elements of business and the rest of society. The problem of suffering and pain is often joined with the problem of evil in confronting theologians with the question of how to explain their existence in the face of an all-good, all-powerful, and all-merciful Deity. Some religions say we deserve our suffering; others join Martin Luther King, who said, "Unearned suffering is sanctifying." Others, like Mother Theresa, seem to face the question by working to include the suffering people in their own lives. Elizabeth Heitman, in Chapter 7, will have a deeper analysis of this impact of theology, but it is sufficient to note here that religious belief systems can influence society's reaction to suffering.

THE GALLUP-HARRIS SOCIETAL HAMMERLOCK

The sixth prism, the Gallup-Harris Societal Hammerlock, emerged from the opinion of some social theorists like Max Weber and his disciple Sam Beer that the modern democratic society will ultimately come under the domination of the survey technologists. Beer's fear is that these techniques, for rapidly and accurately finding out what we think we think about almost any subject, will become so prevalent that we shall have a sort of a collective mental grid-lock, by which progress through leadership and new ideas will be effectively forestalled. The marriage of these survey technologies with the mass media has allowed us to come to know our own median collective mind almost instantaneously. Our tastes and our preferences influence politicians and their behavior. Because of an instance when the presidential campaign got dirty and one of the candidates was perceived to have lost an advantage and ultimately the election because he did not respond in kind, many subsequent political campaigns are continuing the trend of taking the low road. All of us are surrounded by sex and violence and stories of human venality and we choose to be so surrounded. Surveys purport to show how many of us engage in various degrees of self-destructive behavior; explicit movies graphically illustrate for all to see how to kill, injure, mutilate others or oneself; and finally the media makes major figures of many of the sorriest examples of human degradation.

Frankl (1984) points out the relationship between media blackouts regarding suicide notifications in a certain Swiss canton, a newspaper strike in Detroit (when perforce no public notice could be given to suicide), and a sharply diminished incidence of suicide in those places. The postmodern-day casualness toward killing and death makes it easier and easier to minimize the respect due to individuals and makes it harder and harder to empathize with others who are suffering in some way.

The public mass media in general are not geared to messages that bring a sense of meaning and direction into individual lives. In fact, they usually do quite the opposite, focusing on the mundane, the material, the quick fix, the one time around, leaving unaddressed the suffering lurking in the background, waiting for everyman and everywoman just as surely as is the next Coors Light.

THE LADY OR THE TIGER DILEMMA

The seventh prism is what I think of as the Lady or the Tiger Dilemma, the related issues of freedom of speech and the known deleterious effects of pornography and violence, a quintessential tragic choice as articulated by Guido Calebresi and Philip Bobbitt (1978). Calebresi and Bobbitt have articulated the difficult choices society makes in the distribution of scarce resources, referring to these choices as tragic choices, because with each of them there are winners and there are losers. Calebresi and Bobbitt use the armed forces draft as an example by which some procedural rules are put in place that determine who among us have to go and possibly get killed in a war and who among us do not. A tragic choice indeed, but perhaps no less tragic than the decision in the name of maintaining free speech to continue to allow unfettered access to films of certain types which can indeed affect younger people to undertake definitively self-destructive acts. I do not know what the answer is, but I do know that I never in my wildest dreams thought that we as a nation could conclude that we had the right to prevent people from smoking in public places. It could be argued that the damage done to elements within our society by unethical and amoral usages of our media is far deeper and more pervasive than cigarette smoking.

THE JENNIFER CAPRIATI SYNDROME

The eighth prism is what I think of as the Jennifer Capriati Syndrome. Jennifer Capriati is the quintessential new American heroine, a teen-age tennis star, who enthralled millions recently on network television by extending the great Martina Navratilova in the championship match of a major national tennis tournament, only the third one Jennifer had entered since turning professional when she was 13 years old. We all stared in wonderment as she faced down the challenges of the older, stronger, and more mature woman on the other side of the net, and we fantasized that behind that stoic, laser-like stare there was some super-human force that would one day soon do in both Navratilova and Steffi Graf. The next day the radio sportscaster on the main news station in the nation's capital said, "Jennifer has her own line of clothes, her own brand of tennis racquet and already qualifies as a bona fide millionairess . . . she's set for life; she's got it all already!" He did not point out that she had overruled umpires' calls twice to give points to her opponents; nor did he describe how clear is her understanding that she is just another eighth grader with the exception of her tennis prowess. Instead, the newsman, in his role of delivering comment that is aimed at the perceived average public intellect and value system, presented the meaning of life for the new star in terms of wealth and fame. The Jennifer Capriati Syndrome then is something that exists in our environment which makes suffering and pain and adjustment to adversity a foreign substance; the opposite of youth; health; good looks; bright and cheery personalities; celebrity status;

and great affluence, which it must be granted comes with hard work and perseverance.

THE SELDIN SOLUTION

Our ninth prism allows us to conclude by discussing a more parochial restraint, one that affects primarily the medical profession. This prism is the Newtonian, reductionist, biomolecular orientation of modern medicine, which one might nickname the Seldin Solution, after Professor Donald Seldin (1981) who described the view most clearly some years back. According to this account of biomedical science, it has fallen to the doctor to pursue the disease down to the organ systems and thence to the molecular defect, from which a molecular cure should be found and applied to the patient for restoration from the disease state. The intrinsic difficulty of carrying this out and the intense pressure it brings upon the modern scientific medical specialist to pursue these molecular answers leave the physicians little room in which to deal with the psyches and personalities, the wants and fears, the social problems and familial home situations of the patients. These, says Seldin, should and must be left to others, such as nurses and social workers, to do. If suffering is in fact a sense of real or perceived impending personal disintegration, then clearly the reductionist physician described by Seldin is not of a mind to participate in the relieving of that kind of suffering and is likely not to be concerned with understanding it or recognizing it. Seldin, as a representative of the Newtonian, reductionist, molecularly oriented medical scientists, has taken himself and them out of the suffering game as far as the patient is concerned and suggests that others be called in to deal with these issues. The bottom-line message to the patients and the society is one of exclusion from the purview of modern medicine and its high priests, those to whom we have given the vestments associated with marrying high technology with humanity. For these particular doctors, molecular hope is in; total person suffering is out.

CONCLUSION

There may well be a growing awakening in America to its pursuit of the illusion of happiness as pain- and suffering-free and a concomitant freedom from death. The identification of the idea of suffering as a vestigial taboo by thinking about it and talking about it (as we are doing in this book) is an important step in removing the taboo status and restoring suffering to the rest of the human condition and as a part of the community. Suffering is shared by all of us and should be a uniting or inclusive force among us rather than something which is a divisive or exclusive force.

Just as some interpret some of the Gospel stories as parables about insiders and outsiders and Jesus' mission to bring the outcasts in, the outsiders into the center, so, too, the myth we have created about suffering must be re-shaped to include suffering into the inescapable stuff of life— a part we can work to minimize, seek to prevent wherever possible, but a part of life which will not go away in its entirety from any of our lives. That death and its sometime surrogate, suffering, sharpen the vitality and clarity of our lives, making living in the healthy and nonsuffering state a circumstance to be cherished and remembered, only serves to underscore the need for those of us now not suffering to seek out our suffering brethren so as not to exclude them as they suffer, thus not enhancing their discomfort.

As one tries to answer the question put before us, "Is society insensitive to suffering?", the immediate choices for answers are unsatisfying. In the discussion thus far, we have been emphasizing the various ways in which society is insensitive to suffering, promotes it, and/or fails to ameliorate it. On the other hand, ours is a society which spends more money than any other on the care of the sick and which is capable of spending millions of dollars and riveting national attention for days or weeks on efforts to recover a child who has fallen into a well or a person lost at sea or in the wilderness. We have done as much as or more than other nations to include the disabled in our public and private systems, and have brought about some of the world's most sweeping changes in disease prevention through no-smoking and 55 MPH speed limit initiatives. Granted that critics could properly comment that each of these positive initiatives is flawed in terms of incorporating suffering creatively into our national life; we must nevertheless agree that we are doing some things well.

Thus the question posed to us in the title of this chapter is the wrong question. The right question, the answers to which could be most constructive and creative, is "How can we enhance the sensitivities of our society (and its institutions and people) to suffering?"

Now that we have the right question, let me hasten to recognize how difficult and complicated the implementations will be of the prescriptions provided in the answers.

Recognizing that the answers must come from all of us acting together and will take far more insight, analysis, dialogue, and understanding than I have been able to muster in this chapter, I will conclude with some personal prefiguring of the answers to our new question.

First, we desperately need more and more discussion of the subject of suffering, or its meaning in individual lives and in our societal life. That every moment of life is a dance with death as life's hidden partner is poorly understood by a nation of optimists, expansionists, youth and beauty idolaters; but we can all learn more. We need to understand more clearly the connection between our fear of death and the concept of suffering arising out of a perception of threatened or real disaggregation of one's persona. American culture has dealt within my lifetime with at least two societal taboos, death and sexuality. How well or how completely we have dealt with these matters up to now is another question, but it seems clear that, with the demography of chronic disease before us, it is time for us to open a national discussion aimed at demystifying the taboo subject of suffering. Conferences such as this one are wonderful first steps, but they must be followed up with other educational and investigative efforts.

Second, our society needs to find a new integration of its traditional values in a less superficial understanding of individuality, of hope for a long, pain-free, blemish-free existence, free from the responsibilities and accountabilities of social ties or ligatures of various sorts. Self-sufficiency is an important virtue, but we may have gone too far. Benjamin Franklin's wisdom may not be as important to us in the next century as it has been in the last. We may want to move old Ben and Greta Garbo more into the background, while bringing Jefferson and John Winthrop, those two great advocates of community life, closer to the foreground.

Third, the Business School mentality needs to be expanded by incorporating its left-brain strengths into a bicameral synthesis of human intelligence, making room, therefore, for the emotional, the aesthetic, and the integrative dimensions of personality, individual and institutional. In my mind, the analogue in biomedical science of the linear Business School mentality is the so-called "Seldin Solution"; it, too, must be replaced by a broader, more integrative view of science, of human intelligence, and of the border between the science and art of medicine. Signs of movement in this latter direction abound, and more and more biomedical scientists seem to understand that expanding the paradigm beyond the Newtonian concepts should not compromise their ability to continue to mine the biomolecular, reductionist theory for its as yet undiscovered treasure (Augros & Stanciu, 1987). Such movement in biomedicine (partly because of its insistence that the scientist-observer cannot be an external objective observer, but must be considered a part

of the experiment) will tend to restore behavioral science to full intellectual partnership in the community of academic medicine and will serve to
enhance the importance of dealing constructively with suffering within
the health care enterprise (Adegaard, 1986).

Fourth, we have to look with uncompromising hardness at the belief
structures and symbols or icons by which we, or subsets of our population,
live. If we accept the premise that suffering is inevitable, that incorporating it more fully and creatively into our societal life is a central and
important goal, then we must question the dominance of the survey
technologist/mass media team which can instantaneously elevate the
median societal opinion to something akin to "the political will of the
people" or perhaps more dangerously to the status of an opinion so
widespread that it seems to come from some primordial encoding of the
truth in our genes. This sort of subtle but pervasive mind control traps us
right where our collective average currently is, an alienation and im-
prisonment quite removed from what anyone in our society wants.

I understand the importance of the Fourth Estate and of free speech to
our kind of democracy, and I want to sustain those institutions and values.
I am torn, however, by the tragic choices which require that we allow
violent pornography and its pervasive media implementation to be in a
position to influence and warp so many young minds and lives. If you have
not seen someone raped or killed or have not done it yourself, there are
an array of inhibitions to such activity that are largely removed by seeing
larger than life color movies or videos which not only show you how to
kill yourself or others but convey the message that this sort of stuff is done
all the time and by people just like you. If we must sacrifice in this way
some subset of our population on the altar of free speech and freedom of
expression, then perhaps all citizens can unite in recognizing the tragic,
unintended consequences of our social choices in this area. Raising the
level of awareness might lead to other positive actions.

Last and perhaps least, let me say that I do not wish to destroy our sports
heros and heroines. Vince Lombardi and his toughness and values, just as
the sheer brilliance of performance and commitment to excellence of the
Michael Jordans and Jennifer Capriatis of the world, are all very positive
influences in varying ways on all of us. The superficiality comes with the
flatness of the picture that emerges from the image-makers, which when
manipulated by the popular desires, returns a new modern icon to the
society, an icon, which in terms of enhancing the understanding and
sensitivity toward suffering, more often than not leaves a great deal to be
desired. Being forewarned is being forearmed—and we, through education, can address these matters.

America is growing up emotionally, intellectually, and one hopes, spiritually. The understanding of suffering as an individual phenomenon and in its implications for the society as a whole is central to that continuing growth. Finding the proper balance in that incorporation will be our creative challenge. Mother Russia and suffering have reached an accommodation that would probably be alien to our American buoyancy and optimism. A utopian view that abandons suffering as an acceptable fact of life is equally unworkable for us in the post-industrial world. Our American synthesis is just beginning to unfold. I'm hopeful that Eric Cassell, Stanley Hauerwas, Mother Theresa, and Margaret Mead will each provide a major underpinning for what we as a nation ultimately adopt.

REFERENCES

Adegaard, C.E. (1986). *Dear doctor.* Menlo Park, CA: The Henry J. Kaiser Family Foundation.

Augros, R., & Stanciu, G. (1987). *The new biology: Discovering the wisdom of nature.* Boston: New Science Library, Random House.

Becker, E. (1975). *Escape from evil.* New York: The Free Press.

Bellah, R. et al. (1985). *Habits of the heart: Individualism and commitment in American life.* New York: Harper & Row.

Brody, H. (1987). *Stories of sickness.* New Haven, CT: Yale University Press.

Cassell, E. (1982). The nature of suffering and the goals of medicine. *New England Journal of Medicine, 306,* 639–645.

Dahrendorf, R. (1979). *Life chances: Approaches to social and political theory.* London: Weidenfeld and Nicholson.

Feifel, H. (Ed.). (1965). *The meaning of death.* New York: McGraw-Hill.

Fortunato, J.E. (1987). *AIDS—The spiritual dilemma.* New York: Harper & Row.

Frankl, V. (1984). *Man's search for meaning,* 3rd ed. New York: Simon & Schuster.

Hauerwas, S. (1985). *The suffering presence.* Notre Dame, IN: University of Notre Dame Press.

Heitman, E. The influence on religious values and culture on responses to suffering. In P. Starck and J. McGovern, *The invisible dimension of illness: Human suffering.* New York: National League for Nursing.

Mead, M. (1970). *Culture and commitment.* New York: Doubleday.

Murray, C. (1988). *In pursuit of happiness and good government.* New York: Simon & Schuster.

Osterweis, M., Solomon, F., & Green, M. (Eds.). (1984). *Bereavement: Reactions, consequences, and care.* Washington, D.C.: National Academy Press.

Seldin, D. (1981). The boundaries of medicine. *Transactions, Association of American Physicians*, 97, 75–84.

Vieth, R.F. (1988). *Holy power—Human pain*. Bloomington, IN: Meyer Stone.

6

Suffering as Contrasted to Pain, Loss, Grief, Despair, and Loneliness

C. Stratton Hill, Jr.

A distinction is made in this chapter between human suffering and acute and chronic bodily pains as viewed by a practicing physician involved in the treatment of cancer patients with pain. It is especially important for physicians to make the distinction between suffering and bodily pains because treatment of the two requires distinctive modalities (although some modalities may be common to both) if the patient is to experience relief.

Frequently the terms *suffering* and *pain* are used together, with the implication that they are synonymous or at least inseparable. However, pain can occur without suffering and vice versa; therefore, they are distinct entities. Another phrase frequently heard about the sufferer is that he or she is "long-suffering." Suffering is commonly associated with chronicity, but evidence will be presented that acute suffering can occur. The issues of why these terms seem related to one another and why they are separate will be addressed.

The language of suffering and pain is often vague and confusing. One of the major responsibilities of the physician who treats pain and suffering is to look for the true meaning and feelings behind the language used by the patient. Not infrequently, patients are observed who claim to be in severe pain but who respond poorly to analgesics, including strong narcotics. Many such patients, although they have bodily pains, are primarily experiencing suffering and require other or additional treatment, such as emotional support for problems with family, work, and other social concerns. The caregiver should clearly understand the fluidity of language between descriptions of suffering and pain and make every effort to recognize which problem dominates.

This chapter will examine both clinical suffering and clinical pain, separately and collectively, and offer suggestions for effectively recognizing each.

SUFFERING

Suffering has been defined by Eric Cassell (1982), a medical practitioner/ethicist, as, "extending beyond the physical. Most generally, suffering can be defined as the state of severe distress associated with events that threaten the intactness of the person" (p. 640). A second definition, by American theologian Daniel Day Williams is, "Suffering is an anguish which we experience not only as a pressure to change but as a threat to our composure, our integrity, and the fulfillment of our intentions" (Reich, 1987, p. 117). One is impressed by the common theme of these two definitions. One characterizes suffering as severe distress and the other as anguish, but in both suffering is triggered by a perceived threat of disintegration of the person as a whole, functioning entity. Disintegration implies an inability to maintain composure, integrity, or intactness—essentially a debacle—for whatever reason, internal or external. When the threat is from outside the person, external resources previously available to aid in maintaining intactness are perceived to be eroding away. When the threat is from within the individual, internal resources to cope with problems are perceived to be inadequate. With threats of this magnitude, intactness cannot be maintained and suffering begins.

Clinical Suffering

How does one establish the beginning of clinical suffering (i.e., suffering that is apparent to caregivers)? Chronicity of a problem, whether it be a disease or other stressful condition, seems an implicit requirement for suffering. Cancer patients who have unrelenting pain for months to years and patients with benign painful conditions such as rheumatoid arthritis, osteoporosis, degenerative arthritis, and inflammatory bowel disease are all considered sufferers because of the persisting pain associated with these chronic medical conditions. Persons burdened with the physical and psychological stress of caring for these individuals over long periods are also considered sufferers. But did the illness or the stress create a perception of disintegration of their intactness or a threat to the fulfillment of their intentions in either the individuals experiencing the illness or the caregivers experiencing the stress when the problem began or only after it had been present for some time? Perhaps the perception never occurs, but on the other hand, it may occur at any time during the course of the illness, early or late. Individual personality differences and circumstances influence the onset of these perceptions. Therefore, although suffering often occurs in chronic, progressively debilitating diseases and physical and psychological stress states, chronicity *per se* is not required for suffering to commence.

Acute Suffering

If chronicity is not a requirement, what are examples of acute or self-limiting circumstances or conditions that cause suffering? Statements such as, "She suffered the loss of her husband" or "He suffered greatly from that diagnostic procedure" are heard in association with acute painful situations. Here "suffer" is a verb. Suffering is something a person does instantly; it is triggered by an event. Certainly, total personal disintegration, or loss of intactness, may be perceived by an individual who experiences an acute onset of pain, such as chest pain that is subsequently determined to be associated with myocardial infarction, or an occurrence of other ominous symptoms, such as massive gastrointestinal hemorrhage resulting in vomiting of blood or rectal bleeding. The life-threatening meaning of these symptoms adds to the perception of impending loss of intactness of the individual, and suffering begins immediately, though it may be short-lived.

Two other clinical circumstances illustrate acute, self-limiting suffering that may have lasting psychological effects. First, patients requiring mechanical lung ventilation for serious acute medical and surgical conditions must be given drugs to blunt their upper-respiratory-tract reflexes and to overcome their natural desire to breathe for themselves. These drugs cause skeletal and smooth muscle relaxation by paralyzing the motor nerves where they interface with the muscle. The most notorious of this class of drugs is curare. Although curare itself is not used clinically, analogues of it are; both voluntary and involuntary muscular motor activity, or movement, throughout the body is abolished. Paralysis is complete, and there is no resistance to external ventilation. Being unable to breathe, the patient must rely on someone else to mechanically expand his or her lungs to supply oxygen to the body. If this is inadequate, oxygen to the brain is deficient and death will follow in a relatively short time; or if mechanical ventilation is suboptimum, oxygen flow to the brain is reduced and permanent brain damage occurs resulting in a vegetative state. Because of complete bodily paralysis, the vocal cords cannot function and the patient cannot speak or utter any sound. Grimacing or any other facial expression of pain or displeasure, or any effort to withdraw from a painful or noxious stimulus, are also impossible. Curare drugs, however, have no analgesic or hypnotic effects. Therefore, total body paralysis can occur when the patient is fully conscious and fully able to perceive painful stimuli. This is often compounded by the patient realizing he or she is paralyzed but not knowing why. In this state of total helplessness, patients perceive an acute threat of personal disintegration. If analgesics are not simultaneously administered, this suffering is accompanied by severe pain, but the patient is unable to complain.

Loper, Butler, Nessly, and Wild (1989) reported on a series of patients who were subjected to mechanical lung ventilation in an intensive care unit (ICU) setting. While paralyzed, the patients experienced severe pain for reasons related to their specific illnesses. It was impossible for them to communicate in any way with the medical staff perpetrating this perceived act of terror. Because of the relatively high number of patients reporting this experience, these researchers conducted a survey among personnel who performed these procedures in the ICU and found that 51 percent of those responding either thought the curare-like drug had analgesic properties or had no knowledge about it one way or the other; that 50 percent of physicians and 75 percent of nurses thought these drugs had anxiolytic properties; and that 80 percent of physicians and 50 percent of nurses thought diazepam (Valium), a hypnotic, had analgesic properties. If this lack of knowledge is common in other hospitals (the survey was done in a university-affiliated hospital), the probability of patients being terrorized and made to experience acute suffering in this way is too high.

Second, anecdotal stories emerge about patients subjected to painful procedures, including surgical operations, while in a state of conscious analgesia. Modern anesthesia is provided to patients in the majority of cases, and in virtually all cardiovascular operations, by a combination of an opioid (narcotic) analgesic and a hypnotic. The opioid analgesic provides relief from pain and reduces the level of consciousness to varying degrees, depending on the individual. In some individuals, the level of consciousness may be profoundly depressed, but if a stimulus, usually a painful one, is intense enough, a response can be elicited. In others the same dose of drug may produce only a mild to moderate depression of consciousness. To ensure a complete loss of consciousness, the hypnotic must be added. Patients undergoing serious surgical procedures such as open-heart surgery or lung operations whose consciousness is only mildly or moderately depressed have been able to provide vivid, detailed, and terrifying accounts of their experiences during the operations that are later verified by the medical personnel present during the procedure. The reaction of operating room personnel to mishaps, adverse reactions, and complications occurring during the procedure are most often remembered. As in the case of the paralyzed patient, the patient described above is able to perceive a circumstance in which disintegration of his or her being seems imminent but is experiencing no pain because of the opioid analgesic. The overwhelming sense of helplessness in the face of an onslaught to the body that is probably perceived as open-ended or limitless most certainly can be interpreted as a threat to maintaining one's intactness. The unfamiliarity of the procedure, the sense of being manipulated, and probably the casual conversations of the health care personnel during the procedure add up to a feeling of doom for the patient. As in the first illustration, most of these procedures are successful and the patient survives, though the traumatic memory of the experience may have unpredictable results. These illustrations demonstrate that acute and self-limiting suffering, with or without pain, occurs.

Chronic Suffering

Similarly, chronic medical conditions exist in which suffering can occur without pain. For example, patients with irritable bowel syndrome or ulcerative colitis may suffer because of chronic, frequent, sometimes uncontrolled bowel movements but do not necessarily have pain with them. The patient's uncertainty about lack of bowel control limits his or her social or business contacts. Since the condition is chronic, it can be an impediment to the fulfillment of the sufferer's intention to attain his or her desired goals. Similarly, patients with chronic diseases of the lungs that block adequate oxygen exchange with the blood suffer chronic shortness of breath but do not necessarily have pain. This impediment also restricts physical activity and threatens fulfillment of goals and intentions. These illustrations demonstrate that acute and chronic suffering can occur with or without pain.

The distinction between acute and chronic suffering may be artificial. Patients with chronic illnesses may suffer in episodic or paroxysmal fashion. There may actually be recurring acute episodes of pain over many years (e.g., patients suffering sickle-cell crisis or vascular headaches) and there may be intervals in which the patients may be free of actual pain and suffering. On the other hand, one could argue that the mere anticipation of future episodes or attacks interferes with fulfillment of intentions and produces a constant state of suffering.

PAIN

It was indicated earlier that the words "pain" and "suffering" are frequently used together. Yet is has also been demonstrated that one can suffer without experiencing pain. What is the relationship of pain to suffering? Can pain itself threaten the intactness of an individual or frustrate the fulfillment of goals?

Definition of Pain

First one must examine what pain is. To many, the answer to this question is self-evident. It is, "When I hurt." Certainly that is a good answer, but it does not end there. The ancients had trouble with the concept of pain. It was not considered to originate in the body until the time of Aristotle (Weberi, 1877). Prior to this time, pain was associated with external factors; for example, it accompanied the arrow with which one was hit, or an individual became possessed by an evil spirit that came uninvited to dwell within the body (Clements, 1932). Aristotle considered pain the opposite of pleasure and, therefore, a "passion of the soul." He attributed pain to excessive tactile stimulation of the skin and proposed the heart as the seat of pain perception. Rene Descartes, approximately 300 years ago, was the first to associate pain with the nervous system and proposed the pineal gland as the seat of perception (Carter, 1983). He changed pain from a disease entity *per se* (which it was considered to be prior to his time) to a symptom. His concept of the body functioning like a machine and pain occurring only if the machine malfunctions leaves modern society with the legacy that pain exists only when a physical cause for it can be demonstrated. This, however, is not true, and pain must be treated as the subjective entity it is.

This early difficulty with the concept of pain probably accounts for the fact that there is no root word for pain in our language. The English word "pain" is derived from the Latin word "*poena,*" which means penalty or punishment. *Poena* stresses pain inflicted on the body as the result of malevolent intent. The infliction is for a transgression deserving a penalty or punishment. To explain this, Ivan Illich states,

> In the first millennium, Christians do not focus on the bodily pains suffered by Christ in his passion. Certainly one reason for this is the fact that they had no term fitting the word field of modern English pain. The latter directly denotes an ache in the body, and obliquely emotion or feelings. The Greek words, lype, algos, and nosos directly mean a state of the soul. And the Old Testament, one long story of woes and miseries in which Israel comes to recognize the hand of the living God, simply has no one word which directly refers to the body in pain. [Illich, 1987]

Illich states that of the Greek words listed above, "*lype*" comes as close as possible to the English word "pain."

The International Association for the Study of Pain defines pain as follows: "Pain is an unpleasant sensory and emotional experience associated with actual or potential tissue damage, or described in terms of such damage" (Merskey, 1986). Perhaps Rem Edwards's (1989) definition of pain as "any quality of feeling which we ordinarily desire to eliminate or avoid for its own sake" best encompasses the concept of pain. It assumes a concern about both bodily pains and emotional or mental pains. Bodily pains are experienced in some definite place or region of the body, whereas emotional or mental pains have no definite bodily locus. The task of contrasting suffering with acute and chronic pain can be simplified if emotional or mental pains are included in the definition of pain. Unrelieved bodily pains will indeed elicit emotional and mental pains. Emotional and mental pains caused by unrelieved bodily pains include depression, anxiety, frustration, abandonment, uncertainty, guilt, boredom, sadness, sorrow, fear, anger, alienation, loss, grief, despair, loneliness, and others. The danger, however, of including emotional and mental pains in the definition of bodily pain is the confusion that arises when the patient fails to distinguish these emotional and mental feelings from physical bodily pains. It is the responsibility of the trained health care professional to be able to distinguish among the possible elements contributing to the pain and suffering of the individual. Treatment must be directed first to the most salient problem facing the patient.

It should also be recognized that emotional and mental pains may be caused by psychological stimuli unrelated to unrelieved bodily pains. These may represent intrinsic threats to intactness and fulfillment of intentions and produce suffering in the absence of bodily pains.

Unrelieved Bodily Pains

Bodily pain is most clearly related to suffering when it is unrelieved. It can be considered a noxious stimulus for suffering. Unrelieved pain threatens both intactness and the fulfillment of intentions, for a variety of reasons, but the two most important are (1) pain interferes with and limits function and (2) pain elicits emotional and mental pains that complicate the experience. A priori, one would think that all unrelieved bodily pain could be relieved. Isn't it simply a matter of willingness and resolve? The answer is, partially, yes. Albert Schweitzer said,

We must all die. But that I can save him from days of torture, that is what I feel as my great and ever new privilege. Pain is a more terrible lord of mankind than even death itself. [1931, p. 62]

It must be recognized that currently patients in pain are generally undertreated; that is, pain that could be relieved is not (Marks & Sachar, 1973; Morgan, 1986; Melzack, 1990). It is the customary practice in our society to undertreat pain (Morgan & Winick, 1988). Exceptions to this are patients whose pain responds to treatment measures not involving narcotics (e.g., nerve blocks or hypnosis). Therefore, it is patients whose pain has failed to be relieved by alternative treatment modalities and whose pain is relieved only if narcotics are used (and used appropriately) who suffer undertreatment. The reasons for this are threefold: (1) cultural and societal barriers to appropriate and adequate narcotic use, (2) knowledge deficits of health care professionals about the pharmacology of narcotics, and (3) government regulatory boards' and agencies' influence on physicians' prescribing practices (Hill, 1990). Each of these reasons will be briefly discussed.

Cultural and societal pressures to underprescribe narcotics arise out of myths and mistaken concepts about pain and narcotics commonly held by both health care professionals and the general population (Twycross & Lack, 1984). These concepts are determined from the legacy of associating narcotic abuse, prior to any government controls on narcotics, with sinister and illegal activity (e.g., "opium dens") (Musto, 1987), and by society's current experience with narcotics as drugs of abuse which result in the destruction of many lives. Unfortunately, the experience with drug abuse so dominates cultural and societal thinking that even when these drugs are used legitimately for medical purposes, an illegitimate aura persists. Although the drugs' medical use is intellectually recognized and accepted, societal actions generally reflect the dominance of the illegitimate image, and use is overly restricted.

Knowledge deficits about opiate pharmacology stem primarily from information contained in pharmacology textbooks obtained from studies on subjects not in pain (Twycross, 1988). These studies were done on volunteers who were former drug addicts imprisoned for drug abuse. Drug doses recommended in these textbooks were obtained by studying subjects with postoperative pain, a pain whose intensity is seldom severe, and were single-dose studies. Information available to physicians and other health care professionals, from this source, is restrictive. The consequences of this are (1) drug doses are too low and prescribed for unrealistically long intervals for patients with severe pain, (2) there is overconcern for respiratory depression in determining the dose of narcotic necessary to relieve pain, and (3) narcotics are withheld for fear of causing addition, though patients taking narcotics seldom, if ever, become addicted as a result of the use of narcotics for pain relief. Addiction is commonly defined simply as the chronic taking of narcotics, but there is ample evidence that becoming addicted is much more complex than merely being exposed to narcotics (Robins, David, & Nurco, 1974; Peele, 1989). Addiction has become confused with physical dependence.

A force external to the doctor/patient relationship that contributes to undertreatment of pain is drug regulatory agency pressures. Cultural attitudes and barriers to not have the force of law that regulations do. However, lawmakers and regulatory board members all belong to a society whose attitudes about pain and narcotics are based on myths and misconceptions prevalent in the culture. Therefore, the creation of these laws and how they are interpreted and enforced reflect culturally determined beliefs about pain and narcotics that often result in inhumane treatment for patients.

Following in importance to the above problems is the failure to distinguish pain emanating from a damaged nervous system from that emanating from an intact nervous system. Pain occurring in the setting of a damaged nervous system—neuropathic pain—has different clinical symptoms and other characteristics (Fields, 1987) and responds poorly to analgesic drugs, including strong narcotics (McQuay, 1988). This type of pain responds better to antidepressant and anticonvulsant drugs than to analgesics, but response is slow and often incomplete (McQuay, 1988). Patients experiencing this type of pain may find it necessary to adapt to the realization that optimum relief cannot be attained. There is no "silver bullet" or "potion" that will magically take the pain away. Patience and support are necessary for treatment of neuropathic pain. Failure of the physician to recognize pain as neuropathic, and to make the patient aware of this, is likely to introduce tension into the doctor/patient relationship. The physician offers what he or she considers ample narcotic for pain relief, and relief is expected. The patient, however, fails to experience relief, becomes frustrated and perhaps angry, and accuses the physician of withholding relief, while the physician accuses the patient of being a manipulator or drug-seeker.

Relation of Suffering to Unrelieved Acute and Chronic Pain

Unrelieved bodily pain, therefore, may result from two factors: (1) underdosing with narcotics because of the reasons noted and (2) failure to recognize neuropathic pain and to understand its poor response to analgesics, including narcotics. If proper therapy is instituted and pain is relieved to the optimum level possible, its stimulus to producing suffering is aborted. However, if treatment is not instituted or is inadequate, chronic, unrelieved pain can lead to any or several of the negative emotional and mental pains listed above. Prolonged stress from the combination of these influences prevents a fulfillment of the things one desires and intends to do and erodes the ability to maintain one's intactness. Language used by patients when this symptom complex matures is often imprecise. "Pain" becomes a generic term to denote a global feeling of misery rather than merely the presence of bodily pain alone. The physician must look beyond this complaint in the evaluation of the situation. If he or she does not, the patient will be inappropriately treated. Analgesics used alone will fail. If strong narcotics are used, the predominant result will be their side effects, such as oversedation, confusion, sleepiness, and hallucinations, rather than pain relief.

CONCLUSION

Human suffering is a more complex experience than the simple experience of acute and/or chronic bodily pains, which include emotional and mental pains. Human suffering occurs when a human being perceives an inability to function as the highly organized being he or she is. Bodily pains may be endured without ever developing this perception and suffering may never occur. Similarly, emotional and/or mental pains may be present for years without the individual ever perceiving a threat to intactness as an organized human being. Usually, however, unrelieved bodily pains will progress into suffering. Currently, the accepted standard of medical practice for purely bodily pain is the customary practice of undertreatment. If suffering caused by undertreatment of bodily pains is to be prevented, improved treatment must be substituted for the current customary practice.

The recognition that human suffering is a multifaceted, complex experience requires that treatment of each facet, or element, be individually addressed. Failure to do this is likely to leave the patient's pain and suffering unrelieved.

REFERENCES

Carter, R.B. (1983). Descartes' medical philosophy: The organic solution to the mind-body problem. In *The Human Body*. Baltimore: Johns Hopkins University Press.

Cassell, E.J. (1982). The nature of suffering and the goals of medicine. *New England Journal of Medicine*, 306, 639–645.

Clements, F.E. (1932). Primitive concepts of disease. *University of California Publications in American Arch. and Ethn.*, 32, 185–252.

Edwards, R. (1989). Pain management and the values of health care providers. In C.S. Hill, Jr. & W.S. Fields (Eds.), *Drug treatment of cancer pain in a drug oriented society*. New York: Raven Press.

Fields, H.L. (1987). Painful dysfunction of the nervous system. In *Pain*. New York: McGraw-Hill.

Hill, C.S., Jr. (1990). Relationship among cultural, educational, and regulatory agency influences on optimum cancer pain treatment. *Journal of Pain and Symptom Management*, 5, S37–S45.

Illich, I. (1987, November). Lecture given to faculty, staff, and students of McCormick Theological Seminary.

Loper, K.A., Butler, S., Nessly, M., & Wild, L. (1989). Paralyzed with pain: The need for education. *Pain*, 37, 315–316.

Marks, R.M., & Sachar, E.J. (1973). Undertreatment of medical inpatients with narcotic analgesics. *Ann. Intern. Med.*, 78, 173–181.

McQuay, H.J. (1988). Pharmacological treatment of neuralgic and neuropathic pain. *Cancer Sur.*, 7, 141–159.

Melzack, R. (1990). The tragedy of needless pain. *Scientific American*, 262(2), 27–33.

Mersky, H. (Ed.). (1986). Classification of chronic pain: Description of chronic pain syndromes and definition of pain terms. *Pain* (Suppl. 3), S1.

Morgan, J.P. (1986). *American piophobia: Customary underutilization of opioid analgesics. Controversies in alcoholism an substance abuse.* New York: Haworth Press.

Morgan, J.P., & Winick, C. (1988). Non-customary prescribing, dangerous drugs and medical discipline. *Journal of Drug Issues*, 18(2), 259–269.

Musto, D.F. (1987). *The American disease: Origins of narcotic control*, (expanded ed.). New York: Oxford University Press.

Peele, S. (1989, July–August). Ain't misbehavin': Addiction has become an all-purpose excuse. *The Sciences, New York Academy of Sciences*, 14–21.

Reich, W.T. (1987). Models of pain and suffering: Foundation for an ethic of compassion. *Acta Neurochirurgica* (Suppl. 38), 117–122.

Robins, L.N., David, D.H., & Nurco, D.N. (1974). How permanent was Vietnam drug addiction? *Am J Public Health*, 64, 38–43.

Schweitzer, A. (1931). *On the edge of the primeval forest.* New York: Macmillan.

Twycross, R.G. (1988). The management of pain in cancer: A guide to drug and dosage. *Oncology*, 2, 35–43.

Twycross, R.G., & Lack, S.A. (1984). *Symptom control in far advanced cancer: Pain relief.* London: Pitman.

Weberi, W. (1877). Aristotelis de anima libri tres. Ad interpretum Graecorum auctoritatum et codicum fidem recognovit commentariis illustravot Frider. Adolph. Trendelenburg, Berolini, sumptibus.

7

The Influence of Values and Culture in Responses to Suffering

Elizabeth Heitman

THE RELATIONSHIP OF RELIGION, CULTURE, AND SUFFERING

Since the 1970s, spurred in part by George Engel's (1977) biopsychosocial model of illness, a growing number of professionals have actively sought to reintroduce an essential element of health care all but forgotten during a century of scientific achievement in medicine: illness involves every dimension of human life, and the diagnosis and treatment of disease must involve the whole person.

The diversity of contemporary American society offers a real challenge to caregivers who seek to treat the whole patient, as both patients and professionals come from a wide variety of cultural and religious backgrounds that shape their experiences of illness. As high rates of immigration into the United States make the American health care system increasingly pluralistic, practitioners have never had a greater need to understand the interrelationship of culture, religion, and health.

Regrettably, as nurse-educator Chris Sampson has observed, even practitioners dedicated to the ethical principle of respecting patients' individual values and customs often fall short of their ideals in practice. The problem, Sampson claims (1982, p. 1), is not that caregivers "*deliberately* neglect the customs and spiritual beliefs of their patients," but that "in general, they are much too badly informed in this area to do anything deliberately." Other research echoes her harsh assessment: in one-on-one encounters many practitioners are unlikely to recognize cultural and religious factors that can complicate good treatment (Bochner, 1983; Fitzgerald, 1988; Helman, 1990; Qureshi, 1989).

Understanding the invisible dimensions of illness and translating theoretical knowledge into practical, humanistic skills requires a broad, interdisciplinary focus. In that spirit, this paper has two purposes: to examine the influences of religious values and culture on the experience of suffering; and to provide a framework that the caregiver, irrespective of professional training, can use to interpret individuals' responses to the suffering of pain, illness, and disability.

Understanding Religion and Culture

Culture and religion are such complex phenomena that they are difficult to define and distinguish. Anthropologists recognize over a hundred different meanings of the word "culture" (Roosens, 1989), and the term "religion" is interpreted at least as widely. For the purposes of this discussion, "religion" refers to explanatory models of life's ultimate meaning and purpose, and the specific practices and beliefs that stem from them; some religions focus on a supreme being, but definitions of ultimate reality do not require a deity. "Culture" should be understood as the systems of common attitudes, values, beliefs, and behaviors that spring from shared experiences and worldviews; attributes such as race, religion, and language may be central or inconsequential to culture.

Many fundamental elements of culture and religious belief, such as body language, gender roles, and even dietary practices, are so integral to life that they are largely unconscious, and may be mistaken for "human nature." A vague sense of discomfort, embarrassment, or even anger at the "inappropriate" behavior of a stranger is often the result of "culture shock" and its consequent stress (Qureshi, 1989; Tanaka-Matsumi & Higginbotham, 1989). Because few people are aware of their own religious or cultural assumptions, culture shock can be a serious obstacle to communication. Both parties are likely to condemn the other rather than recognize that their intentions are being misinterpreted.

Culture and religion are clearly interdependent. Group identity often hinges on a religious concept of the purpose of human life, and cultural variation in religious practices is evident in all of the major faiths (Eliade, 1959). Culture and religion are relatively distinct in the secularized, industrialized West, but it is much harder to distinguish between them elsewhere. Islam as a religion, for example, also prescribes a significant number of activities that might otherwise be categorized as functions of culture.

Both religion and culture constantly undergo subtle changes, and their expression can vary dramatically across time, geographic region, and socioeconomic groups. For example, the core beliefs of Christianity have produced radically different practices in Middle-Ages Europe, colonial Mexico, and contemporary Africa. Similarly, "American culture" may refer equally to quite different ways of life in urban Atlanta, small-town Minnesota, and rural Arizona. Unfortunately, a brief essay must overlook the depth and scope of specific traditions, omitting or generalizing important variations as well as ignoring minor perspectives. Readers interested in more detailed information on medical anthropology and the world religions will find several excellent sources listed among the references.

As the ultimate focus of this volume is the individual, it is essential to remember that there are as many expressions of culture and religion as there are people. Most individuals develop their own "operational theologies," which may conflict with, misinterpret, or be ignorant of "official" views of the traditions to which they claim allegiance (Anderson, 1989; Fichtner & McKenny, 1991). An event may provoke similar responses among individuals with vastly different beliefs, or vastly different responses from people with remarkably similar backgrounds. To avoid the pitfalls of stereotyping, there is no substitute for asking for and listening to an individual's own interpretation of events and their meaning.

Suffering—an Eternal Human Question

Many of the essays in this volume reflect or expand on the work of physician-ethicist Eric Cassell (1982), who describes suffering as stemming from the perception of an impending disintegration of the self. Cassell discusses suffering in terms of the loss, or threatened loss, of existence, control, or meaning that often accompanies unexpected, unexplained pain or illness. Pain and illness that disrupt life may not cause suffering if they are understandable, controllable, and perceived to be of limited duration; even extreme pain may be experienced as rewarding if it is perceived to achieve a greater good.

Cassell's focus on the individual's search for integrity, positive meaning, and transcendence in the face of an unexpected or long-term adversity has much in common with theological perspectives on suffering. Because the randomness of adversity challenges the logic of every explanation of life's ultimate meaning (Bemporad, 1987; Carmody & Carmody, 1988), suffering is widely considered among theologians to be both fundamentally a religious problem and the most fundamental problem of religion.

The experience of suffering often prompts people who believe themselves to be nonreligious to ask deeply spiritual questions; many who are avowedly religious question even their most fundamental beliefs when struck with adversity (Anderson, 1989). Yet every traditional explanation of suffering ultimately concludes that part of the final answer remains a mystery beyond human understanding. Each requires a degree of faith to transcend suffering and to live with its mystery.

While religion may provide the basis for understanding the origins of suffering, a broader sense of group identity also affects how individuals face suffering. Cultural practices relating to suffering, particularly to illness and disability, are central to every human society (Helman, 1990). Moreover, many cultures define themselves in terms of past suffering and their response to adversity: the Soviet Union's national identity includes vivid memories of foreign invasion and the death of 20 million citizens in two world wars; a "stiff upper lip" and a high toleration of personal discomfort are fundamentally British; Brazilians typically look for a brighter future beyond their present adversity; saving personal honor or "face" despite personal suffering is vital to many Japanese. These cultural expressions are tied to religious values, but also go beyond them.

To appreciate individual responses to suffering, it is essential to understand the cultural and religious worldview of the sufferer. What is the origin and purpose of human life? How is adversity related to nature? How does the individual's experience of suffering fit into the greater scheme? The following section examines these questions in the standard views of the primary religiocultural archetypes: shamanistic traditions of harmony, eastern traditions based on karma, and Western, theocentric traditions. Remarkably, although each of the major religions and cultural groups has its own interpretation of the mechanism of suffering, suffering is almost universally thought both to be caused by wrongful human behavior, and to provide an opportunity for spiritual growth.

Social Harmony and Shamanism in Preindustrialized Cultures

In the preindustrialized, "tribal" cultures of Africa, America, Asia, and Polynesia, all life is religious life where gods, dead ancestors, and the spirits of animals, plants, and inanimate objects have a social role (Eliade, 1959; Mbiti, 1970). Their mythologies record that the world was created as a place of universal harmony, peace, and prosperity where spirits, people, and animals lived together peacefully (Sproul, 1979).

This primeval social harmony was destroyed when a greedy animal or person tricked another out of a prized possession. This deceit led to anger, retribution, mistrust, and ultimately every form of suffering. Humans lost their ability to communicate with spirits and their relationships with other people became distorted. Only a shaman, a physician-priest chosen by the spirits, retained the insight and original powers of communication required to maintain or restore harmony in the community.

In these societies, all adversity is generally believed to stem from broken relationships, whether as intentional evil, a natural consequence of ill will, or punishment from an offended spirit. Illness may be a jealous rival's curse, the result of interpersonal conflict, a symptom of spirit possession, or a sign that the sufferer has neglected obligations to an ancestor or god (Brown, 1989). Only restoring the sufferer's social relationships can relieve his or her suffering. Even in a shamanistic culture that accepted germ theory, the diagnosis and treatment of infection would consider social issues: Why did the germ choose its victim? What needs to be done to placate the germ and convince it to leave the patient?

While technically not shamanistic, the Chinese traditions of Confucianism and Taoism also center on social harmony and natural balance. Both believe in the *Tao*, an impersonal order that runs through the entire universe, governing human activities as well as nature (Liu, 1979). Harmony with the Tao brings peace, prosperity, and health; acting against the Tao results in imbalance, social strife, and suffering. Confucianism stresses philosophical wisdom and Taoism emphasizes the supernatural, but both rely on astrology and divination to identify the immediate causes of suffering and the demands of harmony. Chinese medicine focuses in great part on the detection and treatment of social and physical imbalances, believed to cause all human illness (Kaptchuck, 1983; Liu, 1979; Tu, 1987).

Today exclusively shamanistic cultures are rare, but their teachings about suffering persist as cultural practices alongside other formal religions. When struck with illness, many devoutly Christian patients of Latin American and Caribbean background might practice *curanderismo*, *macumba*, or *voodoo*, wearing magic strings to choke off disease, placing raw eggs under their beds to draw out illness or evil, washing with special waters, or appealing for spiritual assistance by lighting prayer candles (Brown, 1989; Kay, 1977). Some New Age beliefs about illness and healing are largely shamanistic (Elwood, 1973). Similarly, the Taoist spiritual magic *feng shui* survives in both Buddhist and communist Asia, intertwined with Chinese medicine (Liu, 1979). Moreover, "magical thinking" similar to shamanistic belief is a frequent early response to adversity and is particularly common among children (Siegel, 1985).

Karma and Illusion in India and Asia

The Indian religious culture known as Hinduism is over 4,000 years old, and is composed of several traditions with adherents around the world. Buddhism developed out of Hinduism in the sixth century B.C.E, and it soon spread north and east from India to become a dominant force throughout China and southeast Asia. In the past generation, both Hinduism and Buddhism have become popular among Westerners, and both are influential among adherents of New Age groups (Elwood, 1973). At the heart of these traditions are the concepts of *karma* and the illusory quality of human existence; they are separated by distinct interpretations of that illusion and the reality behind it.

Hinduism and the force of karma. Hinduism is based on an apparent conflict: recognition of human imperfection and universal suffering, and belief in perfect, eternal, unchanging, uncreated, and all-encompassing reality known as *brahman* (B.K. Smith, 1987; H. Smith, 1958). Early Hindus claimed that because the real souls, or *atman*, must be part of *brahman*, it must be similarly eternal, unchanging, and uncreated. Thus, life as it appears today must be unreal, the product of a powerful illusion.

Hindu interpretations of the soul's experience of illusion are based on belief in *karma*—the law of cause and effect, and *samsara*—the cycle of rebirth caused by karma (Mahoney & Kogen, 1987; B.K. Smith, 1987). Through karma, every situation results from previous actions, and every action affects future conditions. Blinded by illusion, human beings create their own bad karma and suffering through their error and ignorance; human illness and injury, therefore, are the self-inflicted consequences of wrongful actions in the past.

Although Hinduism acknowledges that the source of illusion is a mystery, it does not recognize innocent suffering. Souls deserve their fate because they alone create it. Moreover, the effects of many actions extend beyond a single lifetime, and adversity may persist or reappear in future incarnations. Congenital deformity, for example, like all conditions of birth, is the directly proportional result of error in past lives.

Souls remain trapped in the seemingly endless cycle of suffering because they fail to understand their true nature as brahman, and cling to the world of illusion instead of seeking the truth. Hindus believe that most poverty, illness, and disability have no real remedy in the present, but that they offer an opportunity to gain the self-knowledge that makes suffering bearable. To achieve final release from the cycle of rebirth and suffering, the souls must cast off all illusion and reunite with the eternal brahman— a process generally believed to take hundreds of millions of incarnations (Carmody & Carmody, 1988; B.K. Smith, 1987).

Buddhism and the illusion of the soul   Buddhism traces its origins to the Indian prince Siddhartha Gautama who, having witnessed illness, old age, and death, abandoned a life of luxury to seek an explanation for human suffering. His conclusions are known as the Four Noble Truths: all life is suffering; suffering is caused by desire; desire can be broken; the means to breaking desire is to follow the Buddhist eight-fold path of wisdom, meditation, and morality (Pandya, 1987; H. Smith, 1958).

Buddhism accepts the basic Hindu principles of karma, samsara, and illusion. However, it differs from Hinduism in three vital ways. First, Buddhists generally reject the Hindu vision of a substantive universal reality or brahman as an illusion; they maintain that the only real, eternal perfection is nothingness, a blissful emptiness known as *nirvana*. Second, the karma which drives the cycle of rebirth and suffering is caused not simply by ignorance, but by desire born out of ignorance. Third, the most powerful desire, and thus the greatest cause of suffering, is not attachment to the physical world, but the belief in a self at all.

The Buddhist concept of no-self, or *anatman*, holds that what appear to be individual souls are really only hollow bundles of karma. The individual who seeks *nirvana* discovers that all personal existence, including sickness and death, is an illusion (Carmody & Carmody, 1988; B.K. Smith, 1987). Moreover, as the First Noble Truth suggests, even the seemingly pleasurable aspects of life contribute to suffering because their appeal perpetuates the desire that drives *samsara*. Therefore, detachment is the only way to live with life's illusion and the suffering that it creates. Like Hinduism, Buddhism has no explanation for the origins of illusion, but Buddhists, too, believe that its powerful effects may require millions of incarnations to overcome.

Suffering and God's Will in Western Tradition

The religious traditions of Judaism, Christianity, and Islam believe that a personal God created humanity for happiness in a perfect world, and that human suffering is both the result of sin and a sign of God's justice. The three faiths vary significantly, however, in their understanding of human nature and freedom, and the degree to which suffering should be interpreted as God's direct will.

Judaism and Job's mystery. Judaism starts with a firm belief in the goodness of God, the world, and the human beings created in God's image. Although God's will for humanity is a life of joy, human beings sinfully abused their free will and brought a recurrent pattern of sinfulness and suffering into the world. Despite the power of sin, however, Jews generally believe that human nature is fundamentally good (Carmody & Carmody, 1988; H. Smith, 1958). In the covenant established through Abraham, Noah, and Moses, God expresses continued dedication to the people of Israel despite their sinfulness.

The early Jews did not speak of an afterlife, believing instead that God dealt justly with humanity in this world. Early covenantal writings suggest that adherence to God's will brings divine blessings, while sin results in divine retribution (Green, 1987). Typically, God's justice applied to Israel as a nation, which suffered war, drought, and plague for its unfaithfulness, and peace, strength, and abundance in times of loyalty. The fate of individuals was also attributed directly to personal righteousness.

The wisdom literature of the fifth century B.C.E raised the challenge of the suffering of innocents. The story of Job, a devout and wholly righteous man beset by the worst possible physical torment and suffering, is a direct attack on simple causality (Green, 1987). Its answer is that God's justice is ultimately beyond human comprehension, and that the full scope of history demonstrates God's good will and fidelity to the covenant.

As Judaism moved away from belief in immediate justice, it developed a future-oriented concept of God's final judgment at the end of history, when the wicked will be destroyed and the patient suffering of the faithful will be rewarded with everlasting life (Carmody & Carmody, 1988). Scripture from the second and third centuries B.C.E also outlines the concept of the servant of God who, although innocent, readily suffers for the sins of others and is richly rewarded for his sacrifice. This figure is interpreted variously as a prophet, a community of faithful within Israel, and the nation as a whole. The common theme is that suffering serves God by teaching others about the consequences of sin, and that faith in God's justice can make even incomprehensible suffering bearable (H. Smith, 1958).

In the 1,900 years since the destruction of the temple at Jerusalem, Rabbinic Judaism has continued to teach that individual suffering is often self-inflicted, but it emphasizes that adversity provides an opportunity for introspection and a deeper knowledge of God's will (Bemporad, 1987). Pain, illness, and disability offer spiritual growth, self-knowledge, and self-discipline if met with faith.

After the model of the suffering servant, some have taught that suffering is a blessing for the righteous that should be accepted gratefully as God's gift (Green, 1987). Modern scholars consider the Jewish people to be God's suffering servant, but many remain deeply troubled about the terrible suffering endured by millions of individuals during the Holocaust (Bemporad, 1987; Green, 1987). While they struggle to understand such widespread suffering of innocents, Job's lesson is the most lasting explanation: the full extent of divine justice is a mystery that will become clear only at the end of history.

Christianity, the crucifixion, and God's mercy.   Like Judaism, Christianity teaches that suffering is both the result of sin and its punishment. However, by focusing on the crucifixion of Jesus of Nazareth as the sacrifice of God's suffering servant, Christian theology reinterprets human sinfulness, the covenant, and the nature of God's justice.

Christians emphasize that God created the world in an act of love, but that humanity sinfully rejected God's loving will. Christian doctrine contends that that sin fundamentally corrupted human nature; although human beings still have free will, the taint of original sin pervades their every endeavor (H. Smith, 1958). Consequently, suffering results not only from individual acts, but from human sinfulness in general. For Christians, the suffering of illness and physical deformity are not always attributable to specific causes, but is a part of being sinfully human (Bemporad, 1987).

While Judaism maintains that human suffering is adequate punishment for sin, Christianity teaches that there is no penalty sufficient to atone for the rejection of God (H. Smith, 1958). Because of original sin, every human being deserves death and eternal suffering, as well as punishment for individual transgressions. However, like Jews, Christians believe that the covenant shows God to be merciful; God continues to love humanity, and is saddened by the pains that people bring upon themselves. Most importantly, because human beings could never fulfill the covenant nor atone for original sin, God forgave sinfulness and assumed the burden of punishment through Jesus Christ (Carmody & Carmody, 1988).

For Christians, the suffering servant of God was God become man: incarnated through the holy spirit, Jesus Christ innocently suffered persecution and death by crucifixion to atone for the sins of the whole world. Christianity teaches that Jesus' resurrection from the dead signaled God's triumph over sin in history; in death, those who accept his sacrifice will join God in an eternal life of joy, while those who reject him are separated from God to suffer the pain of hell.

Christianity has struggled to explain the continued presence of suffering among believers after the crucifixion (Bemporad, 1987). Early Christian martyrs sought out suffering in an imitation of Jesus. Later, theologians concluded that while original sin had been forgiven in the hereafter, sinful acts still warranted God's punishment in this life. Others argued that God did not want humanity to suffer, but permitted suffering in order to preserve human free will. Still others echoed the Jewish belief that for the righteous suffering was a blessed gift, which tested strength of character, afforded spiritual growth, and served as an example to others. Ultimately, however, Christianity teaches that suffering, like the incarnation, crucifixion, and resurrection, is a part of God's infinite mystery, which will be revealed only at the last judgment.

Predestination and divine compassion in Islam. All Islamic theology starts with the omnipotence of Allah. Everything has a divine purpose in God's will; Allah controls all of creation, and knows the destiny of every individual. For early Moslem scholars the concept of God's omnipotence created conflict over human predestination, sin, and suffering. Like Judaism and Christianity, Islam contends that suffering is the result of human sin. Yet, if Allah is in direct control of human behavior, then it is God who causes them to do evil. If humanity cannot truly sin, then their suffering is undeserved punishment from an unjust God.

Unlike Judaism and Christianity, which developed elaborate theologies of free will, Islam's religious leaders have rejected the entire problem since the tenth century (Green, 1987). Islam insists that humanity has no right to question divine justice, because Allah's ways remain beyond human understanding. Unbelief is the worst form of evil, and the greatest cause of human sin and suffering (Bemporad, 1987; Carmody & Carmody, 1988). Both unbelief and the misconduct that it promotes must be punished, not only in this world but with eternal suffering in the next. Human suffering demonstrates God's power over evil, and can be a source of faith and righteousness for those who seek God.

In general, Moslems believe that although much suffering is well-deserved punishment, it can also be a test of faith that reveals the sufferer's true character, moral strength, and religious dedication. Allah knows what each person can bear and metes out their suffering accordingly (H. Smith, 1958). The worst suffering may be relieved unexpectedly by Allah's compassion; thus no illness should be though of a incurable. Islamic tradition holds that even unexpected death can be a sign of God's compassion, for Allah may intervene to save a believer from otherwise certain sin (Green, 1987). While some Shi'ite Moslems practice mortification of the flesh as a spiritual exercise and value the sacrifice of martyrs, Islam typically does not encourage adherents to seek out suffering.

Like Jews and Christians, Moslems generally recognize suffering to be a part of being human that must be endured when it cannot be relieved. Whatever their earthly sufferings, God will judge the faithful compassionately in the hereafter, and reward their patient endurance abundantly.

The Secular Culture of Western Science and Medicine

Across North America and Europe, a secular culture based in scientific theory offers a rationale for human suffering that coexists and competes with the Western religious traditions. In this system, the origin of the universe is unclear, but nature is impersonal and amoral. Life's ultimate purpose is survival and evolution, and humanity's goal is to control the forces of nature that threaten its well-being (Hardin, 1969). Suffering can have amoral causes, such as destructive physical phenomena or evolutionary competition, or may be the result of human error, greed, or failure to recognize and control outside threats. Because human knowledge and control are incomplete, suffering is universal and often unpredictable; all suffering, however, ends with death, which is presumed to be the end of existence.

This secular system of ultimate meaning is the basis of Western scientific medicine, which, like formal religion, seeks to understand reality in order to improve human life and prevent suffering. While medical science accepts some pain as an important negative reinforcement against greater harm, it finds no meaning in suffering, per se. In this system, suffering that cannot be prevented should be relieved; suffering that cannot be relieved should be controlled (Schoffeniels, 1987). Because suffering has no meaning, uncontrollable suffering challenges the very value of life. It is this culture that has developed arguments for active euthanasia in the belief that unrelenting suffering inherently robs the sufferer of dignity and overwhelms any reason to live (Larue, 1985).

RESPONSES TO THE SUFFERING OF SELF AND OTHER

Around the world, victims of adversity are generally offered two interpretations of their suffering: either they are reaping the fruits of their own actions, or their suffering is an opportunity for spiritual growth. In either context, sufferers are counseled to reflect on their lives and their goals, rectify past wrongs, change their behavior, and accept suffering that cannot be alleviated. Whether suffering is interpreted as the result of natural forces, sin, or karma, a punishment, trial of faith, or gift from God, it is to be met with introspection, reform, and faith that life is not meaningless.

Individuals' Responses to Suffering and Community Expectations

Just as religious values define the meaning of suffering, cultural values define the sufferer's social role, and determine whether and how individuals express affliction. The group dynamics of most societies typically center either on individual self-sufficiency or mutual interdependence, and cultural variations on responses to suffering reflect these categories.

In every social system there are individuals who find personal meaning in adversity, and whose response to suffering serves as an inspiration to others. Their experiences typically demonstrate the best features of their society's cultural and religious beliefs about both suffering and interpersonal relations, as well as the tremendous strength of the human spirit. Unfortunately, the individual's experience of suffering may also be made more painful by others, whether family, friends, neighbors, caregivers, or total strangers, whose interpretations of religious and cultural ideals may place additional burdens on the sufferer.

Cultures of individual responsibility.   The cultures of North America and northern Europe, typically influenced by Protestantism and Western scientific theory, place a tremendous emphasis on individual responsibility and self-determination (Carmody & Carmody, 1988; H. Smith, 1958). The suffering of illness is generally interpreted as an individual problem, particularly in urban settings where community and even family ties may be weak (Parsons, 1979). Because of the cultural emphasis on personal privacy, few people outside a small circle of family and friends may be told of an individual's adversity. Moreover, even with family and friends, the sufferer may be ashamed of the loss of personal control or the moral judgment implicit in suffering (Lazare, 1987).

In Anglo-American culture, where sexual restraint is often considered to be the most important form of self-control, and where Christianity teaches that original sin is fundamentally linked to human sexuality, many interpret physical suffering to be a punishment for sexual transgressions. AIDS has renewed debate about the sexual origins of illness as divine punishment, but patients' operational theologies often involve symbolism that can link almost any ailment to sexual behavior.

Irrespective of culture, parents often blame themselves for not preventing their children's misfortunes. But because original sin is believed to be transmitted from one generation to the next, parents may experience additional guilt because they attribute their child's innocent suffering to their own sexual misconduct. Whether as adult patients or parents of a suffering child, such individuals may harbor serious misunderstandings about the causes of almost any medical condition, suffering in ignorant silence because they are too ashamed of their past actions to discuss their assumptions (Lazare, 1987).

In Western cultures, introspection may lead to increasing isolation and despair. A stiff upper lip prevents many Americans and Europeans from admitting to their need or asking for help—especially for analgesics, as such a request would admit additional loss of control (Zborowski, 1958). They may grow frustrated searching for an adequate moral cause for their adversity, or angry at themselves and others for failing to control its effects. Their suffering may be compounded by guilt over the trouble that they cause for others or over failing the test of adversity. Guilty anger at God for undeserved punishment or an unrequested gift of suffering may lead to bitterness, fear that they have been rightfully abandoned, and despair (Anderson, 1989).

In more communal Asian cultures that value "face," the emphasis on personal responsibility and privacy stems from the limited importance accorded to the needs of individuals in comparison to the needs of the larger community (Chang, 1981). Here, again, adversity may bring shame to the individual, whose needs upset the balance of the group. The threat of a communal loss of "face" encourages the sufferer's silence and isolation, and may lead to self-blame, resignation, and a sense of powerlessness.

Among the Japanese, for example, complaining, or even mentioning pain or discomfort is rare. Japanese women are almost silent during childbirth, even without anesthetics, because crying out in pain is shameful (Chang, 1981; Sampson, 1982). Yet, ironically, the sick role may provide a break from the daily rigor of Japanese social demands. Hospitalization in particular can sanction behavior that would be otherwise unacceptable in a culture of rigid hierarchy, and sufferers may ask for and expect favors from others (Chang, 1981; Ohnuki-Tierney, 1986).

Cultures of communal identity. In Africa, the Middle East, India, Asia, Latin America, and eastern and southern Europe, the individual is typically understood to be a part of an interdependent community whose respective needs and afflictions affect the entire group. Although community identity and interpretations of privacy may vary with the culture, the extended family, congregation, or entire village may know intimate details about a member's affliction, and speculate openly about its causes.

Even in community-oriented cultures, illness and disability are a source of shame to the sufferer if they are attributed to individual misconduct; public scrutiny of personal ailments and their possible causes can be humiliating (Chang, 1981; Lazare, 1987; Qureshi, 1989). Nonetheless, patients from many such cultures typically express their physical pains loudly and openly because of their belief in communal or "shared" privacy (Qureshi, 1989). Within such systems, however, certain subjects remain entirely personal: among Indians and Pakistanis, for example, excretory functions and psychiatric illness are not discussed even between spouses, and may go unspoken to caregivers (Qureshi, 1989).

Group consciousness challenges the Western definition of the patient, the patient's best interests, and informed consent. Whatever personal authority the sufferer may have had is suspended until his or her problem is resolved. In all but life-threatening emergencies, decisions are postponed until an appropriate family authority has been consulted because any action must be in the best interests of the patient as part of the larger family. While family authorities may reject options in the patient's best *individual* interests if they conflict too greatly with family or community needs, few such patients will question the decision-maker's moral authority to do so.

Among Hispanics, Indians, Asians, and Middle Easterners, women and younger members of the family expect the male head of the extended household, typically the older husband, father, or grandfather, to speak for them and to make decisions (Kay, 1977; Qureshi, 1989; Sampson, 1982). When the head of the family is ill, authority devolves to his oldest son or a son-in-law. In many Asian countries, the male head of the extended family might be advised by his wife when decisions involve daughters or daughters-in-law (Qureshi, 1989). In most African and Caribbean communities, older women assume a prominent role in negotiating with medical practitioners of behalf of family members, friends, and neighbors (Janzen, 1978; Qureshi, 1989).

Ironically, individual sufferers may be the only ones not told the details of their afflictions, even when personal reflection on suffering is believed to be essential. Terminally ill Moslems may not be told that death is imminent, both because Allah may intervene and because they are not responsible for decisions regarding their care. Latin Americans and southern and eastern Europeans believe that caregivers and family members responsible for decision making should withhold bad news to prevent the patient from losing hope. Although both Islam and Christianity teach that introspection and suffering can strengthen religious belief, these cultural practices imply that too much knowledge can destroy faith. They may also render the sufferer powerless to the affliction itself; patients may accept their conditions with passive fatalism if they believe that they have no active role in their treatment.

Where group solidarity absolves individuals of responsibility for their own care, sufferers may be isolated by their ignorance despite the companionship of others. They are unable to question others' efforts on their behalf because cultural definitions of the patient role emphasize passivity and gratitude (Chang, 1981; Ohnuki-Tierney, 1986; Qureshi, 1989). Even where patients recognize the conspiracy of silence, cultural tradition dictates that they feign ignorance and maintain good spirits to prevent their loved ones from suffering. This mutual deception means that patients often fear abandonment if they express their worries openly (Anderson, 1989). Additionally, the sufferer's shame and humiliation may result in inexpressible anger and resentment toward family and friends, which may be compounded by guilt over being unable to accept their support (Chang, 1981; Lazare, 1987).

Community Responses to the Suffering of Others

In addition to practices shaped by the culturally defined roles of patients and caregivers, four universal responses to the suffering of others also warrant consideration. Indifference, anger, punishment, and compassion have important cultural and religious features, and are common among health care professionals as well as others in the lives of patients.

Indifference. The belief that irresistible forces—whether karma or divine will—govern life implies that no one can affect the ultimate outcome of another's adversity. Fatalism and the acceptance of powerlessness can lead to widespread indifference about the suffering of others, which may be compounded by the belief that suffering in this life is rewarded in the next. Moreover, where suffering is interpreted as punishment, a necessary lesson, or an inevitable consequence of nature, the intervention of outsiders may be rejected as interference with the mechanisms of cosmic justice.

Western medicine, for example, was so influenced by the belief that suffering was essential to God's justice that when the anesthetic properties of ether were discovered, many doctors and patients refused to use it. Their argument was that pain was a natural effect of surgery, and therefore, as part of God's will, must be part of any acceptable cure (Kern, 1987). Similarly, secular "life boat" ethicists have argued that providing emergency food supplies to relieve famine only disrupts the natural Malthusian process of population control, and inevitably leads to greater, more widespread suffering in the future (Hardin, 1969).

Where terrible suffering becomes the norm, as in the case of the endemic poverty in developing countries or the overwhelming caseload of trauma patients in many urban American emergency rooms, observers' indifference may also result from desensitization. Long-term exposure to masses of people in extreme need makes their desperation seem much less appalling because it is so common. In such situations it becomes easy to disregard the suffering of an individual because there are so many others with equally or more compelling problems.

One of the most dangerous pitfalls of the professional commitment to care for the desperately sick and chronically suffering is that their constant demand for help may overwhelm even the most dedicated caregiver. The emotional exhaustion, desensitization, and indifference that are commonly known as "burnout" are often the result of a sense of personal powerlessness that stems from the feeling that helping individuals makes no difference in the long run (Moss, 1989). While burnout can be prevented, the ability to provide personal care while maintaining professional detachment is a skill rarely taught in formal training programs.

Anger. Anger at the suffering of others is a common response that often reflects frustration or grief. When adversity first strikes, the primary targets for others' anger are the sufferer, whose behavior created the problem; the experts who identify the affliction and its causes; and others—including God—who may have imposed the suffering (Anderson, 1989). When the suffering is prolonged, anger may be directed at the sufferer who has not improved, the experts whose treatments have not succeeded, or the God who has not intervened; each of these responses may also reflect self-directed anger at being unable to cope with the burden of care.

Despite the Western religious belief in God's mercy, anger at God is often interpreted as a terrible sin, and consequently may remain unspoken. For family members and friends especially, anger at God may turn to guilt, and subsequently to fear that their loved one will suffer additionally as God's punishment for this anger. Unresolved guilt may also result in a fear of God's abandonment, and overwhelming despair (Anderson, 1989).

Caregivers may respond to their patients' suffering with anger in much the same way that they reject their patients' need: patients who do not improve as expected may be blamed for the failure, and patients who complain or express hostility or frustration may be blamed for failing to accept their suffering nobly (Gorlin & Zucker, 1983). Practitioners' hostility toward patients whose conditions do not improve often stems from their fear of appearing inadequate or incompetent. An unwillingness to acknowledge personal and professional limits may lead caregivers to avoid or reject their "problem cases," or deny the patients' legitimate but unmeetable needs.

Caregivers, too, may wish to curse God for the suffering of the patients whose pain they witness daily. Because many therapeutic interventions seem only to add to patients' suffering, practitioners may grow angry at their patients, colleagues, or professional standards for "making them" impose anguish in the guise of therapy. In settings of tremendous need, practitioners may grow angry at their own inability to care adequately for everyone who needs help, blaming their supervisors, the institution, or "the system" for failing to provide adequate personnel, equipment, or funding. If unresolved, this anger can also produce incapacitating guilt, resentment, bitterness, and ultimately, burnout.

Punishment.   When suffering is interpreted as divine punishment or the result of bad karma, its association with evil may prompt others to reject the sufferer as contaminated. Aspects of each of the world's religions suggest that sin and human adversity are contagious, and that sinners should be cast out of society for everyone's protection. Rejection may take the form of abandonment, or may include humiliation, ridicule, or physical abuse, which may be justified as part of the sufferer's rightful punishment.

Unfortunately, health care providers are not beyond rejecting or even punishing their patients. The needs of "difficult" patients who do not "cooperate" with their caregivers may be discounted or ignored on the grounds that they do not really deserve attention (Anstett, 1980; Gorlin & Zucker, 1983; Stockwell, 1972). Equally, practitioners may unconsciously punish patients who appear slow to recover, noncompliant, or overly dependent by engaging in treatment that is inappropriately aggressive or unnecessarily painful.

Patients most often subject to punishment at the hands of health care professionals are those who afflictions are the result of such socially unacceptable practices as drug abuse, drunk driving, or sexual promiscuity (Gorlin & Zucker, 1983). Caregivers may condemn outright what they view to be willfully self-destructive behavior, especially in settings where there are other "more deserving" patients in need of attention. Such practitioners may also deny adequate pain control to patients with "self-inflicted" injury or disease, claiming that the patients' suffering reinforces the negative consequences of their behavior and serves as a form of preventative medicine.

Compassion. The nature of compassion is evident in the very word: "compassion" means "to suffer with." Compassion is considered almost universally to be the highest virtue and the purest form of personal relationship. In Hinduism, compassion is held to be one of the soul's highest aims, and a reflection of the love of Brahma; in Buddhism it is one of the universal virtues, and the fundamental attitude behind all good behavior. In Judaism, Christianity, and Islam, compassion is recognized as an expression of the image of God, and basis of the covenantal love. Even in secular Western philosophy, compassion has been called the basis of all morality (Blum, 1980).

Although it is impossible to share wholly in another's experience, the person who responds with compassion recognizes and respects the depth of another's suffering. Whereas pity often subsumes the sufferer's needs into the observer's interpretation, compassion is not judgmental, and preserves the sufferer's individual dignity and autonomy. Acting compassionately means offering remedy wherever possible, but even when nothing else is available, compassion means support, comfort, and human presence (Glick, 1985).

In karmic systems, individuals who respond to another's need with compassion create good karma for themselves and reduce their own suffering in the future. In the West, responding to another's suffering with compassion is to imitate God and incur God's blessing. Healers throughout history and across cultures have invoked compassion as not only a primary motivation, but also the source of their curative abilities.

Not surprisingly, compassion is widely interpreted to be the lesson that suffering offers both to the sufferer and those who witness others' adversity. As suffering is universal, it is an experience that can draw together people with little else in common, even when their suffering differs. Although the same experience of adversity or expression of suffering may mean radically different things to different people, compassion means an openness that can give both sufferers and those around them new insight and new sources of strength.

COMPASSION IN THE HEALTH PROFESSIONS: A QUESTION FOR THE FUTURE

The past two decades have witnessed renewed interest in professional ethics and professionalism in health care. Central to this revival has been an emphasis on compassion and the personal relationship between patient and practitioner. Professional organizations and educators have called for a greater emphasis on compassion in the training of health care professionals, and accrediting boards have even begun to call for proof of compassion as well as technical expertise (American Board of Internal Medicine, 1983; Dult, Giffin, & Patton, 1984; Glick, 1985).

In considering the future of health care, we must go beyond a simple call for more compassion to understand its complex nature and diverse manifestations. Cross-cultural, interreligious studies into the expression of compassion can enhance our understanding of its role in clinical practice. For example, Islam's focus on compassion for the stranger in need speaks to a common problem in urban hospitals and clinics, where patients and practitioners typically meet as strangers. The Buddhist concept of detached compassion stresses that no one can help another without that individual's active participation, and balances the role of healer with that of teacher; this view may prevent both paternalism and emotional exhaustion for the caregiver, and offers an alternative to abandoning the patient when physical intervention is no longer effective.

Greater still is our need to discover the origins and essence of compassion in order to foster its growth. Why are the men and women who make the "helping professions" their life's work *able* to care for and about others? Our knowledge of this vital dimension of human life is as incomplete as our understanding of suffering, and the insights of each of the world's traditions will be essential to any definition.

What makes compassion possible? It is a fundamental and timeless question, whose answer will both reflect and challenge humanity's most cherished religious and cultural values.

REFERENCES

American Board of Internal Medicine Subcommittee on Evaluation of Humanistic Qualities in the Internist. (1983). Evaluation of humanistic qualities in the internist. *Annals of Internal Medicine, 99,* 720–724.

Anderson, H. (1989). After the diagnosis: An operational theology for the terminally ill. *Journal of Pastoral Care, 43,* 141–50.

Anstett, R. (1980). The difficult patient and the physician-patient relationship. *Journal of Family Practice, 11,* 281–286.

Bemporad, J. (1987). Suffering. In M. Eliade (Ed.), *The encyclopedia of religion,* Vol. 14 (pp. 99–104). New York: Macmillan Publishers.

Blum, L. (1980). Compassion. In A.O. Rorty (Ed.), *Explaining emotions* (pp. 507–517). Berkeley, CA: University of California Press.

Bochner, S. (1983). Doctors, patients, and their cultures. In D. Pendelton & J. Hasler (Eds.), *Doctor-patient communication* (pp. 127–138). London: Academic Press.

Brown, K.M.C. (1989). Afro-Caribbean spirituality: A Haitian case study. *Second Opinion, 11* (July), 36–57.

Carmody, D.L., & Carmody, J.T. (1988). *How to live well: Ethics in the world religions.* Belmont, CA: Wadsworth Publishing Co.

Cassell, E.J. (1982). The nature of suffering and the goals of medicine. *New England Journal of Medicine, 306,* 639–645.

Chang, B. (1981). Asian-American patient care. In G. Henderson & M. Primeaux (Eds.), *Transcultural health care* (pp. 255–278). Reading, MA: Addison-Wesley Publishing Co.

Dult, B.W., Giffin, K., & Patton, B.R. (1984). *Interpersonal communication in nursing.* Philadelphia, PA: F.A Davis Co.

Eliade, M. (1959). *The sacred and the profane: The nature of religion. The significance of religious myth, symbolism, and ritual within life and culture.* New York: Harcourt Brace & World.

Elwood, R.S. (1973). *Religious and spiritual groups in modern America.* Englewood Cliffs, NJ: Prentice-Hall, Inc.

Engel, G.L. (1977). The need for a new medical model: A challenge for biomedicine. *Science, 196,* 129–135.

Fichtner, C.G., & McKenny, G.P. (In press). Interpreting patient values: A new model for hospital ministry. *Religion and Health.*

Fitzgerald, F.T. (1988). Patients from other cultures: How they view you, themselves, and disease. *Consultant, 28(3),* 65–77.

Glick, S.M. (1985). The component elements of compassion. *Pharos, 45* (Winter), 9–14.

Gorlin, R., & Zucker, H.D. (1983). Physicians' reactions to patients: A key to teaching humanistic medicine. *New England Journal of Medicine, 308,* 1069–1063.

Green, R.M. (1987). Theodicy. In M. Eliade (Ed.), *The encyclopedia of religion,* Vol. 14 (pp. 430–441). New York: Macmillan Publishers.

Hardin, G. (1969). *Population, evolution, and birth control* (2nd ed.). San Francisco, CA: Freeman.

Helman, C.G. (1990). *Culture, health and illness* (2nd ed.). London: Wright.

Janzen, J.M. (1978). *The quest for therapy: Medical pluralism in Lower Zaire.* Berkeley, CA: University of California Press.

Kaptchuk, T.J. (1983). *The web that has no weaver: Understanding Chinese medicine.* New York: Congdon & Weed.

Kay, M.A. (1977). Health and illness in a Mexican American barrio. In E.H. Spicer (Ed.), *Ethnic medicine in the Southwest* (pp. 99–166). Tucson, AZ: University of Arizona Press.

Kern, E. (1987). Cultural-historical aspects of pain. *Acta Neurochirurgica*, Suppl. *38*, 165–181.

Larue, G.A. (1985). *Euthanasia and religion: A survey of the attitudes of world religions to the right-to-die*. Los Angeles, CA: Hemlock Society.

Lazare, A. (1987). Shame and humiliation in the medical encounter. *Archives of Internal Medicine, 147*, 1653–1658.

Liu, D. (1979). *The Tao and Chinese culture*. New York: Schocken Books.

Mahoney, W.J., & Kogen, M. (1987). Karman. In M. Eliade (Ed.), *The encyclopedia of religion*, Vol. 8 (pp. 261–268). New York: Macmillan Publishers.

Mbiti, J.S. (1970). *African religions and philosophies*. Garden City, NY: Doubleday Anchor.

Moss, V.A. (1989). Burnout. Symptoms, causes, prevention. *AORN Journal, 50*, 19710–1072, 1074–1076.

Ohnuki-Tierney, E. (1986). Cultural transformations of biomedicine in Japan—Hospitalization in contemporary Japan. *International Journal of Technology Assessment in Health Care, 2*, 231–241.

Pandya, S.K. (1987). Hindu philosophy on pain. *Acta Neurochirurgica*, Suppl. *38*, 136–146.

Parsons, T. (1979). Definitions of health and illness in light of American values and the social structure. In E.G. Jaco (Ed.), *Patients, physicians, and illness: A sourcebook in behavioral science and health* (pp. 120–144). New York: The Free Press.

Qureshi, B. (1989). *Transcultural medicine: Dealing with patients from different cultures*. London: Kluwer Academic Publishers.

Roosens, E.E. (1989). *Creating ethnicity: The process of ethnogenesis*. Newbury Park, CA: Sage Publications.

Sampson, C. (1982). *The neglected ethic: Religious and cultural factors in the care of patients*. London: McGraw-Hill Book Co. (UK) Ltd.

Schoffeniels, E. (1987). Pain understanding and suffering considered by an agnostic. *Acta Neurochirurgica*, Suppl. *38*, 154–156.

Siegel, B.S. (1985). Helping children cope with death. *American Family Physician, 31*, 175–180.

Smith, B.K. (1987). Samsara. In M. Eliade (Ed.), *The encyclopedia of religion*, Vol. 13 (pp. 56–57). New York: Macmillan Publishers.

Smith, H. (1958). *The religions of man*. New York: Harper & Row, Publishers.

Sproul, B.C. (1979). *Primal myths: Creating the world*. San Francisco, CA: Harper & Row, Publishers.

Stockwell, F. (1972). *The unpopular patient*. London: Royal College of Nursing.

Tanaka-Matsumi, J., & Higginbotham, H.N. (1989). Behavioral approaches to counseling across cultures. In P.B. Pedersen, J.G. Draguns, W.J. Lonner, & J.E. Trimble (Eds.), *Counseling across cultures* (3rd ed.) (pp. 269–298). Honolulu, HI: University of Hawaii Press.

Tu, W-M. (1987). A Chinese perspective on pain. *Acta Neurochirurgica*, Suppl. 38, 147–151.

Zborowski, M. (1958). Cultural components in response to pain. *Journal of Social Issues*, 8, 16–30.

8

The Responses of Caregivers to the Experience of Suffering

Gwen Sherwood

*T*he *Giving Tree* is a poignant story of giving and receiving written by
Shel Silverstein (1964). In this story a boy comes to play on his favorite
tree. He plays with the leaves, eats the apples, climbs the branches, and
sits in the shade. The tree shares all she has through many seasons of the
boy's life. After the boy grows up and moves away, he returns asking for
money. The tree tells him to sell her apples to get the money. The boy is
again absent for a long time. He comes back wanting a house for his
family. The tree offers her branches to build a house. Again the boy is
gone for awhile. This time his return is marked by a wish for a boat. The
tree gives him her trunk to build a boat. When again after an absence the
boy returns, the tree has no apples, no branches, and no trunk. Only a
stump now, she has nothing left to give. But now the boy is old and tired
and only needs a place to sit and rest, which the stump provides. The tree
has given all.

One could wonder why the tree kept on giving even after the tree was
completely in an altered state and without the ability to renew its re-

sources. As caregivers, how long do we keep on giving? Do we, too, give until we are in an altered state unable to renew our resources?

Because we are in caregiving professions, it is expected we will care and give of ourselves. We have a moral duty to care. Our basic human philosophy is based on the intrinsic worth of every individual. We recognize basic human dignity with respect for personhood. We have a moral duty to care for the person's welfare because we have accepted the role of caregivers. Most of us have taken some oath of that declaration. For nurses, it is the Nightingale Pledge; for physicians, it is the Hippocratic Oath; for ministers, it is a Covenant and Ordination. What effect does this constant moral obligation have on us? How do we as caregivers respond to the experience of human suffering?

Let us first explore what it is to care. To care is to produce positive change. Care is encouraging growth of the other. Care is having mutual connectedness and giving existential presence to the other. Our purpose as caregivers is to improve the human condition, to produce positive changes, to encourage growth, to enable others to live life to its fullest, to alleviate suffering.

In our professional practice, we seek to instill hope, empower others, encourage independence, and help improve the other's condition. When we are unable to achieve that, unable to alleviate suffering, we often experience a sense of frustration and failure. Can we, like The Giving Tree in the story, give until we have given it all? What happens when we *give care* every day? How do we balance the stress of constant exposure to suffering with our moral duty to care amid concern for our own well-being?

The inner self can be torn by conflicting professional and personal concerns. Concerns often arise when professional activities require a level of dedication threatening to the welfare of one's personal life. Professional caregivers have extensive opportunity for open-ended dedication. There is always a client in great need for whom not enough can be given. Our professions call for dedication to the welfare of clients; it is considered a high calling. It is considered an ordinary duty, even a selfish act, to take care of oneself, however. We expect clients to observe this ordinary duty to take care of self. We expect them to follow treatment protocols and instructions for self-care leading toward recovery. We feel it is their moral duty to do so.

Why do we not feel a moral duty to care for ourselves? We can see a conflict of duties to self: one dedicated to care of others, the other to self-care. While we are to act with an informed moral conscience, we are taught that needs of the client supersede needs of the caregiver. The caregiver must not compromise the integrity of the client relationship with behavior that is self-serving. The struggle to care for self and others at the same time is not simply a conflict between duties to self and duties to others: the problem for the professional is to strike a consistent balance between these two competing duties (Jameton, 1987).

To maintain our caregiving abilities, it is important morally to treat oneself well (i.e., to treat oneself as an autonomous individual, avoiding degrading situations, not depriving oneself unduly, and filtering out the meaningless demands of our professions). The commitment to care for oneself can create a dilemma. In our current prevailing bureaucratic structures, the personal needs of caregivers are rarely considered. We treat the caregiver with insensitivity and without rights, while expecting the caregiver to treat the client with sensitivity and with regard to basic human rights. How can we expect the caregiver to respect the dignity and needs of others if such is denied to the caregiver? Where is the moral obligation of the institution to the caregiver?

We have been taught psychosocial concepts as applied to the patient experience. However, with increasing pressure from our information explosion and use of high technology, there is very little in our already overcrowded curricula to enable meeting the psychosocial needs of the caregiver. Educators are torn between producing graduates who are employable in the health care marketplace and educating caregivers capable of withstanding the stress of daily practice.

Caregivers do not burn out when good relationships are experienced in the workplace, only when poor relationships prevail. It seems, therefore, that teaching students in the caregiving professions ways to establish and maintain caring and compassionate relationships, not only with clients but also with each other, would help equip the practitioner for the rigors of the real world.

We can give until we reach the end of our resources—the daily toll of human problems, misery, and defeat can produce caregivers who no longer care, who can no longer produce positive change, no longer encourage growth, or make transcendent connections with others. We can become depressed, burned out, withdrawn, guilty, fatigued, irrational, irritable, angry, and impersonal. Recognizing these symptoms is important to maintaining one's inner self.

Most of us are familiar with Herzberg's (1966) motivation-hygiene theory of job satisfaction. He asked engineers and accountants to recall a time when they felt particularly good about their job and to describe the events, what made them feel as they did, how the feeling of satisfaction affected job performance, personal relationships, and well-being. He also asked the nature of the events which served to neutralize or return their attitudes to normal. Then he asked the same about negative times. He identified five factors which were strong determinants of job satisfaction: The first two, achievement and recognition, relate to the self, the person. The last three have more to do with the work environment and are more important for lasting attitude changes: the work itself, responsibility, and advancement. These five determinants of job satisfaction are seen as motivators. Interestingly, the converse of these five do not become the dissatisfiers. Rather the major dissatisfiers, viewed as maintenance or hygiene factors, include: company policy and administration, supervision, salary, working conditions, and interpersonal relations. While much of Herzberg's theory has been debated, it appears that much of the caregiver's response to the intensity of his or her work is tied very closely to concept of the self and the environment in which the work is done.

Within our inner world of perceptions, we are able to find our sense of purpose. Quite often that sense of purpose may be our vocation. When that is the case, we find involvement, commitment, and motivation—three separate aspects of the sense of vocation within the self-concept. As caregivers, we have ample opportunity to experience purpose and meaning through our vocational choice. The problem becomes, how do we balance our competing duties to clients and self?

In a series of interviews conducted by this author with a variety of professional caregivers, many stories were told, stories of how these caregivers respond to the constant witnessing of suffering in their daily work. A common theme for all was a reaction of awe and feeling of privilege to being allowed to enter the world of the suffering, to be invited into this private world. To be included as a member of the caregiving team was itself an opportunity to make a difference in the world of the other. A hospital chaplain explained her response this way, and, in many ways, hers was a typical response:

Some days it is a real privilege. They invite me in almost immediately and immediately start talking about what is going on. Other days it is a real draining experience. Especially if that person reminds me of someone I know, like my grandmother or a neighbor, or is close in age to me. It becomes more personal and it becomes an internal struggle to separate my feelings from theirs, so it is important for my part to focus on their feelings and not try to put words into their mouths or think how they should feel in that situation or how I would feel in that situation. So the overriding word is, it is a real challenge but very rewarding because you learn about the wonder of opportunity—not just the physical aspects but also the emotional and then the spiritual part and how resilient these people really are. I am lucky to have other chaplains to talk with, otherwise I think I might get depressed and let it internalize. We may just go down and get a yogurt or just get together and talk it out. Sometimes it helps just to know someone else has had to do what I've just had to do with a patient.

Something that has meant a lot to me is journaling. Sometimes there is something that is really difficult that I've dealt with that words don't touch on, and it may be a couple of days before the full impact hits me and all the different aspects of the situation dawn on me; and it helps me to write it down to capture my feelings, my reactions to it. Then later I can come back and read that response when it was fresh, and it helps me in another situation that is similar if I can remember my response and how I dealt with it and how I got over the hump. Working with people who suffer makes me appreciate life so much more. I'm so much more aware of the little things. Sometimes I have trouble with certain conversations. I just don't care about the price of tomatoes when I am thinking about the life and death situations I've been dealing with. I just have trouble staying with those trivial conversations.

In his book, *All I Really Need to Know I Learned in Kindergarten*, Robert Fulgrum (1988) lists 14 things essential to living a full life.

Share everything, play fair, don't hit people, put things back where you found them, clean up your own mess, don't take things that aren't yours, say you're sorry when you hurt somebody, wash your hands before you eat, flush, warm cookies and cold milk are good for you, live a balanced life—learn some and think some and draw and paint and sing and dance and play and work some every day, take a nap every afternoon, when you go out into the world watch out for traffic, hold hands and stick together, be aware of wonder.

Fulgrum considers these basic principles, which can be applied throughout life. They are broad lessons which have to do with living comfortably with self and others. It seems feasible that some broad lessons could be taught in beginning courses (the kindergarten of professional education) that are fundamental to our respective practices and offer a lifelong reference for those of us responsible for the care of people (Parse, 1990).

A list of basic principles essential for maintaining self in caring for others could be of help to newly practicing caregivers as well as experienced caregivers. Such a list could help put the demands of a caregiving vocation into a more balanced perspective with the search for meaning and fulfillment.

1. *Be knowledgeable.* The caregiver must first be competent and confident of his or her own knowledge and expertise. Only then can the caregiver be released from the anxiety of "what to do now" to be able to be therapeutic. Davidson (1990) reports on interviews with sexual assault nurse examiners to describe the interaction of the examiner and the sexual assault survivor. These expert nurses deal with the intensity of these emotional encounters by approaching the encounter fully prepared, focusing and centering on the pending interaction based on knowledge of the patient, and by using each interaction as a learning experience incorporating outcomes into their body of knowledge and expertise.

    Knowledge gives confidence. Only a competent caregiver can meet with the client in an atmosphere of trust and mutuality. When the caregiver is able to successfully give competent, knowledgeable care, renewal of energy, not burnout, results. In an interview with this author, a head nurse on an oncology unit reinforced this idea of competence. As she provided the knowledge the staff needed through staff development, anxiety decreased while quality of care increased.

2. *Value the other as a human presence.* Respect differences in views, personalities, and cultural expressions. Recognize individual differences as the uniqueness that makes the world such an interesting place to be. Practice grounded in the intrinsic worth of the individual yields satisfaction and reward.

3. *Be accountable for your actions.* Don't fall into the trap of blaming others for what happens. A professional is able to take responsibility even for failure.

4. *Be open and creative to new ideas.* Don't be afraid to try new ideas and strategies. Learn something new every day. The injection of a new idea into the routine can be a stimulus adding challenge to the job. If you haven't tried keeping a journal, try it. It may be a way of stress management and emotional release which works for you. Don't be afraid to try a new idea.

5. *Connect with others.* Talking stressful situations over with other people helps relieve tension and can put the situation in a new perspective. Take the time to go get a yogurt with a co-worker and talk about the difficult situations you are encountering. If you are in a private practice, schedule lunch with a colleague. Not taking a

break from the routine does no favor to anyone, least of all your clients. Nurses often say they just cannot leave the floor, and indeed there are crisis times when clients come first, but don't routinely deny yourself the opportunity to release your mind and body for a moment from the pressure.

Support your colleagues. We tend to ostracize those who make mistakes by never forgiving and forgetting. Because we are dealing with critical situations, we tend to think there is no room for error. When mistakes happen, why not rally around that colleague and support that person with our presence rather than offer condemnation? We could be next. Think of how you want others to respond to you and let that guide your actions.

6. *Take pride in yourself.* This means take care of yourself. Manage your grooming—make yourself look good. This means that awful "E" word: *exercise.* Exercise everyday. In the interviews with caregivers, it was the most frequently mentioned mode of dealing with stress. It not only lessens tensions and anxiety but it also will make you look better and feel better. The self-discipline exercise requires will make you feel pride in yourself. Remember, you value the basic dignity of all human beings, and this does include you.

7. *Like what you do.* This is essential. Don't sit around daily complaining about your job. Take charge and do something about what needs changing. Use Herzberg's questions to discover your feelings about what you do. Take stock of what gives you satisfaction about what you do. Then consider what is negative and why this is so. You may discover ways to make changes in your situation to deal more effectively with the pressure.

8. *Recognize the moments of joy in the struggles of living.* Every caregiver interviewed by this author talked about the privilege of working with people who suffer. Each felt it a special place to be, to be admitted into the client's world. One minister described it as awesome, to be asked to come at a moment that is so precious, so intense, to be a part of a special team caring for this person.

Oncology nurses echoed this sentiment. They felt it a joyful responsibility to be there, to see the struggle, to be able to make a difference. According to all those interviewed, making a difference is the key to finding satisfaction in caring for those who suffer. This recognition that their own particular skills, abilities, and self can make a difference in someone's life is the element which keeps them coming each day to the job to do it all again with someone else. Seeing the joy of recovery as well as seeing the comfort and peace of those unable to recover was the critical difference. In respecting life, in seeing the joy and the struggle, knowing that *you* make a difference in the world of the suffering is what makes the job meaningful.

9. *Recognize your own limitations.* Not everything in life can be explained. You will not have all the answers. Do not be afraid to ask for help. Expert professionals know their own limitations and recognize when to call for assistance. Don't feel guilty when your interventions are not successful. You won't be 100 percent effective, but recognize the ways you did help and were successful. Incorporate what you can learn from mistakes and failures and continue striving for excellence.

10. *Rest and begin anew.* Physical rest is just as important as physical exercise. A fatigued and worn out caregiver just cannot be expected to pull out the necessary resources in a time of crisis. Even Jesus went away to rest and pray. As one minister described, being alone and contemplating can be a valuable renewal. Solitude can be therapeutic as a retreat from daily pressures. The Trappist monk Thomas Merton wrote,

It is in deep solitude that I find the gentleness with which I can truly love my brothers. The more solitary I am, the more affection I have for them. [Nouwen, 1975]

Solitude did not separate him from his contemporaries but instead brought him into a deep communion with them. Finding peace within ourselves deepens our affection for others and allows real community to take place. For some this will be a religious experience, with prayer and communion with their God a source of renewing energy.

In summary, these precepts for coping with a caregiving profession reflect values emerging from a basic belief that all life is precious, the client's *and* the caregiver's. It is our moral duty to care not only for others but also for ourselves. Caregivers who can employ these fundamental principles for living are more likely to come to the practice arena comfortable with themselves, proud, competent, and available to persons in their changing patterns of living. Recognizing each person as a human presence, these caregivers respect different views and are nonjudgmental. They focus on the client's own view of life. They are open to new discoveries in their practice, willing to examine and test propositions, valuing the mystery in each person with whom they come in contact. They own their beliefs, rise to confirm their convictions in advancing knowledge, and move on to the new. There is an open interchange among these caregivers in a network that fosters diverse thinking. They like what they do, recognizing the moments of joy in the struggles of working with other professionals and clients. Knowing the importance of personal vitality, they take time to rest and begin anew through recreation and contemplation. The challenge is to care for self so that you can care for others.

REFERENCES

Davidson, L. (1990). *A description of certified sexual assault nurse examiners' interactions with sexual assault survivors*. Unpublished master's thesis. The University of Texas Health Science Center at Houston School of Nursing, Houston, TX.

Fulgrum, R. (1988). *All I really need to know I learned in kindergarten*. New York: Random House.

Herzberg, F. (1966). *Work and the nature of man*. New York: Thomas Crowell Company.

Jameton, A. (1987). Duties to self: Professional nursing in the critical care unit. In M. Fowler and J. Levine-Arisf (Eds.), *Ethics at the bedside*. Philadelphia: J.B. Lippincott.

Parse, R. (1990). Essentials for practicing the art of nursing. *Nursing Science Quarterly*, 2(3), 111.

Silverstein, S. (1964). *The giving tree*. New York: Harper & Row.

9

Therapeutic Interventions for Suffering: Professional and Institutional Perspectives

Jan van Eys

Suffering is an affliction, a syndrome, which is in theory amenable to intervention. Persons who are suffering have support structures through their circles of family and friends. Church communities may rally around the one in need. Religion can give a perspective on suffering that may be helpful. The traditions of the community can reassure the person in daily life. In our complex society, however, we think in terms of purchased help from professionals and institutions whenever we are afflicted. This idea suggests a medical model for suffering with scientifically determined intervention strategies.

That view is not really appropriate. Suffering is a human burden that may not be truly avoidable. In fact, it may be the price we pay for being human.

In order to put that view in perspective we must examine suffering in a form as isolated from self-inflicted behavior as possible. The suffering of a child is one such example. Furthermore, the cause of suffering must be considered controllable in order to isolate the etiology. The medical center based care with modern technology and research-laced intervention creates such an environment. Because my profession is pediatric oncology, the example I know best is the child with cancer. In a sense, cancer in a child is a social experiment of nature. We learn from young children with cancer not only about the disease but also about ourselves (van Eys, 1989).

The discussion to follow, therefore, is about children with cancer. It gives an eloquent example of our perceptions of suffering in children. In many ways it is a prime paradigm for the suffering of all children worldwide and yet it is also a uniquely Western example of problems generated both in spite of, and because of, an affluent and technologically advanced society.

Children can and do get cancer. In fact, cancer in children is not that rare a disease. More are cured than not. Cure, however, is bought at a price of much iatrogenic disease, psychological trauma, and social complications. The treatment is often done in an experimental mode, and the cost of care is enormous. A significant number of children are not cured by the current methods available, but that is not predictable; there are very few instances in which the physician can foretell a poor outcome. Therefore, all children with the same type and extent of tumor are treated initially the same.

Parents are informed about the treatment offered and are warned about the side effects. Generally, great pains are taken to protect the child from unnecessary psychological trauma without forgoing truthful disclosure. Families are helped with the social and financial burdens, but there is no denying that the treatment will be onerous on child and family alike. Because cure is so real a possibility, the family almost invariably agrees to the treatment.

Initially the treatment is accepted and hope is high. Side effects are taken in stride. That does not mean that the parents and the child have little problem with the therapy, but it does show that the therapy and its consequences are acceptable. Many a mother has her time of breakdown, but only because of the difficulties faced, not because the cause is seen as hopeless or futile.

Sometimes something goes awry. The tumor recurs, the treatment fails and a new treatment is offered, often with lesser margin between safe and effective dose levels. This may happen again and again. The child enters the investigative-palliative downward spiral. Experimental drugs are accepted for their inherent hope, but realistic expectations are that the best outcome is no more than a prolongation of life with excessive effort and cost at all levels—physical, psychological, social, and financial.

Sometimes a child dies while this investigative route is being tried. More and more often, however, parents refuse that last effort, that newest drug, that touted biological. They suddenly say, "My child has suffered enough." Usually the transition from moderate to severe iatrogenic disease is not sharply demarcated. It is a gradual process. The parent makes that decision as often as not without compelling data that make a change in the cost-benefit ratio obvious. What was deplorable but necessary pain for a child up to then suddenly has become suffering.

The word *suffering* is rich in meanings and heavily value-laden. The meaning can range widely: allowing or tolerating, enduring or undergoing, sustaining an injury and finally, undergoing or feeling pain and distress. None totally describes the choice of suffering when used in the setting of advanced cancer in a child. Suffering in this situation means feeling pain and distress, but a mere definition does not describe the effect of suffering when perceived in this way.

It is not just pain, malaise, or deprivation of the joys of childhood. Often that is present from the beginning before the word suffering is ever used in regard to that child. It is my understanding that suffering in that context, and probably in general, means *the perception of undeserved adversity*. It is the parent or caregiver who uses the word suffering. The child does not have that rich a vocabulary. In other words, for the child, *suffering is an adult concept.*

To elaborate on this thesis that suffering is the perception of undeserved adversity, I will first discuss the adult views of the child in our society. While the concept of suffering is general, the adult-child relationship gives it a special focus. I will then elaborate on that transition from acceptance of onerous therapy to the perception of suffering. I will address the problems that the perception of undeserved adversity brings for modern medical care and clinical research. Finally, I will return to the child and examine this interpretation of suffering in the child's view.

THE CHILD IN 20TH CENTURY AMERICA

It is only very recently that children have been seen as children instead of as miniature adults. Child labor was commonly accepted as being socially productive and individually salutary. Children were considered expendable by society even when individual families cared for their offspring. In his history of American pediatrics, Cone comments that,

> As the nineteenth century began . . . children when ill were still cared for almost exclusively by parents, grandparents, and neighbors. Physicians were rarely consulted, nor, save for a few, did they make any effort to seek out infants and children as patients. [Cone, 1979, p. 69]

The drive to establish pediatrics as a specialty was social conscience. The infant mortality rate was appalling, and inadequate feeding of children was a major cause of infant mortality as it still is around the world. Nutritional science, public hygiene measures, freedom from disease-fostering environments transformed infant and child mortality rates to the modern numbers.

The practice of pediatrics remains accepted. As late as 1970, however, John Apley, the staunch defender of pediatrics, felt compelled to remind the medical and psychiatric professions that children are not mini-adults, mechanistic medicine is incomplete, and detaching child from family does not make sense (Apley, 1984, p. 96). There is a widespread feeling that the conscience of the nation is clear when it comes to our treatment of children. There are compulsory education laws and reasonable standards of required knowledge; there are child labor laws; children often can get public assistance before any other groups; and child protective services are generally well established. That does not equate, however, with a view of the child as one who is a uniquely different human from the adult but inherently equal as a valued individual.

There is an enormous amount of violence to children. It is often said to be the expression of frustration from modern stresses and, therefore, a new phenomenon. That is hardly the case. It was again Apley who said that, "Violence is nothing new, and to children is surely not a' problem peculiar to our time, even though the awareness of it may be" (Apley, 1984, p. 145). Children are not always seen as individuals. Children are seen, at best, as wholly dependent and totally beholden to the adult in whose care they find themselves. They are at the mercy of the adult values by which they are judged. The ambient value system is not always at the level we like to imagine it is.

There is a children's rights movement in this country that tries to support the social acceptance of children as equal participants in society at the level of their competence. In a volume of essays on the subject, the editors wrote in their introduction:

A good case can be made for the fact that young people are the most oppressed of all minorities. They are discriminated against on the basis of age in everything from movie admissions to sex. They are traditionally the subjects of ridicule, humiliation, and mental torture by adults. Their civil rights are routinely violated in homes, schools, and other institutions. They lack the right to trial by jury before being sentenced to jail.

These oppressions are inherent in being too young in this society. If a child is spared then it is because of special privilege and the sufferance of adults, not because as a human being he or she has an inviolable right not to be damaged, sentenced, incarcerated, or discriminated against. [Gross & Gross, 1977, pp. 1–3]

This is very strong and even pejorative language and by most measures rather overstates the case.

There is some truth in it, however. It is the extreme expression of the idea that the child is seen as wholly dependent and under the charge of parent or guardian. That view had the strength of law. For instance, the question of children's competence to give or refuse consent is of largely recent origin (Melton, 1983, p. 1). It was not until 1967 that the Supreme Court stated that "neither the Fourteenth Amendment nor the Bill of Rights is for adults alone" (*In re* Gault, 387 U.S. 1, 13, 1967). That legal precedent is not generally acknowledged and is only slowly working its way down into society's conscience.

Yet there is also a general neglect of children by these selfsame parents and guardians who feel that their children are beholden to them under full authority. The narcissistic trends in today's society make many parents appear indifferent to the needs of today's children, and, even more frighteningly, to those of future generations. The social historian Lash considers this neglect of children part of a broader neglect and reckless exploitation of all natural resources (Lash, 1986). The exploitation of children is still with us but has taken on new forms.

The child in need, as a child with cancer is, does call forth the urge to protect and nurture. The majority of parents have the well-being of their sick child at heart. The parents that bring their children to be treated for as burdensome a disease as cancer are sacrificing a great deal for their child. They want to protect their child from all harm. They do not see the child as the independent person he or she is, but they do accept the child as fully human, worthy of protection by the human herd to which he or she belongs (van Eys, 1981). Any harm to the child is seen as a failure by the parents in the discharge of that duty.

THE ONSET OF SUFFERING

The corollary to this view is that the child is also seen as helpless—incapable of self-help and independent decision. The affliction of cancer is an unacceptable assault on the helpless and innocent child. The parents cannot allow that to happen. The child is stricken in an unjust way, but the parents are convinced they are going to rectify that injustice. They will do what is recommended. They hope that, like Elijah, the physician can restore life to their child. In a sense they let the physician call God down on the injustice, and ask for a repeat of the example of Elijah:

"Give me your son," [Elijah] said. He took the boy from her arms and carried him up to the roof-chamber where his lodging was and laid him on his own bed. "O Lord my God, is this thy care for the widow with whom I lodge that thou hast been so cruel to her son?" Then he breathed deeply upon the child three times and called on the Lord, "O Lord my God, let the breath of life, I pray, return to the body of this child." The Lord listened to Elijah's cry, and the breath of life returned to the child's body, and he revived; Elijah lifted him up and took him down from the roof into the house, gave him to his mother and said, "Look, your son is alive." Then she said to Elijah, "Now I know for certain that you are a man of God and that the word of the Lord on your lips is truth." [1 Kings 17:19–24 (New English Bible)]

God is merciful after all—the recovery of the child is God's doing. There is no need to invoke justice or injustice anymore. Calling on the right prophet has allowed peace with God. That same mother had accused Elijah, her boarder, to have come to bring her sins to light and kill her son. (1 Kings 17–18 [NEB]). There is always that nagging self-recrimination in the parents that it was something they did or omitted that brought the cancer on the child.

In modern medicine, the cures are as often as not bordering on the miraculous as sure as did Elijah's resuscitation. Modern medicine is very powerful. It also demands an enormous amount of physiological insult in order to being these cures about. The issues here are not the excesses modern medicine can cause nor the ethical quandaries that can arise at times when further efforts should be curtailed. It is merely a statement of fact that the side effects of major cancer surgery, radiotherapy, and chemotherapy can be very severe and often a greater cause of morbidity than the cancer itself in the early stages of the disease.

The widow trusted Elijah to take the child to his room and it was implied that she did not follow. She entrusted the child to him. In the same sense parents entrust their child to the physician. The child is admitted to the hospital chosen by the physician, and while one parent, usually the mother, is encouraged to stay with the child, much of what happens is seen but not really understood. All explanations are accepted and informed consents are signed because that is the way the child has access to the cure that God placed in this world to show His mercy to that child.

That mother observes and allows the medical cure, and, when again at home, must execute it herself. She cannot allow herself to doubt the necessity and the ultimate benefit of the treatment even when she observes physical changes, extreme nausea, vomiting, overwhelming infections, bleeding, and transfusions. She has to answer pleas for protection against all those painful procedures with reassurance that it is all necessary.

When all turns out well, and the therapy can be stopped, many parents actually worry about that too. They fear that stopping will bring back the cancer. They fear the new loss of control the cure brings. Up until then they were actively doing something, and they had faith in their physicians to have ordered the best possible care. Suddenly, they are again at the mercy of an uncertain future. There are no longer the incantations to summon God's mercy by reminding the child to take the chemotherapy pill. If cure is real, that fear eventually fades and life goes on again.

A smaller group of children fail the therapy before completion, however. A new treatment is proposed. The side effects become more severe and the chances for success diminish with each succeeding new treatment. Sooner or later cure is no longer a realistic goal. Palliation, symptom abatement, and comfort become the goal.

When that happens, the side effects of all that treatment are no longer acceptable. It changes the perception of what is happening; the parents suddenly see themselves as the ones who make their child sick by either allowing the medical team to continue new attempts at fighting the cancer or by being the persons who actually give the treatment to the child themselves. What was the best way to show love suddenly becomes only the infliction of more pain.

Suddenly, they are convinced that the child deserves better from the persons who have taken upon themselves the total responsibility for and protection of that child. The parents become unjust in their own eyes. What is happening to that child is suffering—they see the child as having undeserved pain. They know they are the perpetrators. It is no longer divine injustice tempered by mercy—it has become human injustice through powerlessness.

It is then that it is said that the child has suffered enough. The direction is a new one. No more pain will be inflicted, only comfort will be sought. There is a feeling of guilt that pain has been inflicted for no good purpose. Even when the child has died and the physician requests permission for an autopsy, the first refusal is frequently, "no, my child has suffered enough." The parents cannot allow anything more to happen, especially something that is perceived as totally futile. When they perceive that there is benefit in the autopsy to other children and for themselves because lingering questions can be answered, they more often give permission.

Ken Vaux summarizes the perception of injustice and mercy in this setting very well:

> The fundamental problem in pediatric oncology is theodicy: caring in the face of the absurd. Why me? Why my child? Justice and mercy are human . . . symbols to construe cruel happenstance and to make sense of a God who cares, yet allows beautiful children to become sick and die. From the human perspective, justice and mercy are defense mechanisms, rationalizations, insights that allow us to continue to believe and act in the face of the inscrutable. [Vaux, 1985]

When we try to be conduits of God's mercy, we can become the perpetrator of human injustice. The necessary pain becomes unnecessary suffering. The total dependence of the child accentuates the human role in this transition.

SCIENTIFIC MEDICINE AND SUFFERING OF CHILDREN

A child suffers when noxious ministrations prove futile. It is not fair— it is unjust and the injustice is perpetrated by those in whom children should be able to place their trust. Just as the trust of the child is in the parents, however, so is the trust of the parents in their child's physician.

In spite of all the stress on informed consent and independent decision making for the consumer of health care, the reality is that the final stage is always placing trust in someone who will and can help. The parents start with almost complete faith and trust in the power of medicine and, by inference, the physician. The physician, however, knows that there are limitations, that failure is quite possible. No promises are made. In fact, even experiments are proposed to try to reach certainty where none exists.

Clearly, when a pediatric oncologist tries to enroll a child in a prospective randomized clinical trial, a message is given that there is no certain way to optimize the chance at cure for the child. The parents may be given all the details about the trial, they may learn the principle of double blinded study, they become aware of the idea that the child will be randomly assigned a specific therapy. After all that is done, they can often retell the rationale and the specifics of a study very well. When the question is asked, however, "do you want your child to participate in this study?" the answer is as often as not, "I don't know doctor, you do what you think is best."

The parents retain the hope for a good outcome and the security that what they have chosen for their child is best. The burden is now on the physician, who must justify the experiment. The concept of justice reappears at another level. If the experiment is not justified, if the science is not impeccable, the child suffers. The physician has the struggle to be the bearer of justice while seen as the conduit of mercy. It is an enormous stress.

When there is no known therapy and the disease is likely to be fatal, the patient is better served with a well-conceived novel idea than with a traditional and futile approach. Research therapy becomes the best therapy. As treatment becomes more effective statistically, however, there is less and less compelling need to use humans as investigational subjects. Care and research become divergent.

Vaux (1987) suggests the image of the physician as sacrificing priest. The priest-physician serves a higher purpose for society beyond the ministrations to the individual. This is the doctor's dilemma. Frankel summarized well the struggle of the physician-investigator. It is difficult to keep the value of the individual patient as the focal point of research endeavors (Frankel, 1987).

The threat to physicians to see their patients as suffering is always there. Sometimes such thoughts are overshadowed with an exaggerated defense and promotion of the benefit and quality of the clinical research. Many excesses in research have been promoted precisely because of that fear of doing harm. However, more often research quality is compromised for patient care. The individual patient wins out, as it should be.

SUFFERING AND THE CHILD

Suffering is an adult concept. Justice and mercy are the noblest human concepts, perhaps the most noble ever to have engaged the human spirit (Vaux, 1985, p. 68). At the same time, they are difficult concepts that are not easily thought through. They came late to human society in the sense we see them now as divine impulses. Similarly they come later to the child in development.

The child's notion, "it is not fair," is initially a notion of distributive justice. The child does not yet subscribe to the idea that reward and retribution are both part of justice. As often as not, a child decides that mercy bestowed on others is not fair.

There is an innate feeling that there is a right to life. In a sense, annihilation is the ultimate injustice. Cassell sees suffering as occurring only when impending destruction of the person is perceived (Cassell, 1982). This is suffering as perceived by the sufferer. This impending destruction, Cassell said, did not have to come physically. It could be played out psychologically or socially. This notion of suffering is close to the idea of a perception of undeserved adversity. It always focuses on the affective meaning of the experience. It is not the pain but the reaction to the pain that changes it from experiencing to suffering.

Children do not have adult reasoning. They do not have adult knowledge. When it comes to feelings, however, children are no different than adults. Children understand abandonment, loneliness, separation, pain, fear, and angst. They feel rudeness, condescension, being ignored. They suffer when they experience these emotions because they rightfully expect that the adults should support them in their needs.

Children must interpret the world with the help of adults. They do not have the time to rediscover all of human achievement on their own. That means help in interpreting the affective meaning of their world and the events in it. Elkind has shown us that before the ages of 11 to 12, most children are unable to understand religious concepts as they are understood by adults (Elkind, 1978). The same idea is seen in the child's view of prayer. Affective content does not enter until the child is older. Emotional responses become more modulated and mature as prayer takes on a personal affective meaning while becoming more impersonal in its objectives and goals.

We are prone to consider feelings childlike and reasoning adult like. Therefore, we try to make the child reason through our religious and philosophical constructs in order to receive the same benefit from them that the adult does. This does not work. A child could understand the meaning of the psalms:

> O Lord, my God, by day I call for help,
> by night I cry aloud in thy presence.
> Let my prayer come before thee,
> hear my loud lament;
> for I have had my fill of woes,
> and they have brought me to the threshold of
> Sheol. [Psalm 88, 1–3 (NEB)]

However, that psalm would be directed to the parent and not to a God that cannot be imagined as relevant except in fantasy.

Many parents hear the words later in that psalm from their children:

> Thou has taken all my friends far from me,
> and made me loathsome to them.
> I am in prison and cannot escape;
> my eyes are failing and dim with anguish.
> I have called upon thee, O Lord, every day
> and spread out my hands in prayer to thee.
> [Psalm 88, 8–9 (NEB)]

Cancer in a child brings pain, separation from the normal childhood, hair loss, and other physical changes. It is the response of the parents and the conviction that whatever is done is all right that helps the child.

Children who undergo painful treatments deserve not to be abandoned by the adults in whom they place their trust. The world of the child with cancer is different than it was before the cancer struck. As I said elsewhere,

> There is absolutely no demand that a child should like a bone marrow aspiration. Rather the converse, a healthy normal situation should allow him to dislike the dislikable. But a normal situation implies that the necessary is accepted as such. [van Eys, 1977, p. 93]

If the reality is distorted, if what happens has no purpose, the child suffers, just as the parents see a child as suffering when they lose faith in the purpose and success of the onerous treatment inflicted on their child.

Suffering is, therefore, inflicted on the child whenever it is projected upon the child by adults who lose faith in the righteousness of the interventions. Suffering is done by the persons who feel the just world and its security disintegrating, and the adult caregivers are the shapers of the child's world.

No apologies are necessary for our medical care if we really believe it is the best we can devise for the child. Whatever it takes is not suffering until we feel it undeserved and no longer is the best interest for that child. The child understands that and suffers. It was John Apley (1984) who said, "If any child cries it is my fault."

REFERENCES

Apley, J. (Ed.). (1984). *If a child cries . . . Collected papers*. London: Butterworth.

Cassell, E.J. (1982). The nature of suffering and the goals of medicine. *The New England Journal of Medicine*, 306, 639–645.

Cone, T.E. (1979). *The child's reality. Three developmental themes*. Hillsdale, NJ: Lawrence Erlbaum Associates.

Elkind, D. (1978). *The child's reality: Three developmental themes*. Hillsdale, NJ: Lawrence Erlbaum Associates.

Frankel, L.S. (1987). Personal dilemmas of care by trial. In J. van Eys & J.P. McGovern (Eds.), *The doctor as a person* (pp. 61–70). Springfield, IL: Charles C. Thomas.

Gross, B., & Gross, R. (1977). *The children's rights movement. Overcoming the oppression of young people*. Garden City, NY: Doubleday.

Lash, C. (1986). The children of narcissus. *The Rochester Review*, Fall, 12–15.

Melton, G. (1983). Children's competence to consent: A problem in law and social science. In G.B. Melton, G.P. Koocher, & M.J. Saks (Eds.). *Competence to consent* (pp. 1–18). New York, NY: Plenum.

The New English Bible (1972). Cambridge, MA: Cambridge University Press.

van Eys, J. (1977). What do we mean by a truly cured child? In J. van Eys (Ed.)., *The truly cured child* (pp. 79–98). Baltimore, MD: University Park Press.

van Eys, J. (1981). *Humanity and personhood*. Springfield, IL: Charles C. Thomas.

van Eys, J. (1989). We learn more from our children than they learn from us. In J. van Eys (Ed.)., *Cancer in the very young* (pp. 135–146). Springfield, IL: Charles C. Thomas.

Vaux, K. (1985). Justice and mercy: The moral requirement of heaven and earth. In J. van Eys & E.J. Mahnke (Eds.), *Life, faith, hope, and magic. The chaplaincy in pediatric cancer care* (pp. 65–74). Houston, TX: The University of Texas System Cancer Center.

Vaux, K. (1987). The physician as priest. In J. van Eys & J.P. McGovern (Eds.), *The doctor as a person* (pp. 127–134). Springfield, IL: Charles C. Thomas.

10

The Management of Suffering in a Nursing Home: An Ethnographic Study

Patricia L. Starck

The golden years are supposed to describe the later years in life when one's career work is completed, when major family responsibilities are fulfilled, when financial security is in place, and when leisure time activities can be enjoyed. Rabbi Ben Ezra said "Grow old along with me, the best is yet to be; the last of life for which the first was made . . . " (Oxford, 1980, p. 104). Yet in today's nursing homes, these years are tarnished by suffering from inevitable losses. This chapter is a report of a study conducted by this author to examine how suffering work takes place and how suffering is managed in a nursing home setting. Suffering may be thought of as being in the eye of the beholder, since it is a perception or interpretation rather than an actual set of objective signs

The author wishes to acknowledge the assistance of Dr. Joseph Kotarba, Professor of Sociology, the University of Houston.

127

and symptoms. Unlike a hospice, which is a place where suffering work is the sine qua non, a nursing home purports to offer quality of life for elderly residents in an atmosphere which values socialization with one's peers, group activities, and normalization. Yet, the losses which occur as persons age and give up meaningful symbols of life's achievements create unavoidable human suffering. Without a support system to recognize suffering and to manage its devastating effects, there can be no complete quality of living. Management of suffering then becomes a key factor in nursing home care. Because of the nature of suffering, its work and management must be shared between resident and staff, and sometimes also with the family.

DEFINITION OF SUFFERING

Suffering is described as being an ineradicable part of the human condition (Frankl, 1959) and as affecting the whole person, not just the body (Cassell, 1982). Suffering touches upon the various dimensions of the human, including the physical and psychosocial. Furthermore, the spiritual or noetic dimension of the human is involved in suffering, and in fact, the dynamic power of the human spirit is often the key factor in overcoming suffering (Frankl, 1959). Suffering is also conceptualized as threat to the self or to the intactness of the self (Kahn & Steeves, 1986). Suffering is a subjective experience which is unique to an individual and varies from simple transitory discomfort to extreme anguish and despair. Suffering is also a teacher about life. In this study, suffering is defined and operationalized as loss (i.e., losses affecting the human body, the human mind, and the human spirit). Suffering work is defined as coping with inevitable losses, and suffering management is defined as an interactional process between staff and resident/family in support of coping with and promoting quality of life.

Unfortunately, neither medical nor nursing diagnosis nomenclature has any reference to suffering per se. The closest diagnosis to the concept of suffering is found in the nursing diagnosis of "spiritual distress (distress of the human spirit)," which is defined as a disruption in the life principle that pervades a person's entire being and that integrates and transcends one's biologic and psychosocial nature (Doenges & Moorhouse, 1985; Kim, McFarland, & McLane, 1987). This diagnosis is said to be related to the inability to practice spiritual rituals or to a conflict between religious or spiritual beliefs and the prescribed health regimen (Carpenito, 1983).

This conceptualization of spiritual distress does not capture the essence of suffering as used in this study.

DESCRIPTION OF NURSING HOME ADJUSTMENT

It is generally accepted that becoming a resident in a nursing home is one of life's most difficult transitions. It is often an extremely difficult decision for a family and is frequently accompanied by much guilt. It is usually the "last resort" when there seems to be no other choice. It signals the end of independence, loss of freedom to follow a personal schedule, and forced adjustment to group living. Coupled with other generalized losses experienced as one ages, these "golden years" can be years of significant suffering.

Ideally, a nursing home views itself first and foremost as a home where residents live comfortably and happily. Social interaction is seen as facilitating quality of life. The home attempts to meet both basic physiologic and security needs as well as to meet many emotional needs. Nursing homes also provide treatment and care for individuals with chronic health problems. Keeping residents functional is a high priority.

The adjustment period is likely to be one of the most intensive suffering periods experienced by the resident while in the home. Yet, this adjustment period is very routine for staff who witness a variety of responses to it and have determined the most effective strategies of coping. These patterns of responses to adjustment also typify responses to other types of suffering encountered in the home. Thus, suffering work done by residents can be identified by those in closest contact—the caregivers. Likewise, these caregivers learn to manage the suffering of the residents as part of their own daily work. The caregivers learn to distinguish true or legitimate suffering from other types of behavior, and they respond accordingly.

LITERATURE ON SUFFERING AND THE ELDERLY

The existing literature on suffering focuses on the individual experience and not on how a system of care delivery might affect or respond to suffering. Existing literature on nursing home care addresses various problems and needs of the elderly, but fails to address the individual suffering work of the residents and the management of that suffering by staff. As a basis for integrating these two sets of literature to study the management of suffering in a nursing home, literature on the existential perspective of suffering as well as literature on care of the elderly will be summarized.

The Existential Perspective of Suffering

Existential philosophy takes the view that humans are living beings, creating reality in the here and now with freedom to choose, and having responsibility for those choices. This view is in opposition to reductionism which conceptualizes the human as drives, instincts, and libidos that can be studied and treated by reducing down to the isolated part that needs fixing.

The existentialist sees suffering as a part of the reality of life which affects the whole person, not just a part or dimension. Existentialists believe that life has purpose and meaning; in fact, a primary motivation of human behavior is to seek for meaning and purpose. Meaning can be found in all life experiences, even in those experiences of unavoidable suffering. Meaning can be found in three ways—in tasks or life work; in experiences such as truth, beauty, and love; and by choosing an attitude toward a fate which cannot be changed (Frankl, 1959). Suffering then, from an existential perspective, is part of living and its management needs to acknowledge that in an interactional approach.

Meaning or meaninglessness of suffering is an important component of understanding this experience. Steeves and Kahn (1987) state that the goal of nursing care is to help to establish and maintain the conditions necessary for and helpful to experiencing meaning. Pursuit of, or the actual experiencing of, meaning to life is recognized as a spiritual component of the whole person; and, therefore, loss of the sense of meaning in life has a negative effect on the health and well-being of the whole individual (Trice, 1990).

Kotarba (1983), using existential social theory in a study of chronic pain, argued that an individual's actual strategy for coping with chronic pain is shaped largely by the degree to which an individual accepts the inevitability of suffering. He found that the state of meaninglessness for patients with chronic pain resulted from a loss of cognitive control over the pain and a lack of viable alternatives. This meaninglessness state manifested itself as a sense of depression.

Thus, the existential literature establishes that suffering is an expected component of life, but that individuals have a tendency to seek meaning in suffering.

Care of the Elderly

In 1985, for the first time in U.S. history, the number of persons over the age of 65 exceeded those under the age of 18 (Callahan, 1987). Even though only 5 percent of the elderly population are institutionalized, the numbers are expected to grow dramatically as more and more people live longer. By the year 2050, 69 million Americans will be over 65 years of age. Quality of life will become a more important issue as this segment of the population needs more services.

A study of quality of care in nursing homes conducted by the Institute of Medicine (1986) acknowledges that quality of life for people in nursing homes is intimately related to the quality of resident-staff relationships. Quality of life is related to a sense of well-being, a level of satisfaction with life, and a feeling of self-worth and self-esteem. In nursing homes, this includes a basic sense of satisfaction with oneself, the environment, the care received, the accomplishment of desired goals, and control over one's life. It is enhanced by close relationships and meaningful interchange with others, by an environment supporting independence and incorporating personal belongings, and by the opportunity to exercise reasonable control over life decisions.

The literature on nursing home care cites multiple and complex problems with the care delivery system. As Phillips (1987) points out, elders and their family members tend to describe their relationships with health care professionals as adversarial rather than collegial. Paternalism, a common means of relating, takes the form of deciding what is best for the elderly without listening to their concerns and needs.

Loss is a prevalent theme in the literature concerning the elderly (Burnside, 1988; Garrett, 1987; LaGodna, 1988; Missinne, 1990; Pollick, 1987; Ryan & Patterson, 1987; Storlie, 1982; Tisdale, 1987; Trice, 1990; and Tulloch, 1990). Garrett (1987) describes the sense of loss as an assault on personal integrity. Trice (1990) concludes that elderly residents of a nursing home are at greater risk for losing a sense of meaning in life than are elderly in general. Storlie (1982) describes the constraints and limitations of life in a nursing home. Among problems cited are physiological limitations of growing older, reversal of the parenting role, and acquiring a nonproductive label. Storlie's study documents deprivation of choice—when to wake, eat, toilet, sit, stand, or lie down—as causing the person to lose touch with the person he or she once was. Every aspect of the lives of nursing home residents are spelled out so that they lose the freedom of choice. Storlie calls this system "entrapment," in many cases no less rigid than the systems used in prisons. Contributing further to this personal devaluation is the typical response by staff of condescending communication, both verbal and nonverbal—the scoldings, cajolings, and unkept promises. The caressing, pattings, and fondlings reduce the resident to infant or child status. Even affectionately laughing at aberrant behavior contributes to the dehumanizing process.

Storlie (1982) notes that residents are not allowed to make meaningful contributions to their home. They are not allowed, even when physically able, to make up their own bed or do light chores such as dust or sweep the floor. It is as if they can do nothing of value to contribute to their setting.

Bould, Sanborn, and Reif (1989) define dependence as a loss of self-determination that results from requiring the help of others but being unable to negotiate the terms of the help received. A move to a nursing home represents a loss of self-determination. People who are institutionalized are dependent because they are under the "care and custody" of the institution and its employees. Residents are subject to nonnegotiable restrictions on almost every activity of their lives, including eating, sleeping, and going outside. They cannot lock their rooms and have no control over who comes in, not even a choice of who helps them to the toilet.

Thus, the literature on care of the elderly in nursing homes cites many shortfalls in coping with the losses experienced by the elderly. The system of care delivery fails to promote a sense of meaning. Further, caregiving practices often contribute to rather than help to solve the very problems of suffering.

RESEARCH QUESTIONS

This study examined the extent to which the management of suffering is a feature of the nursing home as an organization. An approach consistent with symbolic interactionism was used to focus on the activities engaged in by nursing home staff to get the care accomplished. In this study the following questions were addressed:

1. What are the types of resident responses to suffering as perceived by nursing home staff?

2. How do nursing home staff manage residents who suffer?

METHODOLOGY

An ethnographic study conducted in a nursing home in a suburb of a large, metropolitan area provided the data for this project. Spring Glen (pseudonym) is one of a chain of seven for-profit nursing homes and houses 180 residents.

The researcher made regular visits to the home over a five-month period and interviewed various staff, including the executive director (1), director of nursing (1), social worker (1), in-service director (1), and staff nurses (4). Staff nurses were licensed vocational nurses (LVNs). Informal conversations were held with the social worker (5), activities director (2), business office staff (2), residents (4). Except for one group interview, all of the interviews were one-on-one. The group interview convened three experienced staff nurses. The researcher also recorded data during four observation periods—an ethnographic tour of the facility and observations in the waiting room, the activities room, and the feeding room (for patients who must be fed). Only one researcher was involved; data were hand recorded and later typed using a standard word processing program. An expert in gerontological nursing and nursing home systems of care delivery also was involved in review of data and findings. Data analysis was based on the data recorded by both narrative description and typologies. Information in Table 10–1 describes methods used in this study. Methodological issues are further described in Appendix 10–A. An Informed Consent form signed by participants was obtained (see Appendix 10–B).

THE SPRING GLEN NURSING HOME

Spring Glen is a 21-year-old structure which prides itself on a combination of old and new—some of the original solid cherry wood beds are mixed in with the new chandelier, silk moiré wallpaper, and custom made draperies. The atmosphere is a curious blend of institution and home. The dominant institutional symbols seen include wheelchairs and walkers,

Table 10-1

Methods Used in Ethnographic Study of Suffering Management in Nursing Home Residents

Question	Data	Analysis
1. What are the types of resident responses to suffering as perceived by nursing home staff?	• Interviews with Executive Director, Director of Nursing, Registered Nurses, In-Service Education Director, Social Worker, Staff Workers, Licensed Vocational Nurses • Informal conversations with residents • Observations in Day Room and Activities Room • Grand tour of facility	• Narrative Description • Typology of Resident Responses • Inventory of Losses • Expert Witness
2. How do nursing home staff manage suffering in residents?	• Interviews with Executive Director, Director of Nursing, Registered Nurses, In-Service Education Director, Social Worker, Staff Workers, Licensed Vocational Nurses • Informal conversations with residents • Observations in Day Room and Activities Room • Grand tour of facility	• Typology of Responses • Narrative Description • Expert Witness

white uniforms, charts, call lights on hospital beds, potty chairs, linen carts, and other hospital-type equipment. The symbols which indicate this is a home are afghans, religious artifacts such as crucifixes and praying hands, and pictures of loved ones. Other symbols that denote more than a home and less than a hospital are bulletin boards with lists of menus, activities of the week, and volunteers. Locked doors and alarms as well as "wandering bracelets" and motion detectors further suggest the type of environment.

The home has three wings plus an administrative corridor. Each wing has a nursing station that is responsible for 60 residents. There is a large dining room where residents gather to have their meals unless they need to be fed or have some other compelling reason not to go to the dining room. The activities room is a large open space used for gatherings to promote socialization and involvement in various activities to engage the mind, body, and spirit.

A typical day for residents includes breakfast followed by morning activities, lunch followed by rest or activities, and the evening meal followed by bedtime. Residents receive a bath every other day, usually in the morning after breakfast. The activities room is the hub of the social life. Observations in this room indicate that a group (25 to 30 people) sit in this room during the day in varying states of alertness. The wide-screen television is playing at all times with no resident access to volume control or channel selection. Only when there are directed activities, such as a sing-along, is the television turned off. Very few of the residents actually participate in the activities or watch the television set. They mostly sit without interacting with their environment or fellow residents. A particularly striking picture of this passive activity was seen on one ward where residents are the least mobile and the least cognitively functional. They are dressed and placed at card tables seating four residents each. The scene is surrealistic; there is not a sound. It is as if they are playing cards without any cards.

Staffing in this nursing home is amazingly stable, given that staff for a nursing home are usually hard to find and hard to keep. Some of the staff have worked here nearly 20 years. The administrator does not have to advertise to recruit new employees; rather, word of mouth has been the chief vehicle for staffing the home. The residents of Spring Glen come mostly from within a ten-mile radius, thus attesting to the community, neighborhood concept.

Spring Glen, not unlike many other nursing homes, is experiencing a striking change in the increasing number of "oldest old." The average age of Spring Glen residents is 88.7 years. There are many residents who are in their 90s, and there are several two-generation family members who are residents (e.g., a daughter who is 72 and mother who is 90). The oldest old are not necessarily sicker, but they do tend to have more disabilities, including cognitive impairment.

Since enactment of the federal regulations prohibiting unauthorized restraint and overuse of sedative medication, the residents who have Alzheimer's disease can be seen pacing throughout the day. At any one time, there are 20 to 30 residents pacing. They also dress and undress all day. It is not uncommon to see them wearing several layers of clothes.

CONCEPTUALIZATION OF SUFFERING AS LOSS

The conceptualization of suffering by nursing home staff determines how it is managed. Suffering is an interpretation, and its management is an interactional process. In general, nursing home staff operationalize the concept of suffering as loss. In the words of one staff member; a 58-year-old vocational nurse,

> Everyone in a nursing home suffers to some extent. They have given up everything—all their possessions, their home, everything they have worked for all those years. They get upset that their children don't visit more often. They get aggravated with the nurse. They have lost control. They just want some TLC (tender, loving care). The first two weeks of adjustment are the worst of their suffering.

Losses observed in this study fall into four categories (Table 10–2). Losses may be physiological, psychosocial, economic, and loss of spirit.

Physiological losses observed in this study include loss of the senses—vision, hearing; loss of mobility, energy level, and endurance/reserve; loss of control of bodily functions; and loss of memory. Psychosocial losses observed were loss of family closeness, friends, and activities (church and community). In addition to the loss of material possessions, including one's home and the control of one's finances, there is a loss of financial security. There is a well-recognized worry of outliving one's resources. The executive director of the home stated that the recent renovation of the home had caused a great deal of anxiety about costs and charges. For example, residents came into her office and asked such questions as "Does this mean that you will be going up on my rent? Will I still be able to afford to stay in this place?"

Table 10-2
Inventory of Losses of Aged in Nursing Homes as Perceived by Staff

Physiologic	Psychosocial	Economic	Human Spirit
• Senses: Vision, Hearing, etc.	• Family Closeness	• Material Possessions	• Autonomy/Authority
• Mobility	• Friends	• Home	• Control
• Energy Level	• Activities—Church and Community	• Control of Finances	• Self-Worth
• Endurance/Reserve		• Security:	• Usefulness
• Bodily Function		— Sufficient resources for lifetime care	• Freedom of Choice
• Memory		— Sufficient resources for burial	• Sense of Masculinity/Femininity
			• Purpose in Life/Meaning
			• Privacy
			• Information (Truth)

On another occasion, a resident sat down beside the researcher in the waiting room and was curious about what was being written down. He asked if his name was on the list, and when asked what was his name, replied, "I'd better not tell you, you'd bill me."

According to the executive director, resident and family resources are often depleted. Medicaid, the social services program most often used to pay for nursing home care, will only pay for three prescriptions per month in this state. The average resident has 6.5 prescriptions per month, plus over-the-counter medication. Many patients have multiple diagnoses, but can only get coverage for three prescriptions. If such a person already on three medications gets an infection and needs an antibiotic, it is a real problem. Everyone worries about it. The residents have a generalized fear of running out of money and of depleting their family's resources.

Losses of spirit perceived by staff in this study included losses of autonomy/authority, control, self-worth, usefulness, freedom of choice, sense of masculinity/femininity, purpose in life, privacy, and information (truth). Additional losses as described in the literature are personal devaluation and having something of value to contribute (Storlie, 1982).

Having a meaning and purpose in life is said by Frankl (1959) to be the most primary human need, and loss of such creates the deepest despair. Having something of value to contribute or being useful gives meaning to the lives of elderly residents, yet nursing home living rarely provides such opportunities. Trice (1990), in a phenomenological study of elderly men and women, found four themes from which they were able to derive sense that their lives were meaningful. These themes were: (a) concern for others; (b) being helpful or useful; (c) taking action on behalf of others; (d) positivism as an overall emotional tone.

The staff in this study recognized that residents have lost their sense of meaningfulness. This discussion triggered memory of previous projects, such as a Welcoming Committee for New Admissions that one resident in particular enjoyed. They had also in the past had a Foster Grandparent Program and acknowledged that the residents had a lot to offer young people.

The concept of suffering seen as loss determines the way that nursing home staff make sense of their often overwhelming job responsibilities. How the staff deals with suffering is a reflection of the overall way the system does its humanitarian work. Suffering is viewed by the staff as a certain kind of problem that leads to a certain response on their part. Staff then must distinguish true suffering or "hurting" from other types of behaviors. Conceptualizing and interpreting suffering becomes a functional way for staff to deal with loss as an everyday and irreversible problem.

STAFF'S PERCEPTION OF TYPES OF SUFFERING

Staff distinguish between residents who are truly suffering and those who are not. They respond differently according to their perceptions. Although staff recognize that all residents suffer and that response to suffering is very individualized, certain patterns of resident behaviors are recognized by staff. Staff generally divide residents into two main categories, those who are truly suffering and those who simply are seeking attention. Those who seek attention do so by complaining or making requests, either overtly or covertly. This categorization led to a typology of Attention Seekers and Sufferers as depicted in Table 10–3. Whereas the attention seekers or complainers make their wishes or needs known and either overtly or covertly ask for help, the true sufferers are quiet and nondemanding. The *overt complainers* are seen as assertive, if not demanding. They typically roll their wheelchairs up to the nursing station and make their desires known. They tend to stay in the general area of the nursing station throughout the day as if keeping an eye on things. They are open in complaining, and have new grievances to add to their lists daily. Their need for attention is overt. The staff tends to respond to these people in ways that placate the immediate problem, but give little real attention to the resident. For example, one female resident called out to the social worker while she was taking the researcher on a tour of the home and asked for a drink of water. She was told, "Okay, Ms. X," but was never given any water. When the researcher questioned this she was told, "Oh, she didn't really want water, she just wants attention." This same resident was described by a vocational nurse as someone who asks to have her wheelchair seat belt loosened when it is not even fastened.

Another overt response was when a confused ambulatory resident reported to the supervisor (in-service director) that her table-mates had falsely accused her of drinking "all their damn milk." She was told to ignore them and say "God, give me the strength." Short answers that take care of the present moment of anxiety are often used to manage such problems.

The most vivid occurrence of the overt complainer was a resident who described herself as a retired nurse. She became belligerent when other residents tried to sit at her dining table. A staff member placated her and in a few minutes the incident was over.

Table 10–3
Sufferers and Attention Seekers as Perceived by Nursing Home Staff (Behavior and Responses)

Attention Seekers		Sufferers
Overt Complainers	Covert Complainers	Quiet Sufferers
Resident Behaviors		
• Loud	• Quiet	• Meek
• Assertive	• Passive	• Accepts Suffering
• Confrontational With Authority	• Non-Confrontational With Authority	• Non-Demanding
• Seeks Solutions from Staff	• Seeks Help Outside Home	• No Family Support
• Demanding of Staff	• Non-Demanding of Staff	
• May/May Not Have Family Support	• May/May Not Have Family Support	
Caretaker Response		
• Placates	• Sanctions When Outside Help-Seeking Behavior Becomes Known	• Buys Gifts for Resident
• Cajoles		• Takes on Role of Extended Family
	• Counsels Family Not To Feel Guilty	• Displays Affection
• Ignores		• Protects from Unpleasant Truths

Covert complainers do not seek help from staff, but rather turn outside the institution, keeping their pleas for help secret from the staff. Residents will frequently call family members or friends saying they have to come take them out of this place immediately. They will tell the family that they are sick or that they have injured themselves and the staff will not do anything about it. This elicits an irritated response from staff. One resident in her desperation called 911, the emergency service. When the attendees arrived, she tried to deny the call, but it had been traced to her room telephone. This type of behavior by residents is the most upsetting to the staff. Negative sanctions are often their response. If family has been called, they are told by the staff not to let the resident make them feel guilty. Phillips (1987) describes this type of response by staff as a form of paternalism where residents are made to feel that they have overstepped their boundaries. Residents often experience the fear of retaliation.

The quiet sufferers are persons who retreat to their rooms and suffer in silence. They are not hidden and they do display their suffering, but they are not demonstrative. They are helpless to affect their own conditions or circumstances. Often, these residents have no family. They seem to accept their sad state and ask nothing from their caregivers. They do not appear to actively seek solace. These residents engender staff responses by the way they suffer. The caregiver response is one of compassion, including physical demonstrations of affection, such as hugs or saying "I love you." The caregivers adopt such residents as "pets" and think of themselves as extended family of the resident. There may be some identification with the resident, such as, "I thought about what if I was in this condition with no family." The work ethic reflected is that no one should suffer alone.

Another finding was that none of the staff perceived a fear of dying from the residents; conversely, the perception is that residents are ready and waiting for their own death with a sense of relaxed anticipation. Nevertheless, staff engage in attempted cover-up when a resident dies. One staff member stated that if a resident is dying, she will take him or her out of the room, explaining to the roommate that he or she needs to be quiet, or needs to go to the hospital. Official word is not given when a resident dies. However, the staff acknowledged that residents know and pass the word informally, Staff have observed activities as if the group is having a wake; one resident will sit at the door and announce the death to everyone who passes by. The process is referred to as passing away, or "my roommate left me."

STAFF'S RESPONSES TO SUFFERING

The philosophy of the home is dedicated to quality of life, and suffering work is not seen as a legitimate task of its residents. Neither is the staff cognizant of thinking of emotional pain as required therapy. Rather, an attitude of denial of the realities of suffering that is a part of aging is the cultural norm. In spite of the treatment regimen of "reality therapy," involving orientation to reality, there is an elaborate cover-up scheme engaged in by the staff to protect a patient from feeling the hurts of life. Staff consistently saw family rejection as the worst of all hurts. The in-service director told of such an incident of hurt and cover-up:

Some families act like they are trying to throw their parent away. One resident whose family had dumped her, called her family, and they hung up on her. Then they called us and chewed us out for giving her their phone number. The resident told me that the phone went dead, and I went along with her. I would never tell her what her family said. I told her I would try to get the line back later. I kept giving her different excuses until she finally quit asking.

Another example of cover-up by the staff, which might more appropriately be called protection, is seen in the common practice of buying presents at holidays for residents who do not have family or loved ones to give them gifts. These patients frequently become adopted by staff as their "pets," and these staff members frequently take their meager pay checks and buy needed articles or gifts for these otherwise abandoned residents. The staff takes on the role of extended family for the resident.

Suffering then is the interpretation given to a resident's experiences or circumstances as viewed by the caregiver. Not all residents are seen as truly suffering, and even with those who do, no formal recognition or diagnosis is made nor is this addressed in the nursing plan of care. The work of suffering for the residents is generally the coping with losses, often multiple and complex. The response to these losses by staff falls into two broad categories. First and foremost is the response of giving, including standard and routine nursing home care, plus "doing the little extra things." Caregiving also includes providing TLC. During the group interview, the vocational nurses described this caregiving:

I tell my residents, "I love you" several times a day. They are so glad to see me after I have been off a day or so.
I hug and kiss them. I give of myself.
They want to be loved and touched. When they are suffering, it relieves them to hear, "I love you."
They tell me that too. I say it every day. I have learned patience and to listen, and to give of myself.

The second type of broad response is *protection*—protecting the resident from bad news, from family problems, or from economic woes. Residents are not told when one of their membership dies; rather there is a conspiracy of silence among the staff, even when they are cognizant that the residents pass the word among themselves. There is no formal service of commemoration. Likewise, residents are protected from bad news concerning the family. A vocational nurse explained,

When a family member is ill, they don't want the resident to know because

it would worry them. The family often feels guilty, "torn up." We try to
tell the residents and the family anything to make them feel better.

Residents may also have worries about sufficient finances to take care
of burial expenses. In one case, a resident expressed a desire for her body
to be shipped to another state so that she could be buried beside her
husband. Upon investigation, the prefuneral arrangements she thought
she had made were not recorded and her meager sum of $1,000 would not
cover shipping of the body. In discussion of this dilemma, there was advice
to the social worker to protect her from the truth and just tell her, "It's
been taken care of." After all, she would be dead and not know the
difference. However, the social worker opted for telling the truth, explaining that she had done all that she could. The resident expressed her
thanks and accepted the decision. This incident is an example of another
form of paternalism described by Phillips (1987) called "selective information sharing" which takes two forms: (a) actual information screening
and (b) pseudosharing.

QUALITY OF LIFE AND SUFFERING

Quality of life was defined by one vocational nurse as "keep them
ambulating, involved in activities, healthy, alert, and happy." She will do
just about anything to keep her residents happy. Sometimes they just need
listening to, or a small thing to show that the nurse cares. One resident
needed assistance with dialing a telephone. She follows up any time a
resident complains. Most caregivers tell the residents, "I love you," and are
generous with hugs.

One caregiver measured quality of life by the following criterion:

When they go out on pass with their families, they can't wait to get back
to find out what is going on here.

Cox, Kaeser, Montgomery, and Marion (1991) describe the Quality of
Life Nursing Care Model which emphasizes control and choice as well as
other features. The goals of care in this model are delineated as optimal
resident functioning, social and psychological well-being, health maintenance and promotion, and control over decisions. The model focuses on
the whole person. Various instruments are used to measure quality of life.

Choice is an important factor in quality of life as described by the

Institute of Medicine study (1986). Choice of mealtimes, activities, clothing, and times to rise and retire all enhance a sense of personal control and sense of well-being. Lack of privacy for visits, for medical treatment, and for personal solitude contribute to lack of self-esteem. Opportunities to engage in religious, political, civic, recreational, or social activities foster a sense of worth. Quality and variety of food are important to residents. Quality of life also includes such life circumstances as personal assets, financial security, physical and mental health, personal safety, and security of one's possessions.

The monthly activity calendar in Spring Glen would lead one to the conclusion that there is never a dull moment in Spring Glen. Exercise classes, sing-alongs, visitor programs, and so forth fill each week. "Keep them active" seems to be the motto. Even if residents are not active in the event, they are encouraged to sit with the group.

The architecture of the home suggests that solitude is not condoned. The chapel has no doors and cannot serve as a refuge from the rest of the home. The chapel is the last door off the administrative wing, next to the closely guarded entrance where there is tight security to prevent wandering off the premises. Only certain residents are allowed to go across the street, which is sealed off from automobile traffic, to a small park. The chapel is seldom used except for the once-per-week religious services. It is available for families, but there is no privacy because of the open entrance way. Neither are resident rooms conducive to solitude and solace. Television or other noises are prevalent throughout the various wings.

Inventory of Rules

The attempt to manage suffering may also be seen in unofficial "rules" or expectations placed on residents. An inventory of these rules which were observed in operation may be seen in Table 10–4. Various levels of staff who were interviewed believed that the adjustment period, which usually takes two to four weeks after admission, is facilitated by no family contact. One staff member also advocated that the resident not be allowed to have a telephone during this period to avoid the common behavior of calling the family at all hours of the night. This "rebellious stage" soon follows with an adjustment period. However, the adjustment period brings other problems. As one vocational nurse put it,

Table 10–4
Inventory of Unofficial "Rules" in Nursing Home

1. Adjustment of newly admitted residents is best facilitated by minimum or no contact with family (2–4 week period).
2. Group socialization is preferable to solitude/privacy.
3. Residents should participate in group activities regardless of individual interest.
4. Television keeps residents in touch with reality and, therefore, should be kept on constantly.
5. Everyone is expected to eat in the dining room to promote socialization.
6. Residents should be protected from emotional hurt regarding families/finances.

You know, they can be partially alert when they come in, and two weeks later, they are just like all the others. They seem to "get" helpless.

Another important rule is eating in the dining room with other residents. This rule is seen by staff as inviolate unless there are compelling reasons for eating in one's room. Storlie (1982), in her interviews with nursing home residents, found that being forced to eat in the dining room is an aggravation for them. One example given was the smell of urine on an incontinent table-mate. It was noted that some residents make a disturbing scene before every meal to express their hatred of communal dining.

Following the rules is interpreted by the staff as being well adjusted. The staff then does not experience the anxiety of witnessing what they consider to be aberrant behavior.

Residual Findings

Suffering, in its holistic nature, comes full circle and encompasses staff in its reality. In discussing their everyday work of managing multiple and complex loss and witnessing the suffering of other human beings, several respondents expressed their own suffering. Ms. B., a vocational nurse, said,

This is a depressing job. I often cry. I feel sorry for them. I am crying and praying and giving of myself so that sometimes I neglect myself. I don't eat or take time to go to the doctor. At work, I forget to take my medicine; I don't take time to drink water like I should. Often I buy the residents a hamburger and a coke out of my pocket—things they don't get here.

In another interview, the in-service director stated,

Sometimes you have to swallow your hurt; you can't say, and shouldn't say, things back. The families get on our back when there is nothing we can do. They want immediate attention when we are busy with someone else. One lady was about to hit me one night. We had to call the administration.

DISCUSSION

The findings of this study center around the conclusion that suffering in the elderly in a nursing home may be operationalized as loss. Losses are physiological, psychosocial, financial, and spiritual in nature. The suffering work required of the resident is to cope with and adjust to these losses. The management of this suffering work is an interactional process between residents and families. Staff interpret resident behaviors according to their perceptions and experiences. These interpretations fall into two main categories—those who truly suffer and those who seek attention by complaining. The true sufferers are responded to with compassion which is manifested by caregiving and protection. Those residents who complain, whether overtly or covertly, receive responses ranging from ignoring to chastising. The study also delineated an inventory of rules, unwritten and unspoken, that specify the expectations placed on residents who are adjusted to nursing home living. Following these rules makes it easier for the staff to accomplish their daily routines. The study also revealed a glimpse of the suffering of the staff as they meshed their work with their life values.

Limitations

This study was limited to one nursing home and further study should be done to develop the concept of suffering work and management of the elderly who reside in such facilities. The study concentrated on staff perceptions and did not include perceptions of families and/or loved ones. Interviews with residents were limited and, therefore, data concentrated on observations.

Relationship of Findings to Existing Literature

These findings add to the literature on the general concept of suffering as an individual experience by operationalizing suffering in the elderly as loss. The findings support the conclusion in the literature that suffering affects the whole person and expands that understanding to specify the dimensions of loss. Nowhere in the suffering literature is it clearer than in this study that suffering is in the eye of the beholder, and the caregiver's perception of suffering determines how the sufferer will be supported in the experience.

This study also adds to the literature on care of the elderly in a nursing home by describing staff's perception of resident behaviors and needs and by delineating staff responses as well as "rules" for well-adjusted residents. It is clear that losses of a spiritual nature are the category most neglected by staff.

IMPLICATIONS AND RECOMMENDATIONS FOR FUTURE RESEARCH

Future qualitative research is recommended to study the work and management of the elderly in nursing homes, in day care centers, and in their own homes. Research focused specifically on the adjustment process is recommended since, for most residents, this is perceived as being the period of the most intense suffering experienced in the nursing home.

Findings from this research suggest that staff need specific assistance with managing the suffering work of elderly residents, especially during the adjustment period. Since staff perceive that the family role is vital in the adjustment, pre-admissions counseling and support groups might ease the suffering. Staff also need help in designing care to help residents meet the needs of the human spirit. More flexibility in rules is indicated to diminish loss of freedom of choice and to enhance a sense of autonomy. Programs which enhance a sense of usefulness and meaning in life should be a standard part of nursing home life for all residents. Of necessity, such programs would be flexible and creative to meet a wide variety of individual needs. Environmental changes to meet individual tastes and preferences, such as a smaller activities room with classical music rather than one large room of television viewing, should be considered. Finally, assistance should be increased to the staff members themselves in coping with the ever-challenging work they do.

It is also recommended that "suffering" as a nursing diagnosis receive further study.

CONCLUSION

In conclusion, the suffering of aging with its multiple and complex losses is a phenomenon with low visibility within a nursing home context. Management of suffering takes place in various ways to minimize overt signs of emotional pain. Often a game of denial is engaged in to protect residents from facing the harsh realities of family abandonment, the most painful of all losses. The work of suffering is not given a legitimate place in the daily routine activities nor in the architectural planning for such an environment. Caregivers engage in suffering-denying behaviors and use platitudes and reassurances to avoid the experience of seeing suffering in the residents in their charge. Residents in nursing homes, just as individuals in the larger society, vary in their ways of expressing suffering. These cries for help may be loud and explicit or quiet and symbolic. Nevertheless, attention must be given to the therapeutic skills that caregivers use to address the inevitable suffering or tarnish that comes with the "golden years."

REFERENCES

Bould, S., Sanborn, B., & Reif, L. (1989). *Eighty-five plus: The oldest old*. Belmont, CA: Wadsworth Publishing Co.

Burnside, I.M. (1988). *Nursing and the aged: A self-care approach*. New York: McGraw-Hill.

Callahan, D. (1987). *Setting limits: Medical goals in an aging society*. New York: Simon and Schuster.

Carpenito, L.J. (1983). *Nursing diagnosis: Application to clinical practice*. Philadelphia: J.B. Lippincott Company.

Cassell, E.J. (1982). The nature of suffering and the goals of medicine. *New England Journal of Medicine, 306*(11), 639–645.

Cox, C.L., Kaeser, L., Montgomery, A.C., & Marion, L.H. (1991). Quality of life nursing care: An experimental trial in long-term care. *Journal of Gerontological Nursing, 17*(4), 6–11.

Doenges, M.E., & Moorhouse, M.F. (1985). *Nurse's pocket guide: Nursing diagnoses with interventions*. Philadelphia: F.A. Davis Company.

Frankl, V.E. (1959). *Man's search for meaning: An introduction to logotherapy*. New York: Beacon Press.

Garrett, J.E. (1987). Multiple losses in older adults. *Journal of Gerontological Nursing, 13*(8), 8–12.

Institute of Medicine. (1986). Improving the quality of care in nursing homes (Committee on Nursing Home Regulation). Washington, D.C.: National Academy Press.

Jorgensen, D.L. (1989). Participant observation: A methodology for human studies. *Applied Social Research Methods Series* (Vol. 15). London: Sage Publications.

Kahn, D.L., & Steeves, R.H. (1986). The experience of suffering: Conceptual clarification and theoretical definition. *Journal of Advanced Nursing, 11*(6), 623–631.

Kim, M.J., McFarland, G.K., & McLane, A.M. (1987). *Pocket guide to nursing diagnoses* (2nd ed.). St. Louis: C.V. Mosby Company.

Kotarba, J.A. (1983). Perceptions of death, belief systems and the process of coping with chronic pain. *Social Science Medicine, 17*(10), 681–689.

LaGodna, G.E. (1988). Aging women and depression: Unresolved conceptual, etiologic, and epidemiologic issues. *Issues in Mental Health Nursing, 9*(3), 285–298.

Missinne, L.E. (1990). Reflections on aging: A spiritual guide. Liguori, MO: Liguori Publications.

Oxford Dictionary of Quotations (3rd ed.) (1980). Oxford: Oxford University Press.

Phillips, L.R. (1987). Respect basic human rights. *Journal of Geronotological Nursing, 13*(3), 36–39.

Pollick, M.F. (1987). Abuse of the elderly: A review. *Holistic Nursing Practice, 1*(2), 43–53.

Ryan, M.C., & Patterson, J. (1987). Loneliness in the elderly. *Journal of Gerontological Nursing, 13*(5), 6–12.

Schein, E.H. (1987). The clinical perspective in fieldwork. *Qualitative Research Methods* (Vol. 5). London: Sage Publications.

Steeves, R.H., & Kahn, D.L. (1987). Experience of meaning in suffering. *Image, 19*(3), 114–116.

Storlie, F.J. (1982). The reshaping of the old. *Journal of Gerontological Nursing, 8*(10), 555–559.

Tisdale, S. (1987). *Harvest moon: Portrait of a nursing home*. New York: Henry Holt.

Trice, L.B. (1990). Meaningful life experience to the elderly. *Image, 22*(4), 248–251.

Tulloch, G.J. (1990). From inside a nursing home: A resident writes about autonomy. *Generations, 14* (Supplement), 83–85.

APPENDIX 10–A

Methodological Issues

The researcher kept a personal diary of issues of concern during the data collection process. No problems were encountered regarding entry from the administrative standpoint; rather, the researcher was welcomed with an open invitation to conduct the research.

The aims of this type of study according to Jorgensen (1989) are "to generate practical and theoretical truths about human life grounded in the realities of daily existence" (p. 14). Further, the research process should be minimally disruptive to the system. Schein (1987) states that from a clinical point of view, it is not possible to interact with another human being or group without influencing them to some degree. In this study it was important for the respondents to give information on the reality as they perceived it and not as they perceived it should be. This aspect of interviewing was helped by reiterating that the researcher was an administrator and perhaps far removed from current clinical care in a nursing home and not in a position to evaluate quality of care.

This study regarding suffering work and management in a nursing home depended upon gaining access to the subjective experiences and perceptions of the staff worker. Gaining access to the front-line caregiver or the licensed vocational nurse was the most difficult aspect of the methodology. These caregivers are extremely busy, having tight schedules. On one occasion on a weekend evening, the researcher waited over an hour and the caregiver, who was giving medications, never did find the time for the interview. In two interviews, nurses brought their charts to try to do paperwork at the same time. In one instance, their supervisor set a 30-minute deadline. Because these nurses put in a full day's work, they are eager to go home at the end of their shift to attend to other responsibilities. Therefore, holding interviews after work hours was not feasible.

The solution, or partial solution, was for the researcher to plan to combine the worker's break time with the interview. The researcher brought doughnuts and conducted the interview in a setting which encouraged relaxation. It was hoped that the smell of the doughnuts and coffee would encourage the workers to take a break from their work. The time which proved most effective was late morning (about 11:00) when most of the morning care chores had been completed.

APPENDIX 10–B

Informed Consent

You are being asked to participate in a study conducted as part of a course entitled "Qualitative Research in Nursing." This study is designed to explore the meaning of suffering in the elderly in a nursing home. This may help us to be able to give better care to these residents.

If you agree to participate, you will be asked questions relating to your experience with residents in a nursing home. Your answers to these questions will be written up so that they may be analyzed. This interview should take between 30 minutes and one hour.

Your interview will be conducted by a trained researcher. A possible risk is that you may experience some anxiety or have questions during the interview. To alleviate any possible anxiety, the entire interview will be conducted in a private room with no interruptions if possible. Adequate time will be allowed for you to ask questions or to discuss any concerns you may have. You should feel free to interrupt the interview at any time, either to clarify or to expound on a question/answer. You also may ask questions after the interview. If you think of questions later, please call Dr. Pat Starck at XXX-XXXX.

The indirect benefit from participating in this study is that this information will be used to help residents who need to do suffering work. This information can be used to plan the type of care relevant to residents of nursing homes.

You are free to participate or not participate. The choice is yours. If you choose to participate, you may withdraw or stop the interview at any time without penalty. Your job will not be affected in any way if you do or do not participate. There will be no penalty or loss of benefits.

Confidentiality will be assured. Only initials will be used on written materials; no names will be used. You will not be identified anywhere in the study. The name and location of this nursing home will remain confidential as this information will not be included in this research study. All notes will be destroyed no later than two years after the completion of the study. Findings from this study will possibly be published or presented at scientific conferences.

No injury is anticipated as a result of your participation in this study. However, no financial compensation is available to absorb such costs should injury occur. First aid would be provided as necessary.

11

Suffering in Addiction: Alcoholism and Drug Dependence

Robert L. DuPont
and
John P. McGovern

Suffering is the sole origin of consciousness.
—Fëdor Mikhailovich Dostoevski (*International Thesaurus of Quotations, 1970, p. 620*)

As health care professionals who have seen much suffering, we are impressed that the suffering of chemical dependence, or of addiction, is particularly hard to bear, hard to share, and hard to understand. The suffering caused by addiction is not limited to the addicted person, and it does not end when the addicted person becomes clean and sober.

The suffering from addiction forces the addict, and those who relate to the addict, including health care professionals, to explore their lives. There is a spiritual dimension to both the process of addiction and the process of recovery from addiction.

Just as the suffering from addiction involves the core of the self, recovery from addiction requires a profound change in the self, including the way one relates to others and to God (or a Higher Power).

By understanding addiction, health care professionals can understand the human experience of both suffering and the alleviation of suffering. The mutual-aid programs modeled on Alcoholics Anonymous (AA), known collectively as the 12-step programs, provide a useful model for the understanding of the experiences of suffering and recovery.

This chapter is divided into ten sections focusing on the problems of suffering, addiction, and suffering in addiction, with all sections focused on the perspective of health care workers, especially young health care professionals.

THE AMERICAN CHEMICAL DEPENDENCE PROBLEM

Health care professionals in the United States need a working knowledge of the nature, extent, and trends of chemical dependence in this country to appreciate the suffering in addiction. Addiction is a major problem in families, in schools, in the workplace, and in health care. About 4.5 percent of women and 24 percent of men in the United States will suffer from chemical dependence during their lives, with about 1.5 percent of women and 9 percent of men, or about 20 million people, actively dependent at any time (Myers, Weissman, Tischler, et al., 1984; Robins, Helzer, Weissman, et al., 1984).

The National Institute on Drug Abuse (NIDA) and the National Institute for Alcohol Abuse and Alcoholism (NIAAA) produce regular reports to Congress summarizing the most recent knowledge about drug and alcohol problems, including results of research studies. Copies of these reports and other information can be obtained from the National Clearinghouse for Alcohol and Drug Information, 6000 Executive Boulevard, Suite 402, Rockville, Maryland 20852, telephone (301) 468-2600.

The most recent national survey of drug and alcohol use in the United States showed that in 1988 there were 106 million regular users of alcohol, 57 million cigarette smokers, 12 million smokers or marijuana, and 3 million users of cocaine. The use of other commonly abused drugs, including the nonmedical use of prescribed analgesics, hypnotics, and antianxiety medicines, was about one million (National Institute on Drug Abuse, 1989). All these numbers were down from the previous survey in

1985. Alcohol use had dropped 6 percent, cigarette use by 5 percent, marijuana use by 33 percent, and cocaine use by 50 percent. However, drug-caused problems have risen in recent years, particularly problems caused by smoked cocaine known as "crack," and drug problems in the workplace.

Among high school seniors, the following percentages reported use within the 30 days prior to the survey of each of these drugs in May of 1989: alcohol, 60 percent; cigarettes, 29 percent; marijuana, 18 percent; and cocaine, 3 percent (Johnston, Bachman, & O'Malley, 1989). Alcohol and cigarettes are used more widely than marijuana and cocaine, the most widely used illegal drugs, because their use is legal. This is powerful evidence that legalization of marijuana, cocaine, and other drugs would lead to large increases in their use.

Young people use more illegal drugs than older people because drug habits are typically acquired in the teenage years or in the early 20s (DuPont, 1984). In general, the younger a person starts drug use, the more likely that use is to be severe, prolonged, and problem producing. Americans over the age of 40 were seldom exposed to illicit drugs during their vulnerable youth (DuPont, 1989b).

Drug use is declining generally in the United States because there is a growing sense that drug use is unhealthy and socially discouraged (U.S. Department of Health and Human Services, 1987a). Drug use remains particularly high among youth, among children of chemically dependent parents, and among those of all ages who are willing to engage in behavior that is widely disapproved (DuPont, 1989c). An excellent summary of the addictive drugs covered under the U.S. Controlled Substances Act and the laws relating to these drugs is published by the Drug Enforcement Administration (U.S. Department of Justice, 1988).

Overall, addiction (including use of alcohol, tobacco, and illicit drugs) is a major factor in all nine leading causes of death in the United States: diseases of the heart, cancer, stroke, pneumonia and influenza, all accidents (other than motor vehicle) and adverse effects, motor vehicle accidents, chronic liver disease and cirrhosis, suicide, and homicide (DuPont, 1986b; U.S. Department of Health and Human Services, 1990a). At the beginning of the 20th century, the leading causes of death in the United States were infectious diseases. Death from these infectious diseases, which often killed children at very early ages, was reduced dramatically during the 20th century—especially in developed nations— by better public health practices and by the widespread use of antibiotics and other medical treatments. At the end of the 20th century the leading

causes of death in developed nations are behavioral. The diseases that kill
Americans today are related to lifes-styles and choices made as individuals
(DuPont, 1986b). These health-determining behavioral choices include
exercise, diet, and especially the use of "recreational drugs," or chemical
dependence.

Louis W. Sullivan, MD, Secretary of Health and Human Services, in
a presentation to the National Commission on Children, emphasized that
the new perspective on health promotion was based on "values like
integrity, self-discipline, perseverance, personal responsibility, respect for
others, service to mankind, a sense of moderation, and a love of learning."
He went on to point out that,

> . . . better control of fewer than ten risk factors—such as poor diet,
> infrequent exercise, the use of tobacco, alcohol and drug abuse, and the
> use of seat belts—could prevent between 40 and 70 percent of all prema-
> ture deaths, a third of all cases of acute disability, and two-thirds of all
> cases of chronic disability. [1990, p. 6]

In few cases are the results of these health-related behaviors quickly
and certainly experienced by individuals. The effects of behavior are often
delayed and for particular individuals, uncertain. This delayed, uncertain
feedback makes risk assessment and risk reduction a complex problem that
is hard for health professionals and the lay public to appreciate. If modern
behaviorally caused diseases are to be reduced, as infectious diseases were
in the early decades of this century, health care professionals will have to
find better ways to encourage wise health choices. The central goal of this
new concern in health promotion is the prevention and treatment of drug
abuse, including the abuse of alcohol and tobacco. An understanding of
addiction and the suffering addiction causes will help achieve that goal
(DuPont & McGovern, 1991).

As important as the understanding of the public health facts of chemical dependence is the understanding of the family of mutual-aid organizations promoting recovery from addictions, the 12-step programs modeled on Alcoholics Anonymous (Exhibit 11-1). The first AA meetings
took place in Akron, Ohio, in 1935 when two alcoholics, one a physician
and the other a salesman, created one of the world's most remarkable
movements (Robertson, 1988). Today, there are related programs, including Narcotics Anonymous (NA), to deal with dependence on drugs other
than alcohol, and Al-Anon to deal with the problems of family members
of chemically dependent people. Children of Alcoholics (COA) deals

Exhibit 11-1
The 12 Steps of Alcoholics Anonymous

1. We admitted we were powerless over alcohol—that our lives had become unmanageable.

2. Came to believe that a Power greater than ourselves could restore us to sanity.

3. Made a decision to turn our will and our lives over to the care of God *as we understood Him.*

4. Made a searching and fearless moral inventory of ourselves.

5. Admitted to God, to ourselves and to another human being the exact nature of our wrongs.

6. Were entirely ready to have God remove all these defects of character.

7. Humbly asked Him to remove our shortcomings.

8. Made a list of all persons we had harmed, and became willing to make amends to them all.

9. Made direct amends to such people wherever possible, except when to do so would injure them or others.

10. Continued to take personal inventory and when we were wrong promptly admitted it.

11. Sought through prayer and meditation to prove our conscious contact with God, *as we understood Him*, praying only for knowledge of His will for us and the power to carry that out.

12. Having had a spiritual awakening as the result of these steps, we tried to carry this message to alcoholics, and to practice these principles in all our affairs.

with problems of people of all ages who grew up in families dominated by chemical dependence.

Each week there are more than 50,000 12-step meetings with more than one million members in the United States. The 12-step movement is now global and deals with a wide variety of behavioral problems, including gambling, overeating, and dozens of other problems that are not well handled by traditional health care.

These 12-step meetings are free of charge. The meetings take place at all times of the day and night, but many begin at 8:30 p.m. and last for one hour. They accept no health insurance or government funding. They often use donated space in publicly funded or religious facilities. Twelve-step meetings are run by group members—recovering people—not by health care professionals. When health care professionals join 12-step programs they do so as regular members, not as formal leaders or caregivers.

These are called 12-step programs because of the 12 steps of the original AA program. Today, most health care professional who help addicted people recommend participation in 12-step programs. Typically, 12-step members go to meetings once a day at the start of their participation and then gradually decrease the frequency of meeting attendance to two to three meetings a week after months or years of active program membership. Typically, 12-step program members go to meetings for many years, or even for a lifetime, since the diseases being dealt with are lifelong. Information about 12-step programs can be found by calling the numbers listed in the local phone book, or by writing to the national headquarters of each organization. General information about a wide range of 12-step and other mutual-aid programs is available from the National Self-Help Clearing House, Graduate School and University of the City of New York, Room 620, 25 West 43rd Street, New York, New York 10036.

THE NATURE OF SUFFERING

God will not look you over for medals, degrees or diplomas, but for scars!
—Elbert Hubbard (*International Thesaurus of Quotations*, 1970, p. 620)

Suffering, unlike pain, is not a straightforward biological process. Suffering requires meaning. Without meaning, the ill person, like a sick animal, can be in pain but cannot suffer in the sense that ill people commonly suffer. We do not intend to minimize either the experience of pain or the distress of animals in pain, but we do want to call attention to the uniquely human aspect of suffering: it is bound inextricably with the meaning of the experience for the sufferer. To suffer requires an experience of meaning at a fundamental and highly personal level (Frankl, 1973, 1978). Human suffering includes questions such as "Why me?" "Why now?" "What will happen to me?" "What can I do about my suffering?", and "Can anyone help me?"

There are three common aspects to the experience of human suffering

(Cassell, 1982, 1983; Kahn & Steeves, 1986). The first is that suffering is the result of *distress*. The distress that is a necessary part of suffering can result from such feelings as pain, loss, and fear. Although the person experiencing suffering does not consider the cause of the suffering to be trivial, others, sometimes including health care professionals, may consider the cause to be minor or trivial. When this happens, the suffering is intensified because it cannot be shared or understood by either the sufferer or those the sufferer relies on for help.

Second, suffering usually involves *alienation*. People who are suffering feel a loss of connectedness to others, often including their families and health care workers. Suffering people have crossed an invisible line, cutting them off from others and from their own past. They have entered a new and lonely place.

Much of the sympathy given to suffering people by others only adds to their sense of alienation because these sympathetic people do not seem to understand. They seem to the sufferer to remain in the other place, the place free of suffering. Often nonsuffering people do not even speak of their own past suffering so as not to incur a usually unspoken rebuke from the sufferers who know their pain is not understood by those who have not suffered it (Fabry, 1980).

Third, suffering commonly includes the feeling of *despair*. Suffering people can find no way out of the misery they experience. They feel themselves to be trapped and alone. They have lost the expectation that their plight will prove temporary or that they can find effective help. As suffering people turn to others, often including health care workers, to find help, especially in the early stages of their suffering, they repeatedly experience that help is either missing or insufficient. This reinforces the experience of being hopeless and helpless (Lazare, 1987).

These three elements are commonly part of human suffering. If people have severe pain but have the belief that this pain can be understood by themselves and by others and that it does not threaten their sense of who they are or will be; if their pain does not alienate them from others; and if they feel they will be able to get hep for the pain, then they will not "suffer" because the meaning that is necessary for human suffering is absent.

Suffering has another intriguing dimension revealed in the root of the word: ". . . to submit to pain, distress or grief" (*Oxford English Dictionary*, 2nd Edition, 1989). Suffering is, in this meaning, more closely related to endurance than to victimization. The importance of this volitional and positive element, like the universality of the experience of suffering, has been explored by many great religious mystics, including St. Augustine and St. Catherine of Avila, and more recently by Gershom Scholem (1990).

Cure, or as it is known in the field of addiction medicine, "recovery," is the process of overcoming suffering. To be cured is to know what is wrong and what to do about it. To be cured is to know one is whole and connected to others in a network of acceptance and love. To be cured is to know that one has not lost the meaning to one's life or, as it is said in the 12-step programs, that one has not lost the sustaining relationship to one's personal Higher Power. A similar definition of cure is found in the contemporary cognitive treatment of severe agoraphobia and panic disorder in which patients learn not only that by not fearing their panicky feelings they can live more normal lives but also that their panic itself declines in severity and frequency (DuPont, 1986c; Weekes, 1972, 1987).

This definition of cure is a far cry from the usual view of cure in medicine—the elimination of the illness. The definition of cure used in recovery from chemical dependence reinforces the connection of suffering to religion, a connection that can be seen in the origins of medicine. Modern medicine typically turns away from this definition of cure in embarrassment at the unscientific aspects of the process of helping the suffering person understand and cope with a disease that the health care professional, with the best will and the most modern technology, cannot eliminate.

One of the more remarkable experiences in life, and in medicine, is to spend time with a person experiencing an "incurable," dreadful disease who is not suffering. As health care professionals, we have seen patients with grave diseases, often with severe pain, who have achieved a serenity, a peace, and and an optimism that is truly inspirational. These are people who, while experiencing intense pain, do not experience distress, alienation, and despair. They do not suffer in the usual sense of the word.

One of the central and paradoxical tenets of addiction treatment is that the disease of addiction is lifelong and "incurable" in the traditional medical meaning of the word "cure." One never stops being an addict: "Once an addict always an addict." The quest for freedom from the disease of addiction is part of the denial of the disease, a cardinal symptom of the disease, which keeps the addict suffering. Recovery, or cure from addiction, begins when the addict, and those who care for the addict, abandon this understandable but futile hope and replace it with a willingness to admit powerlessness over addiction.

This chapter explores these issues, including the apparent paradox that the alleviation of suffering requires acceptance of the disease.

THE NATURE OF CHEMICAL DEPENDENCE

Much of your pain is self-chosen. It is the bitter potion by which the physician within you heals your sick self.
—Kahlil Gibran (*International Thesaurus of Quotations*, 1970, p. 620)

The disease of chemical dependence, or addiction, is *cunning, baffling, powerful,* and *patient.* Those words come from the 12-step programs, all of which are based on Alcoholics Anonymous. They are typical of the wisdom that educates addicts and their families about their disease (Robertson, 1988). To understand the suffering of addiction, it is first necessary to understand the outlines of the disease of addiction (Vaillant, 1983).

Although we have studied this disease for years, we also know our own understanding of it remains rudimentary. To study addiction, and to work with addicts, is to learn and then to relearn humility. The disease of addiction is baffling not only for the sufferer but also for others, including health care professionals, who relate to the addicted person.

Addiction means the loss of control over a behavior that one previously could control and that others continue to be able to control. Addiction means continuation of the addictive behavior when that behavior clearly causes problems to the addict and to others. Addiction means denying the addiction and wishing to, as well as believing one can, control the addictive behavior (American Psychiatric Association, 1987).

The American Society of Addiction Medicine (1990) recently redefined alcoholism, the prototypical addiction, deemphasizing physical dependence and reemphasizing the aspects of denial and loss of control over the addictive behavior:

Alcoholism is a disease characterized by continuous or periodic: impaired control over drinking, preoccupation with the drug alcohol, use of alcohol despite adverse consequences, and distortions in thinking, most notably denial. [p. 9]

There are three fundamental stages to addictive behavior. Before we explore these stages we must examine the inner experience of the addict, focusing on typical people who become dependent on alcohol and illicit drugs. The soon-to-be addicts begin the process of addiction with important vulnerabilities. They often come from families that have been dominated by addiction. This predisposes them to addiction on the basis of both nature (genetics) and nurture (experience) (Goodwin, 1976; U.S. Department of Health and Human Services, 1990b). People who are about to become addicts often come to their addicting substances with a high level of confidence in their own ability to handle addicting sub-stances and a willingness to take risks in order to use them .Warning signs about the negative aspects of substance use, including their addictive potential, if they are given by health professionals, family members, teachers, or religious advisors, are characteristically ignored because of the potential addict's exaggerated self-confidence. Initial use of the addicting substances usually occurs among peers who use the substances without apparent problems and in an environment that approves of, or at least tolerates, substance use.

What happens to people whose use of addicting substances leads to addiction? Potential addicts do not want to become addicts. They do not want to suffer from the dreadful consequences of addiction. Potential addicts find three important changes in feelings when they use addicting substances. First, they find *reward*, or what is sometimes called "euphoria." More simply, potential addicts find feelings of joy, peace, and pleasure in the use of drugs. This much of the inner experience most nonaddicts appreciate. What they seldom appreciate is that the addict also finds something more, something that for many addicts is even more important than pleasure. They find *relief from discomfort* when they use drugs. They find that feelings of pain, embarrassment, loneliness, anxiety, depression, and fear diminish when they use drugs. Physiologists call the first effect of substance use by addicts "positive reinforcement," and they call the sec-ond, the reduction of bad feelings, "negative reinforcement" (Kalant, 1989). The first two effects of substance use by addicts set the stage for the third positive feeling addicts have. Their use of the substances, combining both pleasure and relief of pain, gives them *courage*. They get from their substance use a feeling of wholeness and the sense of power to live in ways that they could not live without their new "friends." These drug-induced feelings give addicts the sense of power to take risks in interpersonal relationships and situations that they previously were unable to take.

Often younger addicts, addicts to illegal drugs rather than to alcohol alone, and addicts early in their personal histories of addiction are prima-rily motivated by their desire for euphoria (the first feeling change), whereas older addicts, alcoholics who do not use illegal drugs, and people later in their addiction histories are motivated primarily by their desire to avoid pain and discomfort (the second feeling change). These distinctions also relate to the prominence of character disorder in the addictive process. People who are impulsive and who lack feelings for the needs of others have a character defect (American Psychiatric Association, 1987). Cloninger's Type 1 alcoholics, who do not have severe character disorders, are more often seekers of pain relief, whereas his Type 2 alcoholics, who do have character disorders, are more often seekers of euphoria (Cloninger, 1987).

This distinction between types of chemically dependent people is new and important. It separates those addicts who tend to be stable and mature (who have powerful consciences) from those who tend to be impulsive and irresponsible (who have weak consciences). Cloninger focused on alcoholism, but his observations can be extended to all addictions. The high-conscience Type 1 addicts, often older and less likely to be involved in illegal drug use, usually have established, if sometimes chaotic, families and careers. They often suffer intensely from the harm they cause others. They feel shame because of their loss of control over their lives. The second type of addict, Cloninger's Type 2, is often young and likely to have trouble with authority, including the law. Type 2 addicts are less likely to suffer from their addiction or to feel guilt and shame. When they do suffer as a result of their addiction, they suffer because they feel trapped by family, employers, or officers of the law who seek to prevent them from doing what they please.

Both types of addicts cause intense pain to people who love them. The distinction between the suffering of addicts and the suffering of those around addicts is more dramatic in Type 2 addicts because there is often a marked contrast between the lack of personal suffering experienced by Type 2 addicts, especially early in their illness, and the suffering felt by those around them. When Type 2 addicts get well, they become more similar to Type 1 addicts as their consciences develop and they become more aware and responsive to their consciences. Although both Type 1 and Type 2 addictions are the result of the complex interplay of both environmental and genetic factors, Type 1 is more environmental whereas Type 2 is more genetic.

Typically, before addicts experienced substance use, nothing had produced such seemingly great, predictable, and reliable rewards. It is likely that both their genetic and their environmental background predisposed them to this potent experience. Thus, the vulnerability of potential addicts is not "nature or nurture" but "nature and nurture." With these tremendous perceived benefits resulting from the addictive behavior, it is unlikely that potential addicts could resist the subtle addiction process without powerful early preventive measures, which include a strong spiritual base to life and a firm personal rejection of pleasures induced by nonmedical drug use (DuPont, 1984).

Once the process of addiction sets in, the interaction of the evolving addict and the addictive behavior has a life of its own. The substance use becomes the central feature of the addict's life. In this sense addicts fall in love with the addictive behavior, or more properly, fall in love with the changed feelings produced by the addictive behavior. The feelings addicts seek are good feelings produced in ways that cause addicts to lose control of their behavior.

The addictive behaviors also produce a terrible array of negative health and social consequences. Addicts, caught in the love affair with their changed feelings and conditioned to the addictive behavior used to get these good feelings, think of their addictive behavior as similar to that of nonaddicts. Alcoholics, for example, think their drinking is social drinking. Addicts deny the negative consequences and hide their addictive behavior from those who might recognize their problems and act to stop their addictive behavior.

When people who are not destined to become addicts use an addicting substance, they do not have these three reactions (U.S. Department of Health and Human Services, 1987a). They find the substances of little or no interest. In contrast, potential addicts, when they get the substances into their bodies, have powerful and positive reactions to them. This has been called an "allergy" to the addicting substances, but this allergy to addictive experiences produces positive feelings in ways that medical allergies do not (Alcoholics Anonymous World Services, Inc., 1984). The genetic vulnerability to addiction is the vulnerability to this good-feeling reaction to addictive substances (Blum, Noble, Sheridan et al., 1990).

Everyone can learn to get high on drugs, and all people can get physically dependent on drugs, but most people will not use addicting drugs (because of fear or because of personal values that conflict with the drug use). If they do use addicting drugs, they will stop use early because of lack of reward from the use of the substances. In contrast, people who are to become addicts have a different experience when they use addicting drugs. They often report that when they started using the substances they found something of great value, something they had never found before in their lives. This is called "mood-altering behavior," and addicting drugs are called "mood-altering substances" to label the experience of addicts as they find positive feeling, lose negative feelings, and develop courage to live, all as a result of substance use.

Addicts find the addictive substances to be "friends" who can be counted on to help them feel good and to help them do the things they want to do in their lives. Addicts do not fall in love with the "bad" aspects of their drug use, but with its "good" aspects. Unless health care professionals understand this inner experience of addiction, they will think the addict loves "the bottle" or "the needle." Addicts love the feelings the bottle or the needle brings. An even greater error is to think that the addict is inherently self-destructive and seeks the negative results of his or her drug use. Those negative effects—the hangover, the failures at school and in human relationships, for example—are the unintended consequences of what are, from the addict's point of view, the positive aspects of addiction. Sometimes addictive behavior is described as an effort to "escape reality" or to "blot out the world." More realistically and more simply, addicts seek to change their feelings by using the addicting substance.

Fooling Around

The first stage of addiction is fooling around. In this stage the addict often finds pleasure in the addictive behavior and sees few, if any, problems. This is the honeymoon phase of addiction. Fooling around may last for a long period of time or it may be very brief. Sometimes the addict experiences "love at first sight"; that is, the first use of the substance leads to an overwhelmingly positive experience that leads in turn to a rapid, or even instantaneous, loss of control over substance use. In this situation, the addict finds the substance use to be a powerful, positive experience and seeks to repeat it as soon and as often as possible. More often the falling in love takes place gradually after repeated substance use over days, months, or even years. This initial phase of the seduction into the feelings produced by substance use is central to the experience of addiction because the wish to return to this honeymoon phase motivates much of the addict's behavior in later stages of the disease.

Often, this stage of addiction is not innocuous for the addict or for those who relate to the addict. Many people who relate to the evolving addict, even in this early stage, organize their emotions and behavior around their deeply held but erroneous belief that the potential addict can control his or her addictive behavior. Even at this stage, some addicts find their substance use is less to get high than to dampen bad feelings. Also at this first stage some addicts who are seeking to relieve discomfort, rather than seeking to find euphoria, appear to find their objective. For a time they keep pain and anxiety at bay while consciousness and coping ability remain relatively intact.

Being Hooked

The second stage of addiction is being hooked. This stage begins when the addict loses control or falls in love with the feelings produced by the addictive behavior. Everyone knows that people who are in love lose control of much of their behavior and are, in this sense, insane, although they continue to act normally except in relation to the object of their love. The feelings produced by the substance use become the addict's friend and lover.

Loss of control over substance use, however, is seldom complete or universal. It is usually most evident after a long period of time when addicts' continued substance use, despite serious, often painful problems, is baffling to both addicts and those who relate to them. Loss of control is also related to specific settings, feelings, and experiences. Addicts exert more control over their addictive behavior in some settings, at some times, than in others.

As the second stage progresses, the honeymoon ends. Problems pile up because of the substance use. The benefits become less obvious. Substance use becomes a compulsion, a way to survive. It is no longer primarily a way to get high or to have fun.

Because, in this stage, the substance use is often met by social disapproval by others in the addict's family, at work, and in other settings, it becomes secretive, a secret lover. Addicts hide their substance use from others, especially from those closest to them, leading to the lying and the moral corruption that is universal in addiction. Addicts lie to themselves to conceal from themselves how much of the substance they use and what the negative consequences are because they do not want to give up their friend and lover. How can addicts tell others, especially those whom they love and who love them, the truth, when such honesty would lead to strong disapproval of the highly valued addictive behavior?

In this stage of addiction, or even earlier, people who relate to the addict join in the disease as they deny the addictive behavior, deny the consequences of the addiction, and deny their own role in the perpetuation of the addictive disease. They become codependent. As this second stage continues, codependent people come to believe that all of their own problems are caused by the addict's bad behavior and that if the addict's substance use would only stop, then all of the codependent's problems would stop also.

Hitting Bottom

The third phase of the addict's career is hitting bottom. Some event forces addicts to face the reality that they have lost control not only of their addictive behavior but also of their entire lives. They unwillingly come to know that they must change, they must give up their secret lovers, if they are to survive. Bottoms are of many kinds. Sometimes hitting bottom is a health consequence of addiction; sometimes it is a family crisis. Sometimes it is the result of a crisis at work or in the criminal justice system. One thing is clear: bottoms come from outside the addicts. Hitting bottom forces addicts to rethink their lives, to face their own powerlessness over their addiction, and to look outside themselves for help.

Bottoms are at many levels. The experience of hitting bottom is usually repeated by addicted people many times. When addicts hit bottom they usually try desperately to control their substance use rather than give it up. They usually succeed for a while, cutting back their substance use and reducing their problems. This reassures them—falsely—that they can go back to the honeymoon phase when they could use the substances at relatively moderate levels without problems. Addicts try to find recovery their own way, rejecting the advice of other recovering people and of experienced health care professionals.

Inexperienced health care professionals usually accept this denial, this wish of the addict to return to controlled use of the addicting substance, encouraging addicts to try to control their substance use. They often support the addicts' belief that they can stop one drug—cocaine, for example—and continue to use another that they have not had trouble with—alcohol, for example. Approaches that seek to control substance use, although often well meaning, fail. Characteristically, this futile attempt at halfway measures leads to the education of addicts and those health care professionals who seek to help addicts. We call this process "doing personal research on chemical dependence." It can be a long, painful, and dangerous research project, but in our experience it is seldom avoided by addicts or by those who try to help addicts.

When addicts say they will recover their own way, they mean they want to eliminate their drug-caused problems without stopping their drug use. They mean that they want to stop use of some drugs but not of others. This is a phase in the addictive process. It is the exploration of bottoms, of finding out just how far addicts have to go before they have had enough of trying to control their drug use. Some addicts hit bottom when they are told by a spouse or a friend that their drug or alcohol use is a problem. For many addicts it takes far more than this to get them to face the facts about their addiction. For many addicts, hitting bottom requires truly great suffering, such as an arrest, a life-threatening illness, or the loss of job or family. Many addicts die conducting their research project on chemical dependence before they hit bottom hard enough to give up their lover— their substance use.

The tenacity of the hold of addiction on the addict's behavior is one of the greatest puzzles to outside observers of addictive diseases. Addiction is all the more baffling because the addict is often, in other areas of his or her life, an intelligent, rational person.

THE BIOLOGY OF ADDICTION

In recent years there has been a new interest in the biology of addiction (Cohen, 1988; Gregory, 1987; Restak, 1984, 1988). Although the basic science of addiction is still primitive, it is now clear that addiction reflects fundamental brain mechanisms for the creation of pleasure and the relief of pain that primarily involve the brain's limbic system, which controls emotions. The brain manages behavior. All animals move toward what produces pleasure and away from what produces pain.

Freud put it this way: "Our entire psychical activity is bent upon procuring pleasure and avoiding pain." Freud, who spent his long and productive professional life studying the relationships between thoughts, feelings, and behaviors, also identified one of the most important aspects of pleasure as a human experience. Unlike animals, humans can think about the future consequences of their behaviors, and they can relate their feelings to their values. Thus, when Freud wrote that people seek pleasure and avoid suffering, he made clear that the pleasure to be sought was not simply the pleasure of immediate reward. Prudent people work to maximize long-term pleasure, not short-term euphoria. He called this "delayed gratification" (Freud, 1920). This long-term perspective, and the rooting of behavior in deeply held values, is a central concept in the prevention and treatment of addiction.

More recently, Richard Hawley, a poet and teacher, has written wisely on the relationship of youth and drugs in his book, *The Purposes of Pleasure: A Reflection on Youth and Drugs* (1983). Hawley notes that, "Pleasure is intrinsically good" (p. 29). He distinguishes between sensual pleasures (such as sex and food) and nonsensual pleasures (such as elation over mastering a task or enjoying the success of a friend). Hawley also distinguishes between natural pleasures and such artificial pleasures as drugs and alcohol:

> *In the face of so much that is daunting and ominous with respect to drugs, it is good to remember that the young have splendid resources to draw upon. The greatest of these is health itself. No parent, teacher, or psychiatrist has to provide it. Rather, we have only to keep its impressive unfolding from being spoiled until young people have the stability and self-mastery to promote it for themselves. Children will always be curious about altered states of mind, and they will always pursue perceived pleasures with an energy proportional to the intensity of those pleasures. Denying this is futile and dishonest. But even greater than the apparently universal desire for a "kick" or a thrill is every young person's drive to control and master his or her circumstances: to see the point, to understand the mechanism, to be valuable and valued in play, in loving relationships, and in work. These pursuits are also pleasurable, although in a less flashy, more enduring way. Moreover, the pleasures of health and mastery are self-confirming. In the life histories of the world's most revered contributors, only the natural pleasures, never the artificial counterparts, deliver the goods. [p. 169]*

It is no accident that most of the addictive drugs people use are also "painkillers." The brain is tightly organized around the reciprocal relationship between pleasure and pain (Goldstein, 1989; Kalant, 1989; Restak, 1988). The most common nonchemical stimulations of the brain's pleasure centers come from feeding and sexual behavior, two of the most crucial behaviors for any animal. The brain's pleasure centers are activated by specific neurotransmitters: the brain's chemical messengers. When people become addicted to drugs and alcohol, they are using chemical tricks for this pleasure system in the brain by finding chemicals that mimic the natural neurotransmitters of this pleasure/pain system.

There was a time when most experts on addiction thought that addicts pursued their addictions because they experienced withdrawal when they stopped using drugs. We are now learning that what keeps the addict hooked is not physical dependence, although that is sometimes a real problem, but rather it is the repeated experience of chemically induced pleasure. Biological research has shown that "reward" is a separate brain pathway from "withdrawal" and that behavior is determined by the reward pathway, not by the withdrawal pathway (Bozarth & Wise, 1984; Wise, 1988).

Natural pleasures such as feeding and sex have cut-off mechanisms associated with feelings of satiation. Addictive drugs do not. Addicts tend to overstimulate their pleasure centers by their addictive behavior, thereby exhausting these reward mechanisms in their brains. This leaves them depressed and often suffering. This is a sign of addiction (Restak, 1984). The newly understood biology of addiction explains why addicts, especially in the later stages of the disease, are not happy people and why they take less pleasure from the subtler, safer everyday natural pleasures than do nonaddicted people: they have exhausted their natural pleasure capabilities by excessive, artificial stimulation.

Although addiction is a human risk from which no one is spared, it is important to recognize that some people are especially vulnerable to addiction for many reasons, including genetic factors (McGovern & DuPont, 1991). This has been shown in the case of alcoholism by twin studies in which the twins were adopted shortly after birth. Their risk for alcoholism was more strongly determined by their biological parents than by their adoptive parents. The same finding about genetically determined vulnerability to addiction to alcohol comes from animal research where some strains of dogs or rats are alcohol likers and some are not, generation after generation (U.S. Department of Health and Human Services, 1990b).

The simple summary of this short lesson in the biology of addiction is that what produces pleasure needs to be watched carefully, by individuals, by families, and by communities, to ensure that it does not become a behavioral cancer. Vulnerability to addiction is a complex result of both nature (genetics) and nurture (environment and experiences) (Restak, 1988). One does not have to be a Puritan or a masochist to appreciate the universal risks of addiction. Society has simple boundaries for most pleasures. It is generally safer to stick within those routine boundaries than to skate on thin ice outside society's official rules for behavior. The rules of biology and personality and society's rules for pleasure-producing behavior are important to understanding the suffering caused by addiction.

People who are addicted routinely deny their addiction. That explains why it is important for all people seeking to avoid the suffering of addiction to be honest and open about pleasurable behaviors and to work with families, health care workers, and others to monitor their pleasure-producing behaviors. Honesty is the most profound antidote to addiction. When it comes to addiction, "we are only as sick as our secrets."

What is obvious to anyone who works with addicted people is that many of them are risk takers who spend a large amount of their time outside the boundaries erected for ordinary people. Having a risk-taking personality is itself a major risk for addiction (DuPont, 1988b; DuPont, 1989c).

Many people who engage in potentially addictive behaviors without becoming addicted do not indulge repeatedly in these behaviors. They do not become experts in the pleasure the behaviors can produce. Many addicted people, in contrast, have engaged in particular addictive behaviors over and over again, often to substantial excess of society's routine rules, before they become addicted or lose control of that particular pleasurable behavior. Risk taking, willingness to operate outside routine social boundaries, and indulgence in pleasure-producing behaviors set the stage for the tragic suffering of addiction to drugs, to alcohol, and to other addictive behaviors. Usually these personality factors precede the addiction, but they are always present and heightened once the addiction has taken hold (DuPont, 1989c).

Some alcoholics report that they fell in love with alcohol on their first drink. Both patterns for initiation of addiction—gradual falling in love and love at first sight—are common and important. They are two parts of the same problem of the complex vulnerability to addiction. Those people who required years of fooling around before they lost control are relatively less vulnerable than those who fell in love on first experience. Whichever pattern a person has experienced, however, the process of addiction, once it has set in, is the same. The addicts become slaves to their own addiction with predictable consequences for themselves and for all those who relate to them.

It is essential in the process of recovery from addiction for addicts and their families to recognize that many of the addicts' problems preceded their addictive behavior. Many of the problems of the codependents in addicts' lives also preceded the addicts' addictive behavior. Similarly, the needs for help of both addicts and codependents go beyond the addicts' merely stopping use of drugs or alcohol, or engaging in other addictive behavior.

Addiction is, at root, a selfishness and a self-centeredness as well as a loss of connection to caring people and to the spiritual foundations of life. It is common to see a "dry drunk," that is, a person who continues to engage in addictive behavior without continuing to use addictive substances. Such a person has not dealt with the defects of character that preceded the addiction, that were worsened by the addiction, and that persist after substance use ends unless a real recovery program is followed over a lifetime.

There are four central elements of addiction. The first is that the addictive behavior produces good feelings and/or eliminates bad feelings. In other words, the addictive behavior must produce *mood alteration* or *feeling changes* in the person who engages in the behavior. This complex group of feelings was separated into three parts earlier in this chapter: production of good feelings, elimination of bad feelings, and generation of courage to face life.

The second element of addiction is *loss of control* over the addictive behavior, or what we have called "falling in love" with the feelings produced by the addictive behavior. Addicts have lost the ability to set limits on the addictive behavior and have lost the ability to realistically assess the impact of the addictive behavior on their lives.

Third, the addictive behavior *persists despite problems* produced by that behavior. Even when the negative consequences of the behavior are unmistakable, addicts continue the behaviors in reckless disregard for their own best interests.

The fourth central element of addiction is *denial*. The addict and those around the addict routinely deny both the extent and the consequences of the addictive behavior. The phenomenon of denial makes addiction a difficult disease to diagnose and treat, especially in its early stages when it is difficult to distinguish the addictive behavior from normal pleasure-producing behaviors that look similar.

These four central elements are all part of one whole process which is addiction. Addiction is a disease with a natural history, including specific vulnerabilities and predictable consequences. Addiction can be understood, prevented, and treated (American Society of Addiction Medicine, 1990; DuPont, 1984; Vaillant, 1983).

Addiction to Behaviors Other Than Chemical Dependence

Chemical dependence is a model for a wider human phenomenon, the experience of addiction. It is now commonplace to hear health care professionals talk of addiction to sex, food, work, or exercise. Even watching television has been called an addiction. Chocolate has been called an addictive substance (Weil & Rosen, 1983). Unless such terms are to be so vague as to be useless, it is important that health care professionals have a clear understanding of what makes a behavior an "addiction."

The emerging biology of addiction is important to understanding the suffering caused by addiction because it has become increasingly clear that addictions can occur not only to drugs and alcohol but to any activity that produces pleasure (Jaffe, 1985). The more pleasurable the activity, the more potentially addictive it is. Addiction can occur even to good behaviors, such as work and exercising, as long as they are experienced as intensely pleasurable.

The modern biology of addiction offers an important clue for understanding addictions beyond chemical dependence. Not everyone is equally vulnerable to addiction (Deitrich & Spuhler, 1984; DuPont, Goldstein, & O'Donnell, 1979). Some people can drink alcohol or eat chocolate chip cookies without becoming either alcoholics or chocoholics. Others are less fortunate (Platt & Labate, 1976). Many experts have sought the "addictive personality" only to eventually conclude that there is no such thing. Addicts seem to have either more or less of various character traits than nonaddicts, but there appears to be no single or simple characterization of the person who is addiction-prone (Cloninger, 1987; Vaillant, 1983). There may be a genetically determined vulnerability to addiction in general, although this has not been shown in research studies except for early-onset alcoholism, called Type 2 alcoholism (Cloninger, 1987; U.S. Department of Health and Human Services, 1990a). A recent study appears to have identified a gene for alcoholism (Blum, Noble, Sheridan et al., 1990). However, 23 percent of alcoholics in this study did not have the alcoholic gene, and 28 percent of nonaddicts did have the alcoholic gene. This study makes clear that genetic studies show powerful nongenetic factors in the development of the disease of chemical dependence.

Some substances or behaviors are relatively powerful at causing addiction (heroin, cocaine, and cigarettes, for example), whereas others are weaker reinforcers of behaviors (chocolate chip cookies, running, and television viewing, for example) (Jaffe, 1985). Some ways of using substances are more addicting than others. For example, smoking and injecting cocaine intravenously are more addicting than drinking alcohol (U.S. Department of Health and Human Services, 1987a). Much of the heightened vulnerability of particular people to particular substances and to particular patterns of administration of reinforcing substances is biologically based (U.S. Department of Health and Human Services, 1990b).

Using our understanding of chemical dependence and of 12-step mod-

els of treatment to cope with other "addictive behaviors" is a two-edged
sword. On the one hand, the lessons from chemical dependence work in
these other areas. They are, in this sense, uniquely helpful. On the other
hand, comparing alcoholism and drug addiction to addiction to TV,
exercise, or chocolate chip cookies can trivialize the problems of chemical
dependence. These "other addictions," with some exceptions, do not have
the same devastating impact on sufferers and those who relate to them—
especially their families—that chemical dependence routinely, and tragically, does.

Any behavior that is powerfully pleasurable can be addictive. The most
vulnerable people are those who have a genetic and/or a family predisposition to the specific addictive behavior. People who live without strong
internal and external controls over impulsive behavior are also more
vulnerable to addiction. Obesity and alcoholism tend to run in families.
However, most people who are alcoholic are not obese, and vice versa.
Similarly, although children of alcoholics are four times as likely to
become alcoholics as are children of nonalcoholics, most children of
alcoholics do not become alcoholics (U.S. Department of Health and
Human Services, 1990b).

Some people may be more generally susceptible to addictive behaviors
than others, but no one is universally either vulnerable or invulnerable to
all the various sorts of addiction. People differ in their relative vulnerability to addiction generally and in their relative vulnerability to specific
addictive behaviors.

In addition to personal vulnerability to addiction there is a wide range
of environmental vulnerability to particular addictions. Social environments are important to addiction risk. The more available the addictive
substance or experience is in an environment and the more tolerant an
environment is to any particular addictive behavior, the more widespread
that particular addiction will become in that human environment. On the
other hand, there will be less addictive behavior in environments that
have low availability and that are intolerant to particular addictive behaviors, although these behaviors will not be eliminated entirely (DuPont,
1990d). Some people, despite environmental high availability and tolerance, will not succumb to addictions, and some people, despite low
availability and low environmental tolerance, will succumb to particular
addictions (DuPont, 1984).

When it comes to sex, food, work, or exercise, the behaviors are not
merely pleasurable, they are addictive when they meet the four central
criteria of addiction: they produce significant reward; they result in loss of
control; they persist despite problems the behaviors cause; and both the

extent and consequences of these behaviors are denied by those involved in them. To identify addiction often requires a high index of suspicion on the part of the health care professional and a sensitive discussion with the patient and the patient's family members. People who overeat from time to time and those who occasionally watch television are not addicted. People who meet these four criteria, however, are probably addicted, and they probably can benefit from medical assistance with their own particular problem-causing behavior, or addiction. They are not likely to get well on their own because addiction is not a self-curing disease.

When working with a patient, health care professionals need to be aware of the potential for addiction and to help the patient identify addictive behaviors. Once addiction is identified, the health care professional can work with the patient and the patient's family to develop a strategy to overcome the addiction. This is not easy, but it can be done. Successful treatment of any addiction often includes an intervention and the use of "tough love" (DuPont, 1984). Most often, as with chemical dependence treatment, it is done with a combination of professional treatment and mutual aid.

The experience of working in a community of recovery, as the mutual-aid movement is called, to overcome the disease of addiction is unique in medicine. The 12-step mutual-aid programs have the potential not only for transforming the lives of recovering addicts but also for changing for the better medical practice as well as family and community life (DuPont & McGovern, 1991).

Because of the pervasive impact of denial, a careful history is needed, often with information from the patient's family members, to identify addiction (DuPont, 1986a). Two questions in particular can help sort our addictive behavior: "How much do you like to do X?" and "How hard would it be for you to stop X?"

The typical addict's reply to such questions from a health care professional is, "I could stop X if I wanted to, but I don't want to." That answer is usually a signal for further exploration of the behavior to identify its negative consequences, and for the development of a treatment plan if the behavior is found to be addictive.

Addiction Versus Physical Dependence

This broad definition of addiction also highlights patient behaviors seen by health care workers that are sometimes thought to be addictive but that are not. For example, the existence of withdrawal symptoms on stopping a medicine is not a central feature of addiction. "Addiction" needs to be clearly separated from "physical dependence." Thus, when a patient is taking morphine or other narcotic for the treatment of pain, this will, over a period of days or weeks of daily use, produce simple physical dependence in the patient. If the narcotic is discontinued abruptly, the patient will experience withdrawal symptoms. Such narcotic use will not produce addiction unless it involves the four central features of addiction listed previously. Otherwise, medical use of narcotics causes "benign physical dependence," which is treated easily by gradually reducing the dose of the dependence-producing medicine to zero when it is no longer needed (DuPont, 1989a; Twycross, 1983). Because physical dependence and addiction are often confused in health care, it is important for these distinctions to be understood, otherwise truly dangerous addictions will be overlooked (because there are no physical withdrawal symptoms), and appropriate medical treatments will be withheld (because there are physical withdrawal symptoms) (Melzack, 1990).

Most people entering chemical dependence treatment programs do not demonstrate physical withdrawal symptoms, and when withdrawal symptoms are present, they are almost always brief and easily treated. Many drugs that cause severe addiction—cocaine, for example—do not produce typical withdrawal symptoms. Getting an addict off of an addicting drug in a hospital is easy. It is easy to help patients who experience benign physical dependence stay off their medicines once they no longer need them because they do not want to take the medicines. It is hard to help addicts stay off addicting drugs because they love the feelings the drugs produce. Relapse to addictive drug use is not part of physical dependence; it is part of addiction (DuPont, 1989a, 1990b).

Health care workers need to appreciate that not only is the setting important in distinguishing addictive drug use from nonaddictive medicine use but the particular patient also is important. Patients who are chemically dependent, that is, have a current or past history of chemical dependence, react to dependence-producing, mood-altering drugs in different ways than do nonchemically dependent patients (DuPont, 1988a, 1990c). Health care workers need to distinguish between malignant addiction and benign physical dependence. This is sometimes more difficult than it appears, since many chemically dependent people deny their disease. They either lie to health care workers to are genuinely not aware of their chemical dependence. Sometimes patients experiencing benign physical dependence worry that they are addicted (DuPont & Saylor, 1991).

Talking to a family member can help health care workers identify addiction with respect to drug or alcohol use. A simple rule of thumb to identify chemical dependence is that any patient who has more than four drinks of alcohol a week and any patient who reports current or past use of illicit drugs that persisted for more than a few uses of the substance should be considered currently chemically dependent until proved otherwise. Any mood-altering, dependence-producing medicine should be used with great caution with these vulnerable, possibly chemically dependent patients, especially in outpatient settings in which the patient controls the use of the medicine.

Not all medicines are problems in terms of either addiction or physical dependence. Controlled substances, including analgesics and medicines for insomnia and anxiety, are most likely to be problems for chemically dependent patients (U.S. Department of Justice, 1988). Other medicines that are not controlled substances, including other prescription medicines, such as antidepressants, antipsychotics, and antimanic medicines, used to treat psychiatric disorders are not mood altering and thus are not addicting for chemically dependent patients.

When using antianxiety medicines, most of which are controlled substances in medical practice, such as alprazolam (Xanax) and diazepam (Valium), these distinctions between chemically dependent patients and nonchemically dependent patients and between addiction and physical dependence are vitally important. The antianxiety medicines produce physical dependence after daily use for months at a time, but they do not produce addiction, except among chemically dependent people (DuPont, 1990b; 1990c; DuPont & Saylor, 1991; U.S. Department of Health and Human Services, 1987b). Failure to make these distinctions can lead to potentially dangerous prescriptions of antianxiety medicines to chemically dependent people and withholding of these useful medicines from clinically anxious patients who are not chemically dependent out of unjustified fear of addiction. Discontinuation from daily use of antianxiety medicines among both addicted and nonaddicted patients should be accomplished on a gradual basis to avoid possibly severe withdrawal symptoms (DuPont, 1990a).

RECOVERY FROM CHEMICAL DEPENDENCE

Although the world is full of suffering, it is full also of the overcoming of it.

—Helen Keller (*International Thesaurus of Quotations*, p. 620)

The central elements of the experience of addiction in its final stages are bewilderment ("How did this happen?" "Why can't I handle this myself?") and shame ("What's wrong with me?" "What has made me into a liar and a fool?"). Addicts struggle to regain control of their lives and still hold on to their secret, shameful lover. They seek the devil's bargain: if only they can keep their addictive behavior, they will do anything else.

Addicts, at the end of the process, suffer intensely as they feel alone, hopeless, and helpless seeing their lives crumble around them. They do what they need to except the things they most need to do: admitting they have an incurable disease that they cannot control on their own and stopping the addictive behavior.

Other people generally do not understand the addict's plight: "Why don't you behave like you used to (or like I do and like other normal people do)?" Unlike people suffering from heart disease or cancer, neither addicts nor those who seek to help them have a good model for the disease or for what they are to do about it.

These nearly universal reactions add to the addict's bewilderment and shame. They deepen the addict's suffering. This suffering from a poorly understood and invisible illness is similar to many mental diseases, such as panic disorder or schizophrenia. Like them, chemical dependence goes to the core of the person. In this way, mental diseases are different from physical diseases such as heart disease or cancer: they are diseases of the self, not diseases the self has. Addiction is also similar to mental diseases in that it is a stigmatized disorder that is hard to admit to oneself and to others.

Cancer had this quality a generation or two ago, but today the stigma has largely been removed. Now it is comparatively easy to admit one has cancer. This permits better, more candid communication and understanding of the experience for cancer victims and for those who relate to them. One is not blamed for getting cancer. Lung cancer in cigarette smokers is the most common exception precisely because the prevailing attitudes are related to addiction, not to cancer. It is possible to share with the typical cancer sufferer the illness and the fate. Think about why it is so much harder for most people today to say, "I am an addict" than it is to say, "I have cancer."

Addiction is unlike most other mental diseases in two important ways. First, addiction has an unmistakable volitional, willful component: addicts truly have brought their suffering onto themselves by their behaviors. This is true even though addicts did not seek the addiction and even though they knew many other people who engaged in similar behaviors, at least some of whom were not addicted. Addicts are responsible for their behavior even though there is a significant genetic component to their disease, and even though addicts have lost control of their addictive behavior. Addicts are fully responsible for every single act related to their addiction, even though they do not understand their addiction (DuPont, 1984).

Addictive behavior is morally stigmatized by society, especially by the most revered members of society. Such stigma is often painful for addicts, but it reflects the powerful and important force of the community to discourage, or prevent, the out-of-bounds, addictive behavior. Addictive behavior is bad behavior that puts addicts in a never-never land beyond the usual moral boundaries of their communities.

The fact that many others are in that land, and that the larger society often gives mixed messages about the addictive behavior, is small comfort when addicts are forced to deal with the larger society about their addictive behaviors. This is especially true for the use of illegal drugs, which is highly stigmatized by most Americans, especially those over 40 years of age. For this reason drug addicts in the public eye, such as entertainers, athletes, and politicians, when they hit bottom, usually admit to alcoholism and the abuse of prescription medicines but not to the use of illicit drugs. The loss of control over a behavior others can control and the continued use of the substances despite negative consequences are intrinsic parts of the process of chemical dependence that have nothing to do with the legal status of the substances addicts use.

Shame, especially in relation to nonaddicted people, is a major source of suffering for addicts. Shame adds to the alienation, the guilt, and the feeling of being hopeless and helpless, as well as unworthy. Shame also keeps addicts from reaching out for help.

The second way addiction is different from other mental diseases is that health care professionals have relatively little to offer addicts in their efforts to get well. There are no medicines or other treatments for addiction that play more than a peripheral role in recovery, even though health care workers can help, or hinder, the process of recovery. Recovery is something addicts can only do for themselves. Recovery can best be achieved not by working with professionals but by working with fellow sufferers of addiction in a unique community of recovery. Although this is not true today for other mental diseases, the process of recovery from addiction offers a useful model in medicine and psychiatry for the future with applicability far beyond even the broad reaches of addiction (DuPont & McGovern, 1990).

A widely used saying that captures this unique message from the treatment of addiction is "You alone can do it, but you cannot do it alone." Recovery is not "self-help." Self-help is how the addicts got into trouble trying to overcome their drug- and alcohol-caused problems in their own way. Recovery means mutual aid, or working within the community of recovering addicts. It means getting well the programs' way, not the addicts' way.

The term "mutual aid" captures the sense that recovery is something that people do working together. Recovery is mutual in the sense that addicts and codependent people learn about the disease of addiction and are introduced to recovery by other people who suffer from the same disease. Recovery is also mutual in the sense that addicts find recovery through their relationship with their personal Higher Power (addicts are not alone in their recovery even when no other person is around them).

An AA adage puts it this way: "I can get drunk alone but I cannot stay sober alone." Mutual aid also can come from health care professionals working with addicted people in recovery. The disease of addiction, a feeling disease, is often isolating; recovery is a shared experience. Recovery is more than simply admitting one is an addict and then helping others get well. In AA, people who do that are called "two-steppers," meaning that they get to the first step (admitting they are powerless over their drug) and then go immediately to the 12th step (helping others get well) without working through the other ten steps. This is a well-known recipe for return to substance use.

Addicts coming into a 12-step program are in a unique reciprocal relationship. They come to help themselves, and to do that they help others. They must surrender and go through a process of personal conversion. However, they must not let concern for others become yet one more way they deny their own disease and their primary commitment to healing themselves of the disease that they caused themselves—and others—to suffer. This entails both an initial and an ongoing commitment to one's own recovery as the foundation of sobriety. There is a powerful, important, and humbling aspect of real self-help that is missing in the words "mutual aid." Early participation in AA turns addicts' lives and their wills over to the care of God, as they understand that concept, not to the care of other alcoholics. An old AA saying puts it this way: "You carry the message, not the alcoholic." In other words, each individual is ultimately responsible for his or her own recovery, not for the recovery of anyone else.

The role of mutual-aid programs and the relationships of health care professionals to the treatment of addiction are as yet poorly understood by most health care professionals (DuPont & McGovern, 1991). Addiction today is an explosive growth segment within the American health care market. This is true in both public and private chemical dependence treatment programs. These professionally run treatment programs, important as they are, are not the places in which recovery from addiction takes place. Organized addiction treatment programs are places where an addicted person can, for a short time, find a quiet place, free of the mental distractions of active addiction, for thinking and personal growth. These professionally run chemical dependence treatment programs are often the places where addicted people, and their families, are introduced to mutual-aid, 12-step programs. They are less the treatment than they are the preparation for and introduction to the treatment.

Professionally run treatment programs are often the difference between life and death for addicted people and their families. However, recovery from addiction, which is so precious, is not accomplished primarily in the professional chemical dependence treatment program. It is accomplished primarily in 12-step programs, after discharge from the professional treatment programs.

The same conclusion fits outpatient psychotherapy. Mental health therapists often have vital roles to play in helping addicts to regain control of their lives and to fulfill their human potential. Psychotherapy is not addiction treatment; it is human treatment. Because addicts are human beings as well as addicts, many of them need and benefit from psychotherapy. The therapy for addiction itself, the primary disease that is killing addicts, takes place outside professional treatment, whether such treatment is inpatient or outpatient.

The treatment for addiction is also not brief, as is most professional treatment of addicts. Recovery is a lifelong process in which professional treatment is usually a fairly brief, but often a very important, part (Vaillant, 1983).

Recovery from addiction involves learning a new vocabulary and a series of shared, wise messages, many of which are to be found in the books that are the foundation of the 12-step programs (Alcoholics Anonymous World Services, Inc., 1984, 1986, 1987, 1988; Narcotics Anonymous World Service Office, Inc., 1987). Key words include *denial, enabling, intervention, relapse, recovery,* and *codependence.* The goal of treatment is not being clean and sober, although that is a necessary condition for recovery. The goal of recovery is serenity. One of the key features of the search for serenity is the connection to one's personal Higher Power.

THE SUFFERING IN ADDICTION

Returning to the original outline of suffering, after exploring the nature of chemical dependence, or addiction, and its treatment, it is possible to see more clearly the unique nature of the suffering of addiction. Addicts suffer severe *distress* in the terror that comes from realizing that they have lost control of their lives and that they are careening toward personal destruction. The distress of addiction is heightened by the moral dimensions of the crisis. Addicts, prior to recovery, have corrupted their lives, including their highest values and the relationships that mean the most to them. Their lives become a web of self-defeating lies.

Addicts, as they hit bottom, experience extreme *alienation*. They are cut off from everyone else and from their own past and future. They are alone with a problem they cannot see and do not understand. Their selfishness and self-centeredness have both contributed to their plight and been deepened by it.

Addicts feel *despair*. They can see no end to their problems and no one who can offer help. They feel alone and beyond help, bewildered and lost in their shame.

These problems are all deepened by the spiritual impoverishment of the addicts' predicament. Active addicts have no moorings, no anchors to hold them against the storms of addiction.

Addiction has important biological roots. Addicts, like cats futilely chasing their tails, are chasing a chemical mirage. Addicts try to find pleasure in artificial chemical stimulation of their brains' pleasure centers, which, with each stimulation, become more exhausted and unresponsive to the artificial chemical stimulation and to the everyday natural pleasures of life. This produces a profound physical and existential exhaustion, a deep despair and intense suffering.

Addicts got into their predicament out of a willingness to go outside the conventional community rules for behavior. In the case of illegal drugs, their behavior was also outside the law. Addicts went beyond the rules of their family and their religion. The fact that they had a community of fellow addicts does not blunt this important reality. They must accept the spiritual and moral dimensions of their disease and their own responsibility for their behavior, including the hurt they have imposed on those who have most loved and trusted them.

The path to recovery is the path to overcoming this suffering. Recovery means accepting that the addiction is more than "bad behavior," that chemical dependence is an understandable and unfortunately common biological disease with predictable stages and consequences. This awareness comes from joining a community of recovering people, usually in a 12-step program, where the first two steps to recovery are for addicts to admit that they are powerless and to turn their problem over to their Higher Power, as they understand that concept. Because the central element of the disease of addiction is denial, each time drug and alcohol addicts speak in a mutual-aid group, they begin by saying, "I am (first name), an alcoholic (and/or a drug addict)."

In this community of recovery comes what addicts have hungered for, usually for many years: understanding and respect. Although nonaddicted people can never fully understand the suffering of addicts, other addicts can. This sense of community is essential to healing the suffering in addiction. At an even deeper level are the spiritual roots of both addiction and recovery.

Although all addicts had character defects before and during their addiction that prevented them from making major contributions to the welfare of their families and their communities, some active addicts are remarkably creative and productive. In fact, the desire to be "Number One" and to "Have it All" often sets the stage for addiction in these addicts. They are "human doings," rather than human beings. Their recovery involves not doing more and better, but coming to a new relationship with their ambitions so that they can find the serenity in their lives that had eluded them in the frantic quest for the self-glorification that fueled their addiction.

The suffering in addiction is not limited to the addict's loss of control over substance use and the humiliation that causes. Chemical dependence causes a loss of direction and satisfaction in life as healthy goals are replaced by the chemical gratifications in the pursuit of euphoria and/or the relief of pain. Suffering in addiction is caused by the losses in the most important areas of life, including love, work, and self-fulfillment. The suffering in addiction also comes from the problems caused by the substance use itself, including social problems (loss of jobs, arrests), personal problems (loss of the love and respect from family and friends), and physical problems resulting from substance use (the diseases that are secondary to addiction such as cirrhosis of the liver, heart disease, and AIDS).

The great mystery of the suffering from addiction is that despite so much suffering by the addict and by those who care for the addict, the pathological behaviors of both the addict and those who care for the addict (codependent people) persist often for decades. This is a measure of the power of the addiction. Denial, the hallmark of the disease, sustains the suffering in addiction. Recovery begins only when denial is overcome and personal responsibility for problems is accepted by both the addict and those who care for the addict.

CASE HISTORIES

The case histories below exemplify the principles in this chapter focusing on the suffering experienced by addicts and those who love them. Names and some biographical facts have been altered to protect the anonymity of the people involved.

- Bill is a 34-year-old physician who first came to psychiatric treatment because his wife of three years announced, when he brought up his desire to have a child, that her baby would not have an "addict for a father." Bill reported that he had used alcohol and marijuana since he was a teenager. In college he added cocaine. He became a physician and then added prescription narcotics that he got from fellow physician addicts. He vehemently denied that he was "addicted" because he sometimes went several days without any drug use and had no withdrawal symptoms. He confidently said he would stop using cocaine and narcotics if that was what his wife wanted him to do.

  Bill's psychiatrist talked with him about addiction and suggested that he go regularly to Narcotics Anonymous and Alcoholics Anonymous meetings. Bill's psychiatrist also explained to him that he must give up not only cocaine and narcotics but also marijuana and alcohol, since addiction to mood-altering drugs was one disease, not multiple diseases of each separate intoxicating substance. Bill had seen other mental health therapists, but they "only talked about my past and told me I had done a good job of overcoming a difficult childhood. They didn't seem to understand my suffering today or have any suggestions for what I could do to stop the suffering."

  Bill, feeling that he had solved his problem, stopped using cocaine and left psychotherapy when his wife got pregnant. A year later they both returned to the psychiatrist admitting that Bill's wife also had a drug problem, which had intensified when her husband had given her narcotics to use. Bill also saw his narcotics use as a bigger problem than he had at first thought, especially the lying it forced hm into with his wife and others. They both pledged to stop all illegal drug use. They attended several 12-step meetings, with Bill's wife going to Al-Anon when he went to NA and AA meetings.

They came back to treatment a third time two years later on an entirely new basis. Bill said that his brother had admitted he was an alcoholic and joined AA in earnest. Bill had gone to meetings with his brother for a year, to help him stay sober. All the while Bill continued to drink alcohol and to hold on to the illusion that although he had a drug problem, which he felt he had licked, he could drink "normally." Then one evening, when he and his wife had some friends over for dinner, after several predinner drinks, Bill passed out into his soup at the table. The next morning he recalled that only a week before he had "passed out at home at 9 p.m., after drinking." The night after Bill collapsed into his soup he went to an AA meeting with his brother, saying, "I am Bill, a drug addict and an alcoholic. I am a doctor. I thought I was coming here to help my brother. I thought I was better than the rest of you. But last night I realized I was just a dirt-ball addict like everyone else here. From now on I'm here for myself."

Bill told his psychiatrist that with that admission he began his healing, including facing up to the primary nature of his alcoholism, which his drug addiction had helped him deny and hide from others and from himself for many years. Only when he faced his alcoholism did he deal openly with his suffering. He spoke of the times he felt overwhelming guilt about how he treated patients and their families on Mondays and Tuesdays, after his weekend binges when he was irritable and impatient with everyone. He talked about his anger at his wife for forcing him to quit his drug use, but also his anger at his physician friends for helping him continue drug use. Mostly he talked about how alone, afraid, and confused he felt year after year as behavior he considered "in control" was so obviously destroying his life.

Bill compared his suffering to the suffering of his patients, most of whom had chronic diseases that modern medicine could not cure. He observed that although they had pain, it could be shared and understood by others, whereas his pain was inside and not detectable by any physical examination or laboratory study. Neither he nor the doctors he had seen had been able to understand his illness. Worst of all was the lying he had done: lying to his doctors, to his wife, and to himself.

Bill goes to meetings three or four times a week now. He goes no matter what else is happening in his life because he sees his recovery as his top priority. He says the most important part of his recovery is the return of honesty to his life: "I was living a series of ever-expanding lies, and that is all gone. Now I am honest with everyone. Most important,

I am honest with myself in admitting I am an alcoholic and a drug addict."

His wife, who found she had no interest in using drugs once Bill stopped using drugs and alcohol, occasionally goes to Al-Anon meetings. She sometimes is jealous of his commitment to his NA and AA meetings, but she said she also knows that without those meetings Bill is likely to return to his drug and alcohol use. "That would be far worse than any loneliness that I feel when he's at a meeting while I am here alone with the kids in the evenings."

Bill's story shows the limits of his relationship to his psychiatrist. Seeing a psychiatrist was not his treatment for chemical dependence, but Bill found it central to his understanding of his addictive illness, to his finding and using the 12-step programs, and to his work on his relationship with his wife and child.

• Bob is 23 and black. He went o college at 18 on a full scholarship. He had never before been outside his hometown, 2,000 miles away from his college. He was the first person in his extended family to go to college. Bob had been a heavy user of alcohol and marijuana since he was 14. On Halloween in his freshman year, Bob got stoned on LSD and marijuana, becoming seriously paranoid. He threatened the other students in his dormitory. One of them, a good friend Cathy who was a nursing student, had dressed up as a black cat. Bob threatened her, saying that she was "the devil."

The other students in Bob's dormitory considered him the brightest person in the dorm even though he was flunking out of college because of his drug use. His friend, the cat of the night before, sought help the next day for Bob. Cathy did not use drugs and barely drank alcohol. One of Cathy's nursing professors advised her to take Bob to some NA meetings. She had heard of Narcotics Anonymous but never had been to a meeting. Cathy found a listing for Narcotics Anonymous in the phone book and called for the time and location of a meeting. Cathy took Bob to a nearby NA meeting that night and continued to attend NA meetings with Bob every night for two weeks. Then she let him go on his own. Bob stopped using drugs and alcohol for the remainder of his freshman year, and he did well academically. When he returned home for the summer, however, he relapsed to addiction.

He called Cathy, saying he was depressed and had lost interest in returning to college in the fall. When she asked if he had returned to drug use, he said "yes." She encouraged him to go to NA meetings in his home city. He did and once more stopped drug and alcohol use. At the end of his junior year, Bob took Cathy with him to his anniversary NA meeting to celebrate his second year of being clean and sober.

Bob described his suffering this way: As a freshman he had felt confused and helpless at college away from his family and friends. He turned to the only "friend" he thought he had, drugs. Being a member of a minority group had also isolated him from his college classmates, as did his dream of becoming a professional musician. Bob had never known his father, who had died of alcoholism at the age of 25. Bob attributed his gift of music to his father, who had been a talented musician.

Remembering years later his Halloween experience as a freshman—his bottom—Bob said he felt afraid and confused. Bob, in his recovery, faced his suffering. He knew he was letting down everyone who had ever trusted and helped him, but he did not know what else to do because he believed he could not be like his "rich, white" classmates. He felt ashamed and foolish in his drug use. He could think of no one who could help him and no way to find any help. He could not afford to see a doctor and he did not trust the school counselors. He knew he had wasted years of educational opportunity on his drug and alcohol use, but he believed that drug use was an essential part of being a musician, and even of being a "man."

In terms of his recovery, Bob thought that the most important part of his membership in NA was his relationship with his Higher Power, which meant he was no longer alone. Bob's mother had been deeply religious, but Bob had never taken religion seriously in his own life, until he joined NA.

After his junior year, Bob dropped out of college to pursue music full time in his hometown, but he did not return to using alcohol or drugs. He kept going to NA meetings several times a week, saying the meetings "keep me sane." Bob hoped he would have commercial success in music. After a year of working on his music he was penniless. His band broke up over the drug use of some of the band's members. Bob then returned to college to graduate, one year after his initial classmates. He wondered what he would do when he reached the age of 25, the age at which his father died. He said, "I had no role model for what to do after that age, until I joined NA. Now I share my life with people I can understand who are older than that, so maybe I can find some way to live to those older ages."

Cathy said, in retrospect, that she had mixed feelings about Bob's recovery, since he dropped most of his college friends, including her, who were not also members of 12-step programs. On the other hand, she knew that if Bob had not joined NA he would have dropped out of college in his freshman year, or "would have been dead by now."

These two case histories make clear the unique role of 12-step programs in recovery from addiction. They also highlight the suffering that addicts experience in their addiction: the severe distress, the alienation, and the sense of being hopeless and helpless. They demonstrate the loss of personal meaning in life, and the moral and spiritual impoverishment that accompanies addiction.

Both Bill and Bob bear witness to the fact that recovery comes first in their lives. It is the necessary first condition for everything else good that they can dream of having in their lives. Addiction is more than using drugs and alcohol; it is a corrupting, self-centered way of life that threatens the addict for his or her entire lifetime. Recovery, like addiction, is lifelong. It means more than stopping the use of drugs and alcohol. Recovery is not the elimination of the disease of addiction but the acceptance of the disease. Recovery is knowing what is wrong and what to do about it. Finally, the stories of Bill and Bob both show that recovery is not self-help, but that it is found in a unique mutual-aid community of fellow sufferers with a strong spiritual foundation.

These two case histories also exemplify the experience of suffering in addiction as seen by the health care workers who were involved with these experiences. They are typical of the experiences health care workers have when dealing with addicted people, but they hardly scratch the surface of the suffering experience in addiction.

Below are eight brief vignettes that show some of the suffering in addiction:

- Jim is a 65-year-old company owner and president who is a leader in his community. He grudgingly confronted his alcoholism when he was doubled over by "the most severe pain I've ever felt in my life, like a spear in my gut. It just went on hurting hour after hour." His internist diagnosed acute pancreatitis, explaining that Jim's alcoholism was the cause of this disease and that it was likely to recur if Jim didn't stop drinking. He didn't stop.

  Several years later when he drove to his winter home in Florida, Jim arrived barely able to walk because he was so sick with his alcoholism.

His wife admitted him to a local hospital where his doctor told him he might have been dead if he had waited another day before he came into the hospital. Jim was transferred to a 30-day chemical dependence treatment program where he attended AA meetings regularly for the first time. He got out of the hospital and returned to drinking within a month.

Jim's 35-year-old son, Jim, Jr., had been a heroin addict and cocaine addict for 15 years with dozens of hospitalizations and many, many treatment episodes with doctors, psychiatrists, and other therapists. He had been to hundreds of NA and AA meetings. Last summer Jim, Jr. was pulled out of his wrecked car at 2:00 a.m. after he ran it into a bridge abutment. It took the rescue squad 90 minutes to hack and cut his body out of the wreck before they could take him to the hospital where he survived after a six-week stay. He continues to suffer back and leg pain nine months after the accident. Jim, Jr. also continues to drink and to use cocaine, even as his wife prepares to ask him to leave their home.

Jim and Jim, Jr. are two well-educated, intelligent men who are richer than most people could even imagine. Yet they are both dying of chemical dependence. Despite receiving the best medical care in their community and attending many 12-step meetings, they are unable to overcome their denial and their addictions. They are dying, not because they are masochists but because their love for the feelings alcohol and drugs produce and their belief in their ability to manage their illness are more potent than their pain and suffering, more potent even than their fear of death. They both continue to believe that they can "handle" drinking. They are angry with their family members who tell them they must quit. They are unwilling to continue therapy with any psychiatrist or to go to any more 12-step meetings.

• Harry is a thoracic surgeon of much distinction. He is also an active alcoholic. His wife, Sally, is a distinguished university professor of humanities. Harry has been arrested three times for drunk driving. His marriage is a shambles because his wife is so angry at him for drinking to drunkenness every night when he comes home from the hospital. He is not available in the evening to her or to their children, whom they both love deeply. She too is a heavy, regular drinker but she does not drink to drunkenness so she does not think of herself as an alcoholic. Harry socializes with others, many of whom are physicians, who drink heavily. A year ago Sally was preparing dinner and drinking a martini while she talked with Harry and his brother in the kitchen. Harry said something that Sally didn't like. Her chronic rage burst out. Impulsively, without thinking, she threw her martini glass at Harry, breaking it across his face. He cried out in pain. Sally rushed him to a nearby university hospital where an eye specialist discovered that Harry's right eye was filled with shards of glass. Harry lost his eye and his ability to do surgery. He refused, however, to stop drinking, as did his wife, even when, six months later, she was driving them home from a dinner party and was arrested for driving while intoxicated and for assault on a police officer because of a scuffle during the arrest. Sally has been to many Al-Anon meetings because of Harry's drinking. Harry refuses to go to 12-step meetings.

- Laura married a rock star and lived a glamorous international life that included sharing her husband's heroin addiction. Their marriage ended but her addiction did not. She was brought to a social worker by her distraught parents when her weight fell to 80 pounds. She was psychotically paranoid, living in the back seat of an abandoned car and still addicted to heroin when she was admitted involuntarily to a psychiatric hospital. After a six-month inpatient stay her weight went up to 120 pounds and she regained her sanity. A nurse in the hospital helped Laura to see the primary nature of her chemical dependence.

  Laura left the hospital with one central goal in her life: "I'm going to an NA meeting every day for the rest of my life." Four years later Laura remains clean and sober. She got her "first real job" as a bank teller and has worked her way up to an office manager's job. "I love my new life and I'm tremendously proud of my paycheck. My monthly salary now is less money than I would spend in a few days on drugs in my old life, but now I am a free person. Then I was a slave."

- Mary is a 50-year-old wife of a successful but emotionally distant attorney. She has five children; a sixth child died of complications following delivery. Two of her sons became chemically dependent during their adolescent years and "put the entire family through hell." After multiple treatment programs and several painful bouts with emergency rooms and police stations, Mary and her family now are recovering from their "nightmare." "The worst suffering for me was not knowing what was going to happen next. I couldn't trust either boy. Their lying to me about everything they were doing made a cruel joke of all the love I had given them. My baby's death 17 years ago was the hardest thing I ever went through. I still miss him today. But the older boys' drug problems ripped the heart out of the family. It shortchanged the other kids, since my husband and I just didn't have time for them all those years." Al-Anon helped Mary find the serenity she deeply needed.

- Joe, a successful attorney, is 45. He saw his doctor for chest pains, which he later described as "anxiety." To support his cocaine habit, he had stolen from the trust funds he managed. Only by borrowing $200,000 from his aged mother to repay the trust funds did he stay out of jail. His greatest suffering was, however, not his close call with prison, his humiliation in his law practice, or his wife tossing him out of their home for over a year. It was the drug and alcohol problem of his only child, a 16-year-old boy: "I cannot face Tim. I cannot be his father the way I'd like to be and the way he needs me to be because he and I both know that whatever he does because of drugs is nothing compared to what I've done."

- Susan was 16, having set two national age-group swimming records with three teammates in major relay races a year before, when she smoked pot at a friend's house across the street from her home. While walking home, she stepped into the path of a speeding car. Susan was killed instantly. She did not suffer because of her drug use, but her parents were inconsolable. Her sister and her friends suffered for many years from a deep feeling of loss and an unreasonable guilt over what they might have done to save Susan.

- Jill was 17 when she went to a party with her boyfriend to celebrate their high school football team's first victory in three years. On the way back home at midnight, the two teenagers decided to get a hamburger. They never made it. Jill's boyfriend, having borrowed his father's sports car, lost control and hit the wall of an apartment building one block from the McDonald's across the street from their high school. Jill died in the hospital two hours later. Her boyfriend was unharmed in the accident. They had both been drinking heavily at the party earlier that night. Jill's entire high school went into mourning. The principal, fearing legal suits from the children's parents if he mentioned drugs or alcohol, cautioned the students gathered for an assembly in her honor about the need to drive safely and to wear seat belts.

- David, a 34-year-old college dropout with a checkered employment history and multiple arrests for drug possession and sale, was forced to live over 500 miles from his parents' home because he was a fugitive from a parole violation. At a family reunion he told his uncle, a doctor specializing in the treatment of chemical dependence, "I haven't had enough cocaine yet. I'm not ready to quit." Three months later he was killed in a single-car accident at 3:00 a.m. The medical examiner said David was dead of a cocaine overdose before his car hit the brick wall under a bridge where they found him.

These vignettes suggest the range of suffering caused by chemical dependence and the views health care professionals are likely to get of this cunning, baffling, powerful, and patient disease.

OPPORTUNITIES FOR YOUNG HEALTH CARE PROFESSIONALS

Modern health care has moved farther and farther from the basic human connectedness that was the source of the profession's original strength: the healing human touch of the ill person by a health care professional devoted to alleviating suffering (DuPont, 1986b). The growing focus on the 12-step programs offers medicine a way to reconnect to this vital past and to build a more secure future by combining these roots with the newer scientific medicine (DuPont & McGovern, 1991).

When it comes to human suffering in general, a recognition of the specific problems of addiction and of the specific help that comes from 12-step programs offers a model for medical care and for dealing with other sources of human suffering. Suffering flows from three sources: distress, alienation, and despair. Relief of suffering comes from overcoming these three causes of suffering.

America has had a serious chemical dependence problem since the origins of the country more than 200 years ago (Musto, 1987). This is neither an accident nor a shame. It can easily be understood as the inevitable result of the nation being built from cultures from all parts of the world, cultures that gave to the United States the drug-using patterns of the immigrants who built the new nation.

American has also extended personal choices over behavior to more people and to a greater extent than any other nation in the history of the world. American history and values have produced many benefits, but they have put Americans uniquely at risk of addiction. These characteristics, cultural diversity and broad personal choices over behavior, increasingly being adopted throughout the world as part of modern lifestyles sought by people everywhere, have the potential for promoting addiction. Reacting to these risks and to the problems of chemical dependence, America, since the early decades of the 19th century, has been in the forefront of global efforts to prevent, to treat, and to study addictive behavior. In particular, the twin connections of the prevention of addiction to health care and to religion have been continuously at the heart of the American response to the problems of addiction. The 12-step programs, beginning in 1935 in the American Midwest, are an historic American response to the problem of addiction (Robertson, 1988). They are one of America's major gifts to the world.

It is important to recognize that the modern epidemic of drug abuse, and the responses to it, began in the United States quite recently—in the late 1960s (Musto, 1987). As the 20th century draws to a close, the central health concern is behavior, especially addictive behavior. There are unique opportunities for young health care professionals to learn about addiction, its prevention and treatment, so that they can provide leadership in the United States and throughout the world in the decades ahead. There are few other health care areas of such great importance, or where personal experience can be so useful in understanding and helping others. There are also few other areas in health care where deeply held beliefs, including personal spirituality, can play such a positive role.

The study of addiction is an attractive career path for young health care professionals. If they use their compassion and their appreciation for the unique suffering caused by addiction, young health care workers will have a head start on these promising new professional roles promoting healthy life-styles. Addiction is not only one of the major threats to the world's health, it is one of the areas of greatest opportunity in the health care field. New knowledge about addiction is accumulating rapidly in the clinical, public health, and research areas.

While reading and clinical practice are the mainstays of professional education, every young health care professional should attend at least ten meetings of the mutual-aid groups such as Alcoholics Anonymous, Narcotics Anonymous, Al-Anon, Children of Alcoholics, and Overeaters Anonymous. Referrals to these lifesaving programs can be made far more effectively by health care professionals who have been to meetings themselves. Health care workers who have been to many 12-step meetings can truly "talk the talk and walk the walk" in a way that those who have not gone to meetings simply cannot.

In addition, many health care professionals enter the professions out of their own attempts to deal with personal or family experiences with alcohol and drug abuse (DuPont & McGovern, 1990). The 12-step programs can enrich their personal lives, as well as their professional work.

The field of addiction offers many research opportunities, especially in the areas of the biology of addiction (Cohen, 1988; Goldstein, 1989; Restak, 1984, 1988; U.S. Department of Health and Human Services, 1987a). In addition, prevention and treatment of chemical dependence are particularly promising research areas (DuPont & McGovern, 1991; McGovern & DuPont, 1991; U.S. Department of Health and Human Services, 1987a). Research can be expected to produce major benefits, not only in the area of addiction, but also in the greater understanding of the brain and its relationship to behavior (Cohen, 1988; Restak, 1984). Less well appreciated by many health care workers today is the fact that new research into addictive disease will also improve understanding of how human behavior is affected by information, by the caring involvement of other people, and by the spiritual foundations of our lives. These lessons will have important benefits in health care far beyond addiction in the decades ahead.

SUMMARY AND CONCLUSIONS

Addiction, unlike mere physical dependence, is a uniquely human disease. Addicts have lost control of a fundamental human behavior, a behavior that once they had been able to control and over which other people continue to exert control. As part of the mysterious and invisible process of addiction, there is a loss of self-respect and of identity. Addicts also lose their relationships to others, including their families, as well as their spiritual grounding.

The suffering of addiction is particularly intense because it comes from stigmatized behavior and because there is no model for the illness that can be shared with the nonsufferer. The disease of addiction is incurable. It corrupts the moral behavior of addicts. The suffering of addiction afflicts not only addicts but all people who relate to addicts, especially their families.

Recovery from addiction usually requires prolonged, often lifelong involvement with a community of fellow sufferers in one of the 12-step, mutual-aid programs, such as Alcoholics Anonymous. Recovery from addiction includes far more than simply stopping the addictive behavior. Recovery is more than returning to the state of existence before the addiction began. Family members and others are also involved in the 12-step movement, including children who grew up in families dominated by chemical dependence. The 12-step programs are specific antidotes for the suffering of addiction.

The experiences of addiction and recovery have important implications for health care, and for the human experience generally, far beyond addiction itself. The experiences of addiction and recovery make clear the importance of specific communities that provide support and guidance in dealing with specific sources of suffering. Health care workers can help the addict understand what is wrong and what to do about his or her disease, including facilitating the sufferer's participation in mutual-aid programs that provide a lifelong support that no professional treatment program can do.

This mix of professional treatment and mutual aid has the potential for helping those who suffer from other diseases, particularly stigmatized diseases that are not easily seen or understood by people who do not have the diseases. Modern recovery also makes clear the original connection of medicine to religion as the Higher Power, or God, once more comes into the forefront of healing.

REFERENCES

Alcoholics Anonymous World Services, Inc. (1984). *Alcoholics Anonymous comes of age: A brief history of* A.A. New York: Author.

Alcoholics Anonymous World Services, Inc. (1986). *"Pass it on": The story of Bill Wilson and how the A.A. message reached the world.* New York: Author.

Alcoholics Anonymous World Services, Inc. (1987). *Alcoholics Anonymous* (3rd ed.). ("The Big Book," the Basic Text for Alcoholics Anonymous). New York: Author.

Alcoholics Anonymous World Services, Inc. (1988). *Twelve steps and twelve traditions.* New York: Author.

American Psychiatric Association. (1987). *Diagnostic and statistical manual of mental disorders* (3rd ed., revised). Washington, D.C.: Author.

American Society of Addiction Medicine. (March–April, 1990). 1990 definition of alcoholism from ASAM and NCADD. *ASAM News,* p. 9.

Blum, K., Noble, E.P., Sheridan, P.J., Montgomery, A., Ritchie, T., Jagadeeswaran, P., Nogami, H., Briggs, A.H., & Cohn, J.B. (1990). Allelic association of human dopamine D_2 receptor gene in alcoholism. *Journal of the American Medical Association, 263,* 2055–2060.

Bozarth, M.A., & Wise, R.A. (1984). Anatomically distinct opiate receptor fields mediate reward and physical dependence. *Science, 224,* 516–517.

Cassell, E.J. (1982). The nature of suffering and the goals of medicine. *New England Journal of Medicine, 306,* 639–645.

Cassell, E.J. (1983). The relief of suffering. *Archives of Internal Medicine, 149,* 522–523.

Cloninger, C.R. (1987). Neurogenetic adaptive mechanisms in alcoholism. *Science,* *236,* 410–416.

Cohen, S. (1988). *The chemical brain—The neurochemistry of addictive disorders.* Irvine, CA: CareInstitute.

Deitrich, R.A., & Spuhler, K. (1984). Genetics of alcoholism and alcohol actions. In Vol. 8., R.G. Smart, H.D. Cappell, F.B. Glaser, Y. Israel, H. Kalant, R.E. Popham, W. Schmidt, & E.M. Sellers (Eds.), *Research advances in alcohol and drug problems* (pp. 47–98). New York: Plenum Press.

DuPont, R.L. (1984). *Getting tough on gateway drugs: A guide for the family.* Washington, D.C.: American Psychiatric Press.

DuPont, R.L. (1986a). *Benzodiazepines: The social issues.* Rockville, MD: Institute for Behavior & Health, Inc.

DuPont, R.L. (1986b, unpublished). "Doctors, Drugs, and Fun: Modern Medicine Rediscovers Aesculapius' Second Daughter." Presented to the Texas Medical Association, Dallas, TX, May 9.

DuPont, R.L. (1986c). *Phobias and panic: A physician's guide to modern treatments.* Rockville, MD: The Phobia Society of America.

DuPont, R.L. (Ed.). (1988a). Abuse of benzodiazepines: The problems and the solutions. *The American Journal of Drug and Alcohol Abuse, 14* (Supplement 1).

DuPont, R.L. (1988b). Youth at high risk of chemical dependence: Identification and intervention opportunities for the psychiatrist. In F. F. Flach (Ed.), *Directions in psychiatry,* 8 (8). New York: Hatherleigh Company, Ltd.

DuPont, R.L. (1989a, October). Addiction, withdrawal, and the role of BZs. *The Psychiatric Times* VI, p. 1, 28, 29.

DuPont, R.L. (1989b). Don't trust everyone under 40: What employers should know about drugs in the workplace. *Policy Review,* Spring, 52–57.

DuPont, R.L. (Ed.). (1989c). *Stopping alcohol and other drug use before it starts: The future of prevention.* Rockville, MD: U.S. Department of Health and Human Services, Office for Substance Abuse Prevention, OSAP Prevention Monograph-1, DHHS Pub. No. (ADM) 89–1645.

DuPont, R.L. (1990a). A physician's guide to benzodiazepine discontinuation. In Addiction Medicine (Special Issue). *Western Journal of Medicine, 152,* 600–603.

DuPont, R.L. (1990b). A practical approach to benzodiazepine discontinuation. *Journal of Psychiatric Research, 24* (Suppl. 2), 81–90.

DuPont, R.L. (1990c). Benzodiazepines and chemical dependence: Guidelines for clinicians. *Substance Abuse, 11,* 232–236.

DuPont, R.L. (1990d). Introduction to H. Resnik (Ed.), *Youth and drugs:* Preface to *New thoughts on the prevention of alcohol: Society's mixed messages.* Rockville, MD: U.S. Department of Health and Human Services, Office for Drug Abuse Pre-vention, OSAP Prevention Monograph-6, DHHS Pub. No. (ADM) 90–1689, 1–3.

DuPont, R.L., Goldstein, A., & O'Donnell, J. (Eds.). (1979). *Handbook on drug abuse.*

National Institute on Drug Abuse. Washington, D.C.: U.S. Government Printing Office.

DuPont, R.L., & McGovern, J.P. (1991). The growing impact of the Children of Alcoholics movement on medicine: A revolution in our midst. In T.M. Rivinus (Ed.), *Children of chemically dependent parents: Multiperspectives from the cutting edge* (313–329). New York: Brunner/Mazel.

DuPont, R.L., & Saylor, K.E. (1991). Sedatives and hypnotics: Including the benzodiazepines. In R.J. Frances and S.I. Miller (Eds.), *Clinical textbook of addictive disorders* (69–102). New York: The Guilford Press.

Fabry, J. (1980). *The pursuit of meaning.* San Francisco: Harper and Row Publishers.

Frankl, V.E. (1973). *The doctor and the soul.* New York: Vintage Books.

Frankl, V.E. (1978). *The unheard cry for meaning: Psychotherapy and humanism.* New York: Simon and Schuster.

Freud, S. (1920/1964). Beyond the pleasure principle. In J. Strachey (Gen. Ed., Trans.), *The standard edition of the complete psychological works of Sigmund Freud,* Vol. XVIII. London: The Hogarth Press Ltd.

Goldstein, A. (Ed.). (1989). *Molecular and cellular aspects of the drug addictions.* New York: Springer-Verlag.

Goodwin, D. (1976). *Is alcoholism hereditary?* New York: Oxford University Press.

Gregory, R.L. (Ed.). (1987). *The Oxford companion to the mind.* Oxford: Oxford University Press.

Hawley, R.A. (1983). *The purposes of pleasure—A reflection on youth and drugs.* Wellesley Hills, MA: The Independent School Press, Inc.

The International Thesaurus of Quotations. (1970). R.T. Tripp (Compiler). New York: Harper & Row.

Jaffe, J.H. (1985). Drug addiction and drug abuse. In A.G. Gilman, L.S. Goodman, T.W. Rall, & F. Murad (Eds.), *The pharmacological basis of therapeutics* (7th ed., pp. 532–581). New York: Macmillan Publishing Company.

Johnston, L.D., Bachman, J., & O'Malley, P. (1989). "Monitoring the Future: A Continuing Study of the Lifestyles and Values of Youth." (National High School Senior Survey, 1988.) University of Michigan, Institute for Social Research, under a grant from the National Institute on Drug Abuse, Rockville, MD.

Kahn, D.L., & Steeves, R.H. (1986). The experience of suffering: Conceptual clarification and theoretical definition. *Journal of Advanced Nursing, 11,* 623–631.

Kalant, H. (1989). The nature of addiction: An analysis of the problem. In A. Goldstein (Ed.), *Molecular and cellular aspects of the drug addictions* (1–28). New York: Springer-Verlag.

Lazare, A. (1987). Shame and humiliation in the medical encounter. *Archives of Internal Medicine, 147,* 1653–1658.

McGovern, J.P., & DuPont, R.L. (1991). Student assistance programs: An important approach to drug abuse prevention. *Journal of School Health, 61,* 260–264.

Melzack, R. (1990). The tragedy of needless pain. *Scientific American, 262,* 27–33.

Myers, J.K., Weissman, M.M., Tischler, G.L., et al. (1984). Six-month prevalence of psychiatric disorders in three communities: 1980 to 1982. *Archives of General Psychiatry, 41,* 949, 958.

Musto, D.F. (1987). *The American disease: Origins of narcotic control.* New York: Oxford University Press.

Narcotics Anonymous World Service Office, Inc. (1987). *Narcotics Anonymous* (4th ed.). Van Nuys, CA: Author.

National Institute on Drug Abuse. (1989). Highlights of the 1988 national household survey on drug abuse. *NIDA Capsules,* August 1989.

Platt, J.J., & Labate, C. (1976). *Heroin addiction. Theory, research, and treatment.* New York: John Wiley & Sons, Inc.

Restak, R.M. (1984). *The brain.* New York: Bantam Books.

Restak, R.M. (1988). *The mind.* New York: Bantam Books.

Robertson, N. (1988). *Getting better: Inside Alcoholics Anonymous.* William Morrow and Company, Inc.

Robins, L.N., Helzer, J.E., Weissman, M.M., et al. (1984). Lifetime prevalence of specific psychiatric disorders in three sites. *Archives of General Psychiatry, 41,* 959–967.

Scholem, G.G. (1990). Jewish mysticism. In J. Pelikan (Ed.) & C. Fadiman (Gen. Ed.), *The world treasury of modern religious thought* (pp. 537–546). Boston: Little, Brown and Company.

Sullivan, L.W. (1990). Remarks to the National Commission on Children Round Table, Washington, D.C., July 2. (Unpublished paper.)

Twycross, R.G. (1983). Narcotic analgesics in clinical practice. In J.J. Bonica et al. (Eds.), *Advances in pain research and therapy* (Vol. 5). New York: Raven Press.

U.S. Department of Health and Human Services. (1987a). *Drug Abuse and Drug Abuse Research: The Second Triennial Report to Congress from the Secretary, Department of Health and Human Services.* Rockville, MD: DHHS Pub. No. (ADM) 87–1486.

U.S. Department of Health and Human Services. (1987b). Sedatives and anti-anxiety agents. In *Drug Abuse and Drug Abuse Research: The Second Triennial Report to Congress from the Secretary, Department of Health and Human Services* (163–181). Rockville, MD: DHHS Pub. No. (ADM) 87–1486.

U.S. Department of Health and Human Services, Public Health Service. (1990a). *Prevention '89/'90—Federal Programs and Progress.* Washington, D.C.: Superintendent of Documents, U.S. Government Printing Office.

U.S. Department of Health and Human Services. (1990b). *Seventh Special Report to the U.S. Congress on Alcohol and Health from the Secretary of Health and Human Services.* Rockville, MD: National Institute on Alcohol Abuse and Alcoholism, DHHS Pub. No. (ADM) 90–1656.

U.S. Department of Justice, Drug Enforcement Administration. (1988). *Drugs of abuse* (1988 ed.). Washington, D.C.: U.S. Government Printing Office.

Vaillant, G.E. (1983). *The natural history of alcoholism.* Cambridge, MA: Harvard University Press.

Weekes, C. (1972). *Peace from nervous suffering.* New York: Hawthorne Books.

Weekes, C. (1987). *More help for your nerves.* New York: Bantam Books.

Weil, A., & Rosen, W. (1983). *Chocolate to morphine: Understanding mind-active drugs.* Boston: Houghton-Mifflin Company.

Wise, R.A. (1988). The neurobiology of craving: Implications for the understanding and treatment of addiction. *Journal of Abnormal Psychology, 97,* 118–132.

12

The Suffering of Terminal
Illness: Cancer

Lynn W. Brallier

Dying of cancer is one of the most frightening of possibilities existing within the spectrum of human suffering. Fear of the potential suffering associated with dying from cancer is far from neurotic. In fact, despite the efforts of modern medicine, suffering remains a hallmark of the cancer experience. The process of dying from cancer has an extensive and intensely disruptive impact on every aspect of those who are dying and the people who love them.

When cancer is first diagnosed, people may be terrified but often move directly into a task-orientation mode to guide themselves through treatment. They also may become more connective with others around them for support, and pay greater attention than usual to gathering spiritual sustenance. At this point, the attempt to develop and maintain a positive outlook may actually increase a person's sense of involvement in life, creating a kind of emotional "cancer high" (Brallier, 1989). If the disease process becomes clearly terminal, however, suffering may erode the high and eventually replace it. This chapter addresses the suffering that is so often a part of the termination of life due to cancer.

Providing care to people who are suffering as they are dying is an awesome responsibility, calling for the highest level of knowledge, sensitivity, tenderness, compassion, and willingness to be empathic. Those of us who have taken on the challenge of caring for and about persons dying of cancer agree that, although we may feel overwhelmed at times, we most often feel enriched by the meanings we find in our work and by the act of helping relieve some of the suffering we witness and empathically know.

This chapter will first identify the dimensions of suffering of the adult with terminal cancer and will offer philosophical and clinical approaches to address that suffering. Next is a discussion of the suffering of those who are lovingly bonded to the one who is dying. Approaches to help alleviate their suffering will also be addressed. Finally, some issues relevant to the suffering of the professional caregivers who minister to those with terminal cancer will be discussed. Some actual clinical examples, altered only to protect the identity of those involved, will be offered as illustrations of choices health care professionals can make to be either powerfully constructive or powerfully destructive in influencing the suffering of both the person dying from cancer and those closest to that person.

The intensity of suffering from cancer varies widely depending upon what form the cancer takes and whether or not it becomes the cause for termination of life. For someone with cancer, the world of being ill is often filled with feelings of sickness from both the disease and the treatments for that disease. Experiencing a world in which one is ill from both a devastating disease and the treatments for it most often leaves the person feeling extraordinarily vulnerable. In helping relieve this suffering, the vulnerability must be sensitively and empathically recognized and honored by us as health care professionals. Our major healing work with people who are dying is to help them design and create their own safe physical, psychological, social, and spiritual environment to have as a base from which to make their exit.

THE DIMENSIONS OF SUFFERING
FROM TERMINAL CANCER

The primary dimensions from which the suffering of the person dying from cancer may be discussed are the physical, psychological, social, and spiritual dimensions. It is important that we as health care professionals be willing to be aware of the details and subtleties of the suffering accompanying terminal cancer in each of these dimensions and understand how the suffering in each interacts with the suffering in other dimensions. For example, the physical suffering of nausea and lack of appetite may be somewhat influenced by the degree of social isolation or companionship being experienced. We will now look at some specifics of the suffering experienced by those dying of cancer.

The Physical Dimension of Suffering

The physical dimension of suffering when life has become terminal from cancer is usually a primary aspect of the whole picture of suffering. This suffering is often due to the physical devastation and pain caused by the cancer and the side effects of chemotherapy or radiation if those treatments are being used. The enormous degree of physical exhaustion accompanying cancer in its terminal stage is in itself a significant kind of suffering. The experience of exhaustion that is unrelieved by rest or sleep is often a serious problem. For an active person, immobility during the terminal stage of cancer is a form of suffering. Various forms of cachexia and weakness are often part of the pervasive exhaustion. Nausea is often present, due to a combination of the disease and the treatments being administered.

Medication or other treatments aimed at reducing pain can, ironically, cause a significant degree of suffering. Nausea, constipation, and intestinal cramping are common but very distressing side effects of drugs for pain management. When someone is in extreme pain, chemotherapy and/or radiation may be given along with analgesics to help control the pain, again leading to discomfort. Decisions about whether to withstand the pain or the combination of less pain but more side effects are often quite difficult ones for the person who is dying and that person's caregivers.

The severe pain that accompanies many forms of cancer often causes overwhelming suffering. Since, according to Foley (1987), as many as 80 to 90 percent of cancer patients in terminal facilities may have significant pain, control of that pain is an extremely important part of relieving suffering in the person dying from cancer. Bonica (1987) states that there is evidence that, in some situations, as many as 80 percent of those dying in pain from cancer are not receiving adequate pain management. He points out the tragic loss of quality of life inherent in inadequately managed pain for the person with cancer and those family and friends whose suffering is to watch and be unable to relieve the suffering. The pain itself can be unbearable but can nearly always be controlled if the physician and the health care team has the knowledge and a sincere desire to help alleviate suffering.

The Psychological Dimension of Suffering

The psychological suffering of one who is dying of cancer can be another complicated dimension of the total picture of suffering. The sense of being out of control of one's body and nearly every other aspect of one's life is not uncommon as the following poem illustrates.

Broken Body, Broken Trust

Since cancer took up residence in me
So much of my body-self as I knew it and loved it
is gone now or its function radically altered.
I trust it not one whit for not one moment
to do what I intend.

"Be healthy!" I say in my commander's voice.
"Don't be in pain!" I demand earnestly.
"Have enough energy!" I ask.
"Move easily!" I plead.
It just doesn't listen anymore.

"Attention Body!!" "ATTENTION BODY!!"
"DO NOT DIE!!" "PLEASE DO NOT DIE!!"
Will it hear that one?

                         [Brallier, 1990]

This suffering of being out of control peaks in the moment of hearing an authoritative voice say, "There is nothing more we can do to try to cure your cancer." Many experience these words as if they have taken the form of an invisible anvil that swings like a pendulum, slamming directly and forcefully into the solar plexus. This stunned, reeling-out-of-control experience can linger in a curious kind of forever moment and pass, returning intermittently in various thinly disguised forms as the dying process proceeds.

In addition to feeling a loss of control, a sense of alienation from the self often builds as the result of a decline in the ability to be one's usual self. This sense of alienation is heightened when one is re-defined from being a person to being a "cancer patient" or a "case." Caregivers who are able to relate to someone dying from cancer as another adult in the world who is as deserving of full respect as anyone else are helping that person retain personal strength and integrity.

Fear, anxiety, depression, and despair are often present in some form as part of the psychological suffering during a terminal illness. These emotions may vary greatly from one person to another and from one stage to another for the same person. Complex combinations of emotions are often indicative of a grieving process that is present because the person has been and will be experiencing many dramatic losses from every dimension of life as death approaches. Grieving is part of the psychological picture of distress and is a significant addition to the mountain of mental and emotional suffering already present.

The Social Dimension of Suffering

Somewhere along the way of experiencing cancer and treatment for it, people enter what many describe as a separate world. This is the world of illness and suffering as opposed to the usual world of health and fitness. It is often a very lonely world due to some degree of isolation, particularly lack of contact with others who have also entered the illness world and can relate to the common experience. Entering the world of the ill implies some degree of disconnection and alienation from the world of the healthy. No longer is the person involved in going to work, participating in social events, and interacting with friends and family members about the details of their lives. No longer does one have one's usual personal empowerment or social influence in one's family, workplace, or community. Radical changes in appearance or mobility such as hair loss and severely limited energy level can cause a mutual interpersonal withdrawal. The person with cancer may feel vulnerable to being judged ugly or socially unacceptable in some way, and the visitor may feel discomfort about how to relate to someone so radically different than usual.

At the end of life, many of the usual social contacts are weakened for the person with cancer and the caregivers become among the few people with whom the person with cancer is still in contact. The relationship between staff and those suffering in the terminal stage of cancer may be crucial in that it often carries with it the double impact of a social as well as professional relationship from the ill person's vantage point.

Social support may be lacking because others who are healthy often do not dare fully empathize with the suffering of the person who is dying. The consequences of this denial and discomfort by the healthy friends and relatives is that social contacts are such that the person with cancer is pitied and spoken to and about as a child rather than respected as a fellow adult. Also, if family, friends, and co-workers are not empathic, they may deny or discount the dying person's condition and pain. This may be evident as people toss out glib lines that miss their mark because they are overly optimistic. When people in the person's support network are able, in spite of their own pain, to stay attuned to the real experience of the person during his or her entire process of dying, it can be one of the most appreciated gifts anyone can give someone who is dying of cancer.

One of the social hazards of having cancer is that of receiving unwanted advice from well-meaning friends, family, or health care persons. When the word incurable is spoken, most people want their loved one to deny or fight that notion. It is essential that persons who are in a terminal stage of cancer be consulted for their opinions and decisions and that these be respected regarding whether they want to fight or flow peacefully with the currents of dying.

If fighting is the decision, forces may be mobilized to utilize conventional and unconventional methods of treatment with the hope that the person will be an exception and survive. This mobilization may indeed result in the very happy outcome we call a miracle because it was not the expected or usual course of events. At times, people who have been told they are incurably ill try many methods of getting well to feel a sense of hope and control. These efforts may be heartily supported by those who love that person. The activities and social support for them may serve to reduce everyone's suffering for a time even if the person with cancer eventually dies.

In the past few years, more people with cancer have become aware of the possibility that attitudes and personality characteristics may play a part in the onset and course of cancer. As often happens, when these kinds of ideas become popular in a culture, they can be oversimplified and distorted, leading to an essentially distorted perception in which the ill person is judged to be inadequate for having become sick and is blamed for dying. The person with terminal cancer is not served well by this mislaid guilt.

When the belief phenomenon about attitudes and personality appeared in our present culture, some people with cancer used it to their advantage and appear to have helped themselves into remission while others have tried every bit as hard but cannot survive. The response most people with cancer desire from others is that of being offered true empathic support to derive their own meanings from the experience, rather than being directly or subtly chastised for having cancer and not "beating it." Being blamed for having "created" one's cancer and for not adeptly eradicating it can certainly add to the alienation and suffering of the disease.

The potential for suffering exists in the social dimension when the person who is dying and his or her social support system are at odds. For instance, a woman the author interviewed for a research study complained that though she had come to terms with the idea that her death was imminent, had very little energy, and wished to simply die with grace, she was being "hounded" by some friends, family, and even one therapist who were telling her that all she had to do to save her life was to close her eyes and image herself well. She was a journalist and was aware of imagery and some of the occasional apparently lifesaving possibilities of it but was too weak and overwhelmed by the cancer and pain to practice it. In addition, she took pride in being very in tune with nature and had always accepted death rather fearlessly as a part of the way meaning is derived in life. She made it very clear that her suffering was compounded by those around her who insisted on pushing "love, miracles, and the cancer olympics of self-control."

If we are not mindful, similar situations may develop about suffering as about cancer. Since people are basically suffering-phobic, they want themselves and others not to suffer. If we go too far in declaring that it is perfectly possible to have pain without suffering, those who do suffer in spite of their efforts to overcome their suffering may be seen by themselves and others as failures. In an increasingly notable way, ours is a high-tech culture of immediate gratification. Combined with a sense of somehow being entitled to "the good life," being happy and healthy are becoming the only socially acceptable states to be in. Those who suffer are blamed for creating their suffering or failing to be in charge of it to make it disappear. Our secular, technological, individualistic, even narcissistic ideas of self-control can lead to unreal demands upon ourselves and others to manage our attitudes and life-styles in a way that avoids personal power defects like illness and suffering.

The Spiritual Dimension of Suffering

The spiritual dimension of suffering is another substantive element in the experience of dying of cancer. The spiritual part of us can be thought of as the essence of our being. It is our spirit that searches for the meanings in life and in suffering. Frankl (1963), from his experience in Auschwitz, has developed an entire philosophy about finding meaning in any part of life. He claims that even those who are suffering a very painful death are relieved if they find meaning in their suffering. Though that meaning must be one's own, discussions with others about the meanings they find in their suffering may prove helpful.

Being told one is dying of cancer and perhaps already suffering significantly in the process of dying causes many of the usual daily meanings in life to fade by comparison. One spiritual task during the process of dying is to find or create meaning in the very process of experiencing massive changes and suffering. It is often a nearly overwhelming challenge to find both ultimate meaning and meaning in any given moment when one feels very ill, in pain, and relatively useless or even burdensome to others.

Another key element in the spiritual dimension inherent in the process of dying is to define or clarify the meaning of one's own death when one is on the brink of it. To meet this challenge, people may rely on beliefs from their childhood religious teachings, may have recently updated these beliefs since they were diagnosed, or may die being unsure of their beliefs.

SUFFERING OF THE ONE WHO IS TERMINALLY ILL: CLINICAL ISSUES IN PALLIATIVE CARE

Becoming fully aware of the numerous possibilities for severe suffering during a person's process of dying from cancer can provide compelling motivation to formulate clinical approaches that are most efficacious in relieving suffering. We will now focus on approaches designed to reduce suffering. The clinical suggestions in the following section are based upon what people who were experiencing the suffering during the dying process deemed the most helpful or hindering to them.

Goals of Palliative Care

In a discussion of clinical approaches, it is first necessary to understand clearly the goals of palliative care. The word "palliate" is derived from the

Latin word meaning to cloak or conceal. When applied to helping a person who is terminally ill, it means to help reduce the intensity of suffering. This is done at all the dimensional levels of suffering that were just discussed. The following section of this chapter will address the two major clinical issues of palliative care; (1) compassionate caregiving that can be offered when cure is no longer a goal and (2) issues regarding clinical expertise in the management of pain.

The experts at palliative care are most often associated with hospices which offer care exclusively to those who are in the process of dying. Hospices originated in the early 1960s when St. Christopher's Hospice in London was opened by Dr. Cicely Saunders. The reason for creating these homes for the dying is that hospitals are geared to acute care, aggressive treatment, and prolongation of life. This is not the ideology that will allow for the finest care of someone who is in severe discomfort while dying and needs gentle comfort and as much control over his or her care and environment as possible. Benner and Wrubel (1989) validate the impact of the difference in ideologies by recognizing hospices as "an important counter to the terrors of a strictly cure-oriented health care system" (p. 290).

In spite of the fact that a hospice is the place of choice to die, many of the readers of this chapter will eventually care for or are caring for someone who is dying of cancer in a hospital setting. Because many people who are terminally ill and in pain are hospitalized during their dying process, it is particularly important that the hospital staff be able to shift their acute-care ideology to one which allows for adequately relieving the suffering of those who are dying. The clinical suggestions in this section are based upon the notion that it is worth considering what terminally ill people anywhere, including a hospital, want and do not want from their caregivers.

It is of vital importance that we are mindful of the fact that people who will soon die are generally much more vulnerable than people who are in the hospital for acute illness or surgery and have not been robbed of their strength, defenses, and self-care energies. While respectful, empathic care is due everyone who is hospitalized, it is crucial in the humane care of those dying of cancer.

The basic wish of those who are dying in pain from cancer is to be as comfortable as possible. More specifically, people want to have their pain managed effectively and want to be genuinely cared about. We will look first at the many aspects of what it means to those who are dying of cancer to be cared about.

Caring as a Clinical Art

What is caring as a clinical art and how is it practiced? Examining some definitions of caring may be helpful in answering this question. Mayeroff (1971), in his classic book, *On Caring*, states, "To care for another person, in the most significant sense, is to help him grow and actualize himself" (p. 1). Benner and Wrubel (1989), in their textbook for nurses, use the word caring to mean "being connected" and "having persons, events, projects, and things matter" (p. 1). They also make the important point that "it takes courage to be involved and offer what you can, even though it may not be enough" (p. 376). Noddings (1984), in her book proposing an ethics based on natural caring, describes caring as a state in which one is receptive to and respectfully apprehending another's reality as a possibility for oneself, becoming engrossed in that process, and feeling an impulse to act on behalf of the other.

People who are dying of cancer say they want these caring attitudes and behaviors directed toward them. For our discussion, we will consider the concepts of respect, empathy, and compassion to be part of the definition of caring.

A person who is dying of cancer typically wishes to be respected as a competent adult who is a viable member of the social order. When we as caregivers show respect for the real person who is present before us just as we would for anyone else we care about in our lives, much of the suffering of alienation is relieved for both patient and caregiver. Demonstrating to the person dying from cancer that above any other role relationship we may have with them, we honor them as fellow human beings, helps people who may have suffered significant loss of self-esteem to regain or at least maintain what positive feelings exist for themselves. When both the caregiver and the person who is ill care enough to respect the ill person, strength builds to forge ahead with a bit less suffering.

In practical terms, it is important to show respect by speaking to the person who is dying in a normal voice, not shouting as if the person is deaf and not speaking as if the person is of preschool age. When a caregiver simply does not speak to the person who is dying or speaks in ways that do not address that person as a capable adult, the person is dehumanized. The result of dehumanizing communication is to leave dying persons with the feeling that their real selves must be invisible, and that they must expend tremendous energy which they do not have to initiate and maintain relationships. This feeling of invisibility easily translates into feeling that they have just been treated as if they are already dead or as if at some level the caregiver wishes they were. In contrast to dehumanizing communication is the comfort of being cared for by a nurse or doctor who makes personable, warm contact and stays emotionally and spiritually available to help cope with the suffering and perhaps even help discover or create meaning in it.

An aspect of caring that includes both respect and empathy is knowing that someone who is dying is quite naturally pulling away from the world as most of us know it. Understanding this, it is important that we be open to the world of the person with cancer and determine how much information is wanted from the world of the caregiver. For example, early on in the illness, talking with a person about the things of the healthy world such as current events or entertainment may be a process of bringing welcome gifts. Later, however, as the person is closer to dying and his world moves farther from the world inhabited by the rest of us, it is very important to understand that chatter about topics such as current events or the weather or asking a colleague in the presence of the dying person who she has a date with that evening can leave the dying person feeling very isolated and alienated since that is no longer that person's world.

Being willing to be empathically part of the experience and meaning of the dying person's world is the most caring social act we can offer. If the person is not in a state of denying death, being receptive to the dying person's world may mean inquiring about what it is like for that person to be in the process of dying, or it may mean helping the person clarify things about his or her life that help that person detach from life with some comfort or peace, or it may mean simply being with the person as a silent companion.

For most people dying from cancer, finding meaning in death is not as difficult as finding meaning in the suffering along the way. Often, people have had some time to consider their beliefs about death and come to relatively peaceful terms with them. Again, the important task is that of being clear within oneself. We as health professionals cannot supply meanings of life to the person who is suffering. What we can do, however, is be with, listen, and encourage the person who is dying to listen carefully to his or her own inner spiritual voice.

An example of this work is demonstrated by an oncology nurse who, in the process of giving a bath to a woman dying in unremitting pain, was able to initiate a discussion with her about the woman's level of self-actualization. Both were familiar with Maslow's hierarchy of self-actualization and the discussion led to an agreement about the great extent to which the dying woman, only 49 years old, had become self-actualized.

The nurse was able to provide he observations of how "centered" the woman was able to be in spite of the pain that was not being adequately controlled by medication. Though the ultimate meaning of her suffering may not have been discovered, the woman was able to make more meaning of the moment. She appreciated the fact that the nurse wanted to have such an intimate and supportive discussion with her.

Another key aspect of genuine caring is the desire by the one caring to help but not be controlling of the one cared for. Many people dying of cancer agree with Mayeroff's (1971) definition of caring as experiencing power in a relationship ". . . as if I had been entrusted with the care of the other in a way that is the antithesis of possessing and manipulating it as I please" (p. 7).

Many people complain that health care professionals are too controlling and take advantage of the ill person's vulnerability, wielding unkind or even cruel power over the weakened one. Baier (Baier & Schomaker, 1986), who was completely paralyzed from Guillain-Barre Syndrome, writes an eye-opening narrative of being dehumanized and oppressed by health care professionals while in the hospital. This is also a theme in "other side of the bed" books written by physicians who were hospitalized (Rosenbaum, 1988; Widome, 1989) and by Katz (1984) who examines power dynamics in the doctor-patient decision-making process.

People dying from cancer often feel so weakened and vulnerable that they give up some of their basic rights to be the ones who are in charge of their health. They may give up participating in making decisions about their treatment, saying what they want, and asking as many questions as they have, and saying no to treatment suggestions or getting second and third opinions. A common fear verbalized by people with cancer is that if they are powerful rather than submissive, their doctors and nurses and other professional caregivers will feel threatened and abandon them. Katz (1984) makes a strong case that doctors create an authoritarian relationship with patients when they (1) deprive patients of basic information, (2) treat patients as children, not as the adults they are, (3) promote an image of infallibility rather than acknowledging uncertainties they may have about treatment, (4) fail to invite the patient to participate in decision making, and (5) psychologically abandon patients when patients do not accept the doctor's notion of authority in their relationship.

A situation in which people who are vulnerable, in pain, and dying experience anxiety about asserting themselves for fear of being abandoned by their caregivers sounds more like a description of one of Dante's rings of Hell than an institution whose mission is to provide comfort and care to the sick. Clearly, a professional's need to dominate and control a person who is ill and dying is the opposite of caring.

Doctors or nurses whose intent is to have control over the person who is dying are operating from an intrapsychic process that blocks their expression of compassion, one of the very few effective things they can give the dying person at that point. Blocks to compassion are often due to fears about the possibility of one's own suffering and death. Another common source of blocks to compassion is fear of becoming emotionally vulnerable to the dying person. Allowing oneself to be open to empathically feeling the pain of someone who is in the process of dying, then suffer the pain of losing that person when death occurs can be very discomforting. Fear, however, does not seem an adequate reason for a professional person to deny someone the best possible care. Clearly, the alternative is to deal forthrightly with one's own fears. When these are resolved, the full force of one's caring and compassion can be available to energize and give meaning to the caregiving process. Professional satisfaction and excellence in clinical care are the twin positive outcomes.

If we think of caring and compassion as the normal human response to suffering, and further assume that those of us who entered nursing and medicine did so in part because of this response within ourselves, then controlling and oppressive attitudes and acts presumably are not ones that feel good to us. When we are behaving in self-alienated ways, we can harm ourselves as well as the dying person in our care.

Oppressive behavior on the part of caregivers ranges on a continuum from subtle to so overt and offensive as to trigger a malpractice suit. One form of subtle oppression is simple social insensitivity as in the failure to connect with the person in our care in a gracious and empathic manner. In caring for the person who is dying and in pain, it is extraordinarily important to gently and unintrusively ask and be empathically receptive to what the person wants, and follow that person's lead and directions in care. This means entering the room in a consciousness of openness to that person rather than imposing one's own moods, values, and topics of conversations upon the person. It also means being open to collaboration about what to do to help relieve physical discomforts. In this regard, being compassionate means allowing the person to control his or her own medication for pain, never withholding it out of disbelief that the person needs it or an illogical fear about the person becoming addicted toward the very end of life.

Relieving the Suffering from Cancer Pain Syndromes

According to Foley (1987), pain from cancer can be acute and chronic and can be somatic, visceral, and deafferentation in type of syndrome. These syndromes produce sensations of severe and widespread constant aching or gnawing, as well as paroxysmal or burning dysesthesias when there is nerve damage. Experiencing many of these kinds of pain at once when there is widespread metastasis is pain beyond the imagination of most of us. Perhaps that is part of the problem professionals seem to have in taking pain seriously enough to treat it adequately.

As we noted earlier, an estimated 80 to 90 percent of terminally ill people with cancer suffer significant pain, and that pain is thought to be inadequately managed for as many as 80 percent of those people. These figures are alarming considering the number and variety of methods available for managing cancer pain. What are the issues involved in the failure to provide this cornerstone of compassionate care?

As was stated earlier, many dying people are now receiving hospice care either as inpatients or by home visits. Hospices provide specific expert attention to the relief of pain and to dying with as much comfort as possible. Those who die in a hospital, however, where the focus is on acute treatment usually do not fare so well.

Generally speaking, caregivers in hospital settings have yet to master the science and art of relieving the suffering of cancer pain. Wanzer et al. (1989) report in *The New England Journal of Medicine* that people who are dying, their families, and the public suffer a pervasive anxiety about whether or not physicians will allow needless suffering from pain during the dying process. Having reviewed current practices affecting the care of people who are dying, the authors state that "to a large extent, we believe such fears are justified" (p. 847). C. Stratton Hill of M.D. Anderson Cancer Center echoes this observation by estimating that thousands of people with advanced cancer in this country suffer needlessly because physicians do not give them narcotics needed for their pain (Bloom, 1989).

Fagerhaugh and Strauss (1977), two social scientists, studied people who were dying in pain in hospitals and wrote about their observations from the viewpoint of the politics of pain management. They describe the importance of taking into account the organizational settings, political processes among staff and patients, and the inadequacy of an acute-care model for dealing with chronic pain as is seen in the terminally ill population. Fagerhaugh and Strauss describe in some detail how the influences of these factors account for unrelieved pain in people hospital-ized with advanced cancer. For instance, rules develop about the proper ways patients must make their need for pain medicine known to staff. They must do so with politeness and tact, not at change of shift or directly after, and must not request more pain medicine than a staff member thinks they should have. Clearly all these rules for a patient's role are controlling maneuvers on the part of staff, blocking a compassionate process of effective pain relief. When staff can be fearless in relating to the person who is dying as a fellow human being for whom they feel compassion, controlling behavior does not feel appropriate or desirable.

Other rules can develop among staff regarding pain control. A common one in hospitals is that a staff member may be branded as unsophisticated or soft or even a "sucker" for responding compassionately to someone's pain, the assumption being that the professional person has just been manipulated by the person in pain. Clearly, it takes courage to defy the prevailing norms and reach out to the dying person rather than be intimidated by one's professional peers.

Attitudes of health professionals toward people in pain, even those with cancer pain, may be a large part of the failure to relieve the pain of a dying person. Denial of the person's pain is not uncommon. There are many forms of denial of pain. One form is to believe that pain simply comes with the territory of cancer as if it should, therefore, be dismissed as something that should be aggressively treated in and of itself. Another closely related attitude is that the pain is an irrelevant problem compared to the cancer. Again, this line of thinking continues by believing that the pain is not important, only the cancer is.

When the physical suffering of the person who is terminally ill with cancer is extreme and intense, another form of denial is often evident. This is a denial of the pain since it is at times difficult to let ourselves be fully aware of the degree of suffering of the other. This denial state in the practitioner can be identified by the verbalization of doubts about the degree of pain someone is experiencing or negative comments about the patient's inability to tolerate discomfort and pain. This lack of empathic attunement to the one who is suffering can lead to inadequate physical care and pain control, increasing the level of anxiety, fear, frustration, and sense of lack of control in an already vulnerable and overwhelmed person.

In instances in which the suffering is due to treatments, the amount of suffering from the side effects of the treatments may need to be denied or diminished by practitioners since they know of no alternatives and do not wish to think that the treatments are causing a notable portion of the client's suffering. Observing and listening attentively to the physical complaints resulting from treatments is an important part of acknowledging the person's suffering and being willing to do what can be done to alleviate it.

When a person is in the terminal phase of illness and much of the suffering is due to side effects of treatments, it is appropriate if not mandatory to consider discontinuing treatments. This consideration must be done with the person who is dying, giving that person the choice and putting aside one's own neurotic needs to treat someone in order to feel useful instead of helpless.

Who is able to best respond adequately to the pain of one who is dying of cancer? Holm et al. (1989) report their research indicates that nurses' assessments of pain in patients are "significantly influenced by the intensity of a nurse's personal pain experience." Nurses who have experienced significant pain tend to be more sympathetic than other nurses to the person in pain, including recognizing the psychological distress of the pain experience. Findings from a study conducted by Mason (1981) suggest that nurses, with repeated exposure to those in pain, become desensitized and infer less suffering. By extrapolation, the dying person in pain should hope for care from nurses who are not experienced in caring for those in pain or those who are experienced but have not let themselves become desensitized, perhaps because they themselves have experienced intense pain. Cleeland et al. (1986) identify others who respond in a helpful manner to people in pain. These are physicians who are young and have experience in specialized oncology units. Their attitudes are described as liberal. In the Cleeland study, there were only 19 of these physicians compared to 72 who were described as more typical in their approach to the person with cancer pain.

Education about pain control is essential to successfully managing cancer pain. Materials about conventional and unconventional methods of pain management should be made available to people who are in pain and their friends and family members. Not everyone will want to or have the strength to study these materials, but those who do may feel a psychological boost from participating in the decisions about pain management.

There is also a need for more thorough training and continuing education programs for physicians, nurses, and others in the health field who may help those who are dying of cancer receive proper management of their pain. Cleeland et al. (1986) cite lack of knowledge of effective use of analgesics and alternatives to systemic analgesics as one problem. They also cite outmoded concern about addiction and tolerance to analgesics as another barrier to proper treatment of cancer pain. Bonica (1987) reviewed 11 major oncology books and found that only two had chapters on relieving cancer pain. Of the remaining nine books totaling over 10,000 pages, only 62 pages were devoted to pain control. Clearly, much additional education is overdue and excellent articles such as those by Brescia (1987), Foley (1985), Hill (1988), and Portenoy (1988) are readily available to help the clinician provide pain control that reflects a compassionate attitude.

Ethics of Pain Control

Meanwhile, what about the ethical issues involved in allowing people to suffer and die in uncontrolled pain? Wanzer et al. (1989) take a firm position on this issue of suffering from pain by declaring that "to allow a patient to experience unbearable pain or suffering is unethical medical practice" (p. 847). It is ethically mandatory that persons with cancer pain be offered as much pain medicine as they want and have control over the type, amount, and timing of delivery. Only the person experiencing the pain knows the severity of that pain and what relieves it.

SUFFERING OF THE SIGNIFICANT OTHER, FAMILY, AND FRIENDS

Bonds of love between human beings help us share in each others' suffering. Bonding also leads to fear of losing the other, especially to death. When we are bonded to another and feel the other's pain, we are motivated to help relieve it. We also do not want the person to die. Those who deeply love a person who is suffering and dying are likely to be very vulnerable while caring for that person. It is important that caregivers be aware of the vulnerability of the significant other, family, and friends of the dying person and offer comfort and support to them. Nature can allow great pain and suffering during death from cancer, but when incompetent or insensitive caregivers add to the suffering, the situation can become unbearable for the dying person and those around him or her. The following poem conveys the suffering a significant other can experience when the dying person receives poor care.

Notes from the Sidelines as Cancer Took Over

She was a moving illustration of humanity at its finest.
Our minds and souls were entirely open to each other.
Watching her go down in searing, unbounded pain was too much.
Like watching Bambi be torn apart limb by limb.
By the disease, the treatments,
and the health professionals who harmed her.
The torture and damage from this evil triumvirate
was agonizing, absurd, unfair, beyond cruel.
Too slow and all too sure.

Cosmic level fury flares like a nuclear blast
in my consciousness still.
Why did this innocent spiritually adept being
have to suffer so drastically?
Why wouldn't they relieve her pain?
The three torturesome elements collected to form
a tight web of suffering wrapped entirely around her.
She could only escape by dying.

The moment of death, then, became a moment of twisted relief
resembling ecstasy in its intensity.
There have been no ecstatic moments since.
Only stills and movies of her outrageous suffering.
Waking in the night to the crash of vivid memories of her pain.
Memories that send sickening tremors throughout my body.
This is the legacy of the evil triumvirate.
One web of suffering begets another.
Can I also only escape my pain by dying?

[Brallier, 1990]

Perhaps if we received more candid feedback from family and friends of the cancer victim, we could gain a deeper understanding of what helps and harms them. Clearly, the quality of care we offer to someone who is dying of cancer will affect the grieving process of the significant other, friends, and family, all of whom are constantly witnessing the suffering and dying process from a close emotional range and will continue to experience their memories of this crisis the rest of their lives. These memories may be shared within a family so that the additional suffering caused by poor care can last for generations in the family.

Providing a sense of a core team of caregivers that includes the significant other, family, and friends is extremely important. This means show-ing respect for and sharing decision-making power with those who are attending the dying person. No visiting hours should be imposed and around-the-clock attendance should be allowed if the dying person wants that arrangement. Staff must take care not to have stereotypic ideas about how family and friends should behave. Families may have ways of in-teracting that are understood only by other family members and are not readily understood by strangers. In addition, caregivers must be acutely aware of prejudices that could compromise the quality of care delivered. Suffering during the process of dying from cancer is quite enough to bear without having to be battered by a staff person's discriminatory behavior based on negativity regarding the dying person's racial, ethnic, or religious background or sexual preference. As with other fears, it is important that caregivers deal with them honestly and resolve them so that the best of human caring can be practiced.

As with any human team that has a mission, there must be a high degree of trust for a successful outcome to be possible. The significant other, family, and friends need to be able to trust that the caregivers will provide compassionate attention to their loved one even in their absence. It is not unusual to hear those close to someone who is dying in a hospital setting indicate that an advocate of some sort must be with the dying person at all times in order to see that the person receives good quality care. This is a sad reflection on caregivers' sense of desire and ability to give their finest efforts out of their own motivation to do so.

The significant other, that person who is the most consistently and closely relied upon by the person who is dying, has probably been present since before the swing of the terminal-diagnosis anvil that hit his or her solar plexus when it hit the person who is dying. This person, while accompanying the loved one through the dying process, is likely to be suffering from a sharp and desperate sense of lack of control over the suffering of the person with cancer. No matter how competent a caregiver the significant other has ever been, he or she is about to suffer the defeat of being unable to relieve suffering in any profound way, let alone save the beloved person's life. Many persons with cancer readily say that they believe the suffering of the significant other is just as severe as, if not more so, than theirs, because of the perception of having even less control than the dying person feels.

As with the significant other, the degree of suffering experienced by other family members and friends of the person dying of cancer depends in large part upon the degree of suffering of the dying person. For family and friends, who also watch the suffering of their loved one with varying

amounts of denial, hope, realization, helplessness, and anticipatory grieving, the degree of suffering during the dying process and afterward is
correlated with the quality of care given. The quality of interactions with
all the dying person's loved ones is important for everyone's well-being.
Especially important, as Cameron and Parkes (1983) point out, is that the
family and friends be made aware when death is imminent. This is
essential in allowing all involved to resolve issues if possible and express
love and thankfulness or whatever people still need to do with each other
before the moment of death occurs.

When caring for the person who is dying, it is wise to bear in mind how
the care will affect the grieving process of the significant other, family,
and friends. Those who are grieving often recall and speak of the care their
loved one received. When the care was excellent, remarks such as, "One
thing I am very thankful for is that even though he suffered for so many
weeks, the staff did everything they possibly could to help. They were so
kind and really cared and always took his pain seriously." When this is not
the case, the grieving, rather than being softened by comforting memories, is sharpened by memories that are very upsetting and rightfully bitter
about staff insensitivity, thus adding to the suffering.

Cameron and Parkes (1983) conducted a study of significant others
whose loved ones died in a palliative care unit (PCU) with a matched
control group of significant others whose loved ones died on other wards
of the same hospital. The palliative care unit provided optimal symptom
control for the dying person, whereas physicians on other wards were
reluctant to order medicines in a way that would adequately manage the
dying person's cancer pain. One year later, interviews with significant
others in the control group indicated that, for half of the group, the most
difficult aspect of the year of grieving was experiencing the distressing
memories of their loved one's unrelieved pain. None of the PCU group
reported this. Also, 85 percent of the control group and only 5 percent of
the PCU group reported persisting irritability and anger. One conclusion
by the researchers is, "Our study indicates that relatives of patients who
have suffered severe, unrelieved pain before death are left with intense
feelings of anger which disturb their sleep and impair the process of
grieving" (p. 76).

Foley (1987) also recognizes the enormous suffering for the family
when their loved one dies in unrelieved pain due to inadequate pain
control. She encourages physicians to remember the impact on bereavement of survivors when treating people with cancer pain. Stroebe
and Stroebe (1987), in their book on the psychological and physical
consequences of partner loss, emphasize the significance of the impact of

the quality of interaction with medical staff on the bereavement outcome for the partner who attends the loved one during the dying process.

When the significant other has been intimately and quite helplessly involved in watching the agonizing death of a loved one, the experience can result in suffering from a post-traumatic stress disorder in which one is tormented by flashback memories of the experience during the day and may wake crying aloud and sobbing in the night from memories in dream form. Adding this to an already painful grieving process is nearly too much to bear, especially if the pain and suffering that accompanied it could have been relieved if truly compassionate care had been given.

It is important for us as caregivers to fully acknowledge the power of our influence upon the dying person and those who love that person. Only by realizing that power can we keep ourselves attuned to the details of relieving suffering through providing excellent care.

SUFFERING OF THE PROFESSIONAL CAREGIVERS

When a person is suffering during the process of dying of cancer, those around that person, including the professional caregivers, suffer too. Stress, burnout, grief, depression, and despair are likely forms of that suffering. Fortunately, each of these conditions can be improved, healed, and even prevented if we are willing to show compassion and give quality caregiving to ourselves (Brallier, 1982).

Health care facilities are rarely staffed in a manner that supports excellence in caring by allowing time for contact with a client beyond that of providing adequate physical care. The wise practitioner knows the necessity of breaking away from a predominantly high-tech focus on physical care to identify and personally address the psychological, social, and spiritual factors inherent in the context of dying from cancer. Finding the time and energy to do that is something we not only owe the people we care for but ourselves as well, since much of the meaning in our work comes from our unique relationship with each of the people in our care.

Like the person who is attempting to find meaning in the experience of dying, we as professional caregivers will suffer less if we continue to create or discover meaning in the intense and rewarding work we have chosen. One meaning often found is that of genuinely caring about the dying person, those who love that person, ourselves, and the process we are all going through together. One of the greatest challenges for us as professional caregivers is that of initiating and remaining in an empathic

relationship with a person who is dying. Doing so means allowing ourselves to fully perceive their pain and other kinds of suffering. Remaining
open requires expenditure of emotional and spiritual energy but allows us
to respond with approaches that are comforting and effective. When we
know that our interventions significantly reduced a person's suffering, we
can feel enormously revitalized by the meaning we find in our compassion
and acts of caring.

REFERENCES

Baier, S., & Schomaker, M.Z. (1986). *Bed number ten*. Boca Raton, FL: CRC Press.

Benner, P., & Wrubel, J. (1989). *The primacy of caring*. Menlo Park, CA: Addison-
Wesley.

Bloom, M. (1989, April 11). New look in cancer research. *The Washington Post Health*,
p. 7.

Bonica, J. (1987). Preface. Journal of Pain and Symptom Management, 2, 3.

Brallier, L.W. (1982). *Successfully managing stress*. Los Altos, CA: National Nursing
Review.

Brallier, L.W. (1989). *The efficacy of existential beliefs as cognitive resources for coping with
breast cancer*. University Microfilms, Inc. No. 9015774.

Brallier, L.W. (1990). *Sisters and soulmates: suffering and death*. Washington, D.C.:
Consciousness Connections.

Brescia, F.J. (1987). An overview of pain and symptom management in advanced
cancer. *Journal of Pain and Symptom Management, 2*, 7–11.

Cameron, J., & Parkes, C.M. (1983). Terminal care: Evaluation of effects on surviving
family of care before and after bereavement. *Postgraduate Medical Journal, 59*, 73–78.

Cleeland, C.S., Cleeland, L.M., Reuven, D., & Rinehardt, L.C. (1986). Factors
influencing physician management of cancer pain. *Cancer, 58*, 796–800.

Fagerhaugh, S.Y., & Strauss, A. (1977). *Politics of pain management: Staff-patient interaction*. Menlo Park, CA: Addison-Wesley.

Foley, K.M. (1985). The treatment of cancer pain. *New England Journal of Medicine, 313*,
84–95.

Foley, K.M. (1987). Cancer pain syndromes. *Journal of Pain and Symptom Management,
2*, 13–17.

Frankl, V.E. (1963). *Man's search for meaning*. New York: Pocket Books.

Hill, C.S., Jr. (1988). Narcotics and cancer pain control. *CA-A Cancer Journal for Clinicians, 38*, 322–326.

Holm, K., Cohen, F., Dudas, S., Medema, P.G., & Allen, B.L. (1989). Effect of personal
pain experience on pain assessment. *Image: Journal of Nursing Scholarship, 21*, 72–75.

Katz, J. (1984). *The silent world of doctor and patient*. New York: The Free Press.

Mayeroff, M. (1971). *On caring*. New York: Harper & Row.

Mason, D.J. (1981). An investigation of the influences of selected factors on nurses' inferences of patient suffering. *International Journal of Nursing Studies, 18*, 251–259.

Noddings, N. (1984). *Caring, a feminine approach to ethics and moral education*. Berkeley: University of California Press, Ltd.

Portenoy, R.K. (1988). Practical aspects of pain control in the patient with cancer. *CA-A Cancer Journal for Clinicians, 38*, 327–352.

Rosenbaum, E.E. (1988). *A taste of my own medicine*. New York: Random House.

Stroebe, W., & Stroebe, M.S. (1987). *Bereavement and health*. Cambridge: Cambridge University Press.

Wanzer, S.H., Federman, D.D., Adelstein, S.J., Cassel, C.K., Cassem, E.H., Cranford, R.E., Hook, E.W., Lo, B., Moertel, C.G., Safar, P., Stone, A., & van Eys, J. (1989). The physician's responsibility toward hopelessly ill patients. *The New England Journal of Medicine, 320*, 844–849.

Widome, A. (1989). *The doctor/the patient: The personal journey of a physician with cancer*. Editech Press.

13

The Suffering of Shame and Humiliation in Illness

Aaron Lazare

This chapter will explore the extent to which the suffering of patients can be understood as resulting from, or being a manifestation of, their shame and humiliation. The shame and humiliation patients experience in medical encounters is evident if we take into consideration that patients are people, people who commonly perceive their diseases as defects, inadequacies, or shortcomings and who must expose their bodies and minds to strangers to receive the desired help. Yet the subject of shame and humiliation in the medical and nursing care of patients is rarely discussed, studied, or written about.

The medical and nursing literature emphasizes qualities of therapeutic interactions such as sympathetic attention, interest, positive regard, politeness, sensitivity, trustworthiness, dignity, decorum, and respect in

This article was adapted from Lazare, A. (1987). Shame and Humiliation in the Medical Encounter. *Archives of Internal Medicine, 147,* 1653–1658. Reprinted with permission.

dealing with patients. Little attention is paid to antitherapeutic qualities of interactions which include shaming and humiliating experiences. Psychiatrists, psychologists, and sociologists have only begun systematic explorations of shame and humiliation during the past three decades, but not in health care settings.

I will first discuss the semantics, phenomenology, and general psychology of shame and humiliation, and then attempt to show the relevance of these effects to suffering in clinical practice.

SEMANTICS, PHENOMENOLOGY, AND GENERAL PSYCHOLOGY

Shame, humiliation, and related emotions and cognitive states refer to painful experiences (thoughts, feelings, and behaviors) caused by or resulting from perceptions of oneself or one's presentation to others as less than one had thought or hoped. In this state, we feel or believe that we have been acutely exposed (to others and/or to ourselves) as not measuring up to ideals or standards that we have set and accepted for ourselves.

One can list hundreds of words that express these emotions. They include expressions that emphasize visual exposure (blemished, exposed, naked, red-faced, scarred, shamefaced, stigmatized); the subjective experience of feeling reduced in size (belittled, diminished, humbled, put down, slighted, taken down a peg); overall deficiencies (degraded, dehumanized, devalued, dishonored, and insignificant); the subjective experience of being tortured or murdered (whipped, nailed to the cross, trashed, devastated, demolished, destroyed); and avoidance responses (disappearing from the face of the earth, hiding one's face in shame, hiding under the rug, sinking into the ground). Vulgar expressions that are used to humiliate others include parts of the lower gastrointestinal tract and synonyms for excrement, male genitalia, and female genitalia.

Shame and humiliation are often used in parallel or interchangeably. "I was shamed and humiliated." There are, however, differences in derivation and usage between the two words. The etymologic roots of the word shame refer to expressions of hiding or covering up, while the etymologic roots of the word humiliation refer to the ground or being low to the ground. A person is more apt to refer to an experience as one of humiliation if it is interpersonal and if the experience is perceived as being a result of hostile intentions of another. Shame may occur with or without another present, but in this case the other is not perceived as having hostile intent. Shame is more apt to refer to a state of the self, whereas humiliation is more apt to refer to a temporary status of the self.

The experiences of guilt and shame are more easily distinguishable. With shame, the antecedent event is the sudden awareness of a deficiency of the self, a goal not reached. With guilt, the antecedent event is an act committed, a boundary transgressed leading to a sense of badness. Shame shields the self against further exposure; guilt regulates the wish to exert aggressive power. With shame, the response is to hide or disappear. With guilt, the response is to make restitution. Finally, a person can be ashamed not only of himself, but feel shame for those close to him—a child, parent, or friend. It is less common to feel another's guilt.

In everyday encounters, people are not apt to directly acknowledge their experiences of shame and/or humiliation. Instead, they describe the event as embarrassing, the expression as an insult, the perpetrator as insensitive, and themselves as hurt or upset.

The acute shame reaction is usually of sudden onset and short duration. Sometimes there is a delay before the person realizes what is happening. There may be a sense of receiving an unexpected blow, a jolt, or a sting. Accompanying autonomic reactions may include blushing, fainting, sweating, burning, freezing, and feeling weak. On a cognitive level there is a painfulness awareness of oneself as defeated, deficient, exposed, a failure, inadequate, wanting, worthless, and wounded. The deficiency seems all-pervasive. The very essence of the self feels wrong. The person feels alone and estranged from the world; there seems no way to redress the situation. The person wants to sink through the floor, disappear, or cease to exist. When the humiliation experience is perceived as resulting from the hostile intentions of the other, the person may experience a particular kind of anger, "humiliated rage," which may lead to long-lasting grudges, a desire for revenge, and poor social judgment in controlling one's own aggressive behaviors.

The power and significance of shaming and/or humiliating experiences and their relationship to human suffering can be understood by exploring the meaning of the self-concept. (Other expressions that have been used to name this concept are the self, ego, and identity.) Following Rosenberg's (1979) synthesis, the self-concept is the totality of a person's attitudes, feelings, perceptions, and self-evaluations. Rosenberg divides the self-concept into three broad regions: the *extant self-concept* or how we perceive ourselves, the *desired self-concept* or how we would like to perceive ourselves, and the *presenting self* or how we show ourselves to others. When any aspect of our self-concept is jeopardized, *we* are in jeopardy because it is the very essence of our being. It is no wonder that we spend a great deal of time and energy, and even risk our lives, protecting it. Damage to any aspect of the self-concept can give rise to the shame or humiliation experience. The relationship between shame and humiliation and the self-concept is so strong that when one identifies the shame or humiliation experience, one can invariably discover an antecedent event of an assault or threat to the self-concept.

Before exploring the significance of the shame/humiliation experience in medical settings, it is important to comment on the value of shame in human experience. A person's ability to experience shame is healthy. It means that the person has ideals and a sense of pride. It means the person is not shameless. It means the person is a social being who cares what others think about him or her. All of this is necessary for meaningful social interaction. Shame and/or humiliation is maladaptive when a person is so shame-prone that he or she avoids social interaction or participates only at enormous psychologic expense. Shame and/or humiliation is maladaptive even for "normal" people when their defenses have been assaulted by overwhelming social situations such as a betrayal by a trusted friend, being accused of malpractice, or being taken as a prisoner of war. The adaptive-maladaptive polarity of shame may be likened to blood pressure which is necessary for physical existence. Too high or too low blood pressure is pathologic. A normal range of blood pressure depends on a finely regulated hemostatic mechanism.

DETERMINANTS OF SHAME

For the purpose of exposition, I propose that any experience of shame can be understood as resulting from the interaction of three factors: (1) the shame-inducing event; (2) the vulnerability of the subject; and (3) the social context. These factors are a part of any given shame experience, and their contributions are usually additive or complementary. Yet, any one may be so powerful in a particular situation that it alone can dominate the experience.

Shame-Inducing Event

The importance of the shame-inducing event can be illustrated by those occurrences that are shameful or humiliating to most people, irrespective of personality and context. Examples include betrayal by one's spouse, being fired from one's job, being accused of a crime, and being sexually abused or raped. Each of these situations, regardless of social context and personal vulnerability, leads to shame and/or humiliation in our cultural setting.

In health care settings, patients may experience physical or psychological limitations as defects, inadequacies, or shortcomings that assault various treasured images of the self: youth, beauty, strength, stamina, dexterity, self-control, independence, and mental competence. This sense of inadequacy further jeopardizes social roles that give meaning to patients' lives such as student, teacher, physician, parent, sexual partner, and breadwinner. Treatments and their side effects may be sources of further shame and humiliation: mastectomies, loss of hair, and impotence are examples. In psychotherapy, interpretations are potentially humiliating. Here, patients are told truths about themselves that they had previously kept out of consciousness. (Whether the interpretation is perceived as a humiliation depends largely on the nature of the therapist-patient relationship.)

For some patients in certain clinical situations, death is preferable to disfiguring treatment. This issue of dignity in dying was illustrated by Peter Noll, a man who began keeping a diary after learning he had cancer of the bladder. He was informed that he needed surgery which, he understood, would result in removal of the entire bladder, need for a plastic urine pouch on his abdomen, and permanent impotence. He refused surgery with the following comments: "Perhaps my decision to refuse surgery is motivated by too much pride and arrogance . . . . I can't bring myself to submit to surgery that leaves me hollowed out, like a dugout canoe that floats along with no one in control . . . diminished and mutilated . . . .. The urge to survive must never be allowed to become so absolutely overpowering that one submits to all of these indignities" (Noll, 1989, p. 8, 20, 80, 99).

When patients discuss the importance of "dying with dignity," the indignities they refer to are damaged body image (edema, emaciation, deformities, etc.), diminished awareness, loss of control (incontinence), loss of independence (the need to be washed and fed, the need to ask or beg for medicine to relieve pain, the need to ask for a bedpan, the need to be cleaned by someone else after defecation), and the perceived loss of meaningful social roles and social value. In general, there is the loss of one's image to oneself and to the public. Many patients who are dying prefer privacy so that their prior image as a vital and healthy person is maintained to others. A friendly visit, in such situations, may be experienced as a humiliation.

Shame in Different Medical Specialties.   In each medical specialty, there are events and issues which may evoke shame responses. In pediatrics, parents experience shame for their self-perceived genetic contributions to their child's disease or for their self-perceived failure to provide adequate care. In dermatology, the disease is often visible for the patient and others to see. John Updike eloquently describes his feelings about his own psoriasis as "humiliation." In the field of obstetrics/gynecology, the patient may perceive her sexuality as promiscuity or her lack of sexuality (or lack of pleasure in sexuality) as incompetence. Inability to conceive or deliver a normal fetus may be viewed by the patient as further failure. Venereal disease may be perceived as moral failure. Even when there is no pathology, the examination requires undressing, exposing, and allowing penetration of the most private parts of the body. In the field of gastroenterology, some diseases are believed to be stress related with the implication of psychologic weakness (peptic ulcers, ulcerative colitis, irritable colon, Crohn's Disease). Surgery of certain diseases requires ileostomies with experiences of odors, deformities, and incompetence. Similar situations of shame-inducing events and procedures can be described for urology, neurology, cardiology, and other fields.

Names of Diseases.   As if the humiliation of disease, treatment, and dying were not enough, the medical and lay terms assigned to various diseases may be intrinsically shaming. In cardiology, there is cardiac *embarrassment*, heart *failure*, coronary *insufficiency*, hyper*tension*, and in*ferior* infarction. In reproductive medicine, one may be *barren*, *sterile*, or suffering from an *incompetent* cervix. Personality disorders in psychiatry include the *narcissistic*, *dependent*, *histrionic*, and *borderline*. In infectious disease, AIDS is a *deficiency* disease. In orthopedics, there is osteogenesis *imperfecta* and various *degenerative* diseases. All cancers, even the curable ones, are *malignancies*. Patients with certain physical limitations are referred to as *invalids*. This listing has more than academic interest. Patients are troubled by, resentful of, and suffer from these labels.

Stigma.   In addition to the physical and psychological limitations caused by a particular disease, patients may also feel stigmatized; that is, they feel they are socially discredited or branded, and they anticipate unfavorable reactions by others. (The subtitle of Goffman's book, *Stigma*, is particularly poignant: *Notes on the Management of Spoiled Identity*.) I suggest that diseases that are stigmatizing may be categorized according to the following: (1) those which offend others through their sight, odor, contagion, and possibility of physical violence (e.g., leprosy, other dermatologic conditions, gross body deformities, contagious diseases, mental disorder, epilepsy); (2) those which are associated with low social station or poor living conditions (e.g., tuberculosis, lice, and gross dental neglect); (3) those which involve sexual or excretory organs (e.g., venereal disease, cancer of the rectum); and (4) those which are believed to be caused by behaviors that are perceived by others as weak, stupid, immoral, or manifestations of personal failure (alcoholism, mental disorders, obesity, venereal disease, and AIDS). With our current knowledge about the prevention of disease, many individuals who become ill feel ashamed over their failure to behave in a prudent manner—by overeating, smoking, or failing to exercise. Similarly, patients who develop diseases that are believed, at least by the lay public, to be caused by stress or personality defects may feel a sense of inadequacy or personal failure. Such diseases include peptic ulcer, ulcerative colitis, rheumatoid arthritis, asthma, migraine headache, cancer, coronary artery disease, and essential hypertension.

There are exceptions to the principles described above. To some individuals, peptic ulcer or myocardial infarction is a badge of courage, evidence of hard work and success. In earlier times, tuberculosis was associated with sensitivity and creativity. The stigma of epilepsy, tuberculosis, mental illness, and cancer has diminished over time as more is known about their causes and as treatment has become more effective.

Vulnerability to Shame

Attempts have been made to categorize issues over which people may be vulnerable to shame. These include the need to be loved and taken care of, not rejected; to be strong and powerful, not weak; to succeed or win, not fail or lose; to be clean and tidy, not messy and disgusting; to be good, not bad; to be whole and complete in physical and mental makeup, not defective; to be in control of bodily functions and feelings, not incontinent and out of control. A multitude of day-to-day issues involving self-esteem may be subsumed under these categories. The vulnerability to one or a combination of these issues varies from person to person, and the wide range of issues over which a person may be vulnerable makes it difficult to predict how one person will respond to a particular event. For example, an individual arriving 30 minutes late for an appointment because of automobile failure may feel like a social misfit. Another may feel like an inept automobile mechanic. A third may feel no impact on his or her self-esteem.

In the health care setting, it is evident from clinical experience that the self-esteem of people may be associated with their physical attractiveness, strength, dexterity, intellectual acuity, sight, hearing, or other physical or psychological attributes. One can make no ironclad assumptions in advance that a given patient will or will not be humiliated over a given symptom or disease. Adolescents, in general, are more prone to shame than people in other age groups. This sensitivity may be attributed to the rapid changes that are occurring in their bodies and identities. Physicians, many of whom enter the profession to conquer, master, or control disease, and who are expected to know more about disease and its prevention than lay people, may be particularly shamed by their own disease. This may explain, in part, the belief that physicians delay seeking help for their own symptoms.

Social Context of Shame

The last factor necessary for the experience of shame is the social context. The social context includes the nature of the relationship to the person or people perceived as doing the shaming, the nature of the communication, and the nature of the social event. The more the person matters to the subject and the more public the exposure, the more intense the shaming experience. The perceived humiliating communication may take the form of a facial expression, a gesture, a verbal intonation, an innuendo, an explicit criticism, a scathing attack, or a complex symbolic act such as tarring and feathering or having to stand and "face the music" and be "drummed out of the corps."

A person may experience shame and humiliation alone, but such an experience is apt to be less severe than one experienced in the interpersonal realm. In solitary shame, the person may consciously anticipate exposure and ridicule at a later time or may completely internalize the shame dynamic so that the exposure takes place internally (e.g., "how stupid of me to misplace my keys!" or "wait until they realize what a fool I have been!").

In the health care setting, the shame-inducing event (the perceived disease) and the individual vulnerability ultimately interact with a social context once the patient seeks professional help. Patients who visit urban hospitals for the first time often brave unfamiliar traffic, search frantically for parking space in high-priced lots, and make their way through a labyrinth of buildings, passing busy and seemingly indifferent hospital employees as they search for the doctor's office. In the elevator, they hear white-suited house officers openly discuss patients. They hope they do not meet any acquaintances who may ask: "What are you doing here?" These patients may understandably feel bewildered, harassed, exposed, insignificant, and incompetent. They are not quite sure at that moment what preoccupies them most, their disease, their insignificance, or arriving late. In the waiting room, privacy is further eroded. Patients are noticed by other patients and are labeled as people who belong in this office or clinic—oncology, hypertension, arthritis, psychiatry. They may be acutely aware of telephone communications in the waiting room in which other patients' names are mentioned within earshot of strangers. Eventually they are acknowledged by the secretary or other office personnel.

Once in the examining room, patients must reveal personal information about their weaknesses, expose their bodies, place themselves in undignified postures, and accept handling of their bodies including intrusions into orifices. In normal socialization, we learn that such behaviors are shameful except when done in the health care setting. Upon admission to the hospital, there is the giving up of everyday clothes, valuables, freedom, and privacy. For certain diagnostic and treatment procedures, there is the further surrender of glasses, dentures, and hearing aids. In providing detailed histories, patients may be expected to describe their perspectives on their illness. This description may include previous attempts to find lay and professional help, use of home remedies, theories about the cause and pathophysiology of the disease, fears as to what is wrong with them, the reason for deciding to come for help at this time, goals of treatment, and desired methods of treatment. In anticipating such an inquiry, many patients fear they will be laughed at or criticized for their ideas about the nature of the disease, for causing or aggravating the disease, for waiting too long before seeking medical attention, or coming too soon with such trivial complaints and so wasting the doctor's time. Patients may be further humiliated by the physician's pursuit of historical data about the possibility of diseases such as AIDS and venereal diseases. Physicians, in communicating the diagnosis to the patient, may become the messengers who carry the news of the humiliating event: that the patient has coronary insufficiency, heart failure, alcoholism, or syphilis. In effect, the physician may humiliate the patient by communicating the diagnosis.

Emergency room visits are particularly humiliating since patients are apt to be frightened, and privacy is often inadequate, particularly as patients wait unattended in corridors for their roentgenograms, or sit or walk about in johnnies flapping open at the rear. Finally, there is the significance of communications to friends and relatives. Who shall know and what shall they know? A physician friend of mine was hospitalized for several days with lower back pain. The most distressing experience of the hospitalization was an unexpected visit by one of his patients. This led to intense shame over being exposed as not being strong and in control. Confidentiality and privacy is most often a matter of protection from exposure (shame) to others knowing about something that one personally regards as an inadequacy.

REACTIONS TO SHAME AND/OR HUMILIATION

There are a wide variety of adaptive and maladaptive reactions to shame and humiliation. The adaptive response is to overcome one's weakness. In health care, the desire to avoid shame may help the patient lose weight and maintain the exercise program. Three common maladaptive responses are depression, hiding and avoidance, and anger. The depressive response is understandable since depression and the low self-esteem caused by shame and/or humiliation are so intertwined. The second common response is hiding or avoidance. In medical settings, this may take the form of lying to the physician about the severity of the symptoms and failing to comply with the prescribed treatment or self-treatment. The hiding response may take the form of breaking appointments or generally avoiding the physician. (e.g., "I will see the doctor after I have lost weight." "I will make an appointment when my blood pressure is down." "I will see the dentist after I get my gums in better shape.") The two most maladaptive forms of hiding are denial of illness and suicide.

The anger response is a manifestation of humiliated range. Such anger is particularly dangerous since it may lead to long-standing grudges and revenge seeking. Patients respond to humiliated rage by expressing anger indirectly through criticism of other employees in the office or on the hospital ward, by changing physicians, by complaining about the medical or nursing profession as a whole, by filing a formal complaint with the patient care representative, or by suing. In most suits that I have investigated, the patient's perceived humiliation was usually a necessary but insufficient cause.

I believe that most patients who are angry at their physicians or nurses are responding to perceived experiences of shame and humiliation. The specific complaints are not that the doctor makes mistakes, misses the diagnosis, causes too much pain, or charges too much. The complaints are that "the doctor seems too busy for me," "the doctor tells me I am too fat," "the doctor treats me like a piece of meat," "the doctor is sexist," "the doctor insults my intelligence," "the doctor thinks my problem is all in my head." Underlying these complaints, I contend, are the emotions of shame and humiliation.

SHAME AND HUMILIATION IN PHYSICIANS AND NURSES

Physicians and other health professionals, like most people, have self-concepts or sets of ideals and standards that they strive to maintain. In the professional realm, these standards may include qualities such as intelligence, dexterity, honesty, reliability, dignity, integrity, devotion, and compassion.

During the past several years, I have lectured on the general subject of shame and humiliation in health care encounters to physicians and nurses. At the end of lecture I have asked the audience to respond on a blank sheet of paper to the following directions: "Please describe the most shameful or humiliating experience of your professional career." Approximately 20 percent of the audience completes the form. The responses can be organized into five categories: experiences related to humiliations during student or house officer training, experiences related to the person's own illness or illness of a family member, experiences related to feelings of incompetence regarding professional functioning, reactions to criticism by fellow professionals, and reactions to criticism by patients. Most striking about the responses are the detailed descriptions of painful experiences, many of which occurred many years before.

The writing functioned as a catharsis for experiences which had mostly not been previously shared with others. This speaks to the loneliness of our professions and the perceived need for secrecy over sharing shameful experiences.

From a clinical perspective, I have found it useful to assume that whenever a clinician becomes angry at a patient, the clinician is usually responding to a perceived humiliation at the hands of the patient. The physician, unaware of his or her own emotional state, then counterhumiliates the patient.

THERAPEUTIC IMPLICATIONS

Shame and humiliation are common sources of suffering. To optimally manage shame and humiliation in health care encounters, clinicians should assume that any disease (and treatment) can be a shame-inducing event which then interacts with a patient's individual vulnerabilities. With this heightened awareness, clinicians can use their skills to manage the social context of the medical encounter. In this role, clinicians attend to three interrelated tasks: (1) diminishing the patient's shame and humiliation; (2) avoiding exacerbating the patient's shame and humiliation; and (3) recognizing and managing their own shame and humiliation.

To accomplish these goals, physicians and nurses should attempt to develop relationships in which the patient allows them to come inside the protective boundaries erected to avoid shame. Ideally, patients should come to believe that their exposure of physical and emotional weaknesses will be respected and cherished. In this perspective, there are common elements in patients' relationships to their physicians and nurses and to those they love. The lonely anguish of patients over their illnesses and the physicians' and nurses' socially defined roles as nonjudgmental healers make such relationships both possible and desirable. The betrayal of such a trust, once achieved, will lead to humiliation and will usually damage the relationship beyond repair.

What follows are several observations and suggestions on the management of shame which are based on discussions with patients and experienced clinicians.

Ambience of the Hospital and Office

Physicians and nurses have the ability and responsibility to influence patient's experiences in the hospital and office including the admission procedure, emergency attendance, roentgenograms, and blood drawing. Patients commonly feel frightened, depersonalized, and dehumanized, and that their presence and needs are an imposition on the complex bureaucracy, rather than the reason for the existence of the bureaucracy. Physicians and nurses need to work with administrators to create an atmosphere in which patients feel welcome, cared for, and respected.

Promptness and Uninterrupted Interviews

It is important for the professional to see patients on time. Long waits after the designated appointment time or interruptions during the visit devalue the importance of patients' time and worries. A simple apology for significant lateness or unavoidable interruptions acknowledges that the delay or interruption is the professional's problem or a result of unavoidable circumstances and not an indication of the patient's lesser status.

Use of Surnames

Professionals seeing adult patients for the first time should refer to them by their proper titles and last names. Calling new patients by their first names forces a level of intimacy to which the patient has not agreed. It also assigns to patients a lesser status, since they are generally not expected to refer to their physician or nurse by his or her first name. Asking patients how they would like to be addressed puts the burden on them to anticipate what the professional would like to hear. Changes in the way professional and patient address each other are negotiated as the relationship evolves.

Supporting the Patient's Self-Concept

The patient's self-concept is placed in jeopardy by feeling sick, by assuming the patient role, and by the specific medical procedures (removing clothes and other personal belongings). Professionals should support patients' attempts to strengthen their self-concept by bringing personal possessions, such as photographs, to the bedside and by sharing personal stories which emphasize the nonpatient role.

Attention to Privacy

Professionals communicate respect and dignity to patients by attending to the privacy of their body parts, verbal disclosures, and records.

Professional's Self-Exposure

The professional's self-exposure, carefully thought out, can help diminish the patient's shame and humiliation. ("I broke my leg skiing. The recuperation can be dreadful, having to ask people for help all the time.") There are at least three pitfalls in the use of self-exposure. First, patients may feel the professional is burdening them with his or her problems. Second, patients may experience the professional as acting superior and condescending, since they have already solved similar problems. Third, patients may experience the professional as offering insincere support ("I know how you feel").

Shaming the Patient

Shaming the patient can be effective when it is done out of a sense of caring by a professional whose relationship with the patient is positive and secure. Otherwise, the shaming will damage and possibly terminate the relationship.

Acknowledging the Patient's Shame and Humiliation

When professionals suspect that shame and humiliation are important aspects of the patient's experience, they may engage patients by empathically commenting on their distress without referring specifically to shame and humiliation. For example, the health care professional may say, "it is not easy to come and see a physician," or "This disease can place enormous stress on a person," or "What does this illness mean to you?" Such comments or questions invite patients to ultimately share more specific aspects of the stress, including feelings of shame and humiliation. Ultimately, helping the patient identify these emotions helps to dissipate some of the suffering.

Validating and Praising the Patient

It is often helpful to support the patients in their decisions to see a professional ("it was wise of you to come today; pigmentation of the skin like you have can be quite a source of worry"). Such a response diminishes the patients' concerns that their worries are trivial or foolish and that they are wasting the doctor's time. It may be equally helpful to praise patients on the management of their disease. In the lonely struggle with chronic and/or deteriorating disease, patients often feel that they are failures. Their families may feel helpless, discouraged, and angry. The physician or nurse may be the only one who can see courage and heroism in the patient's coping behavior.

Clarifying the Patient's Perspective on the Problem

Professionals may be able to diminish patients' shame and humiliation by eliciting and responding to their perspective on their illness: the patients' definition of the problem, including their theories about the nature of the illness; their goals of treatment; and their requests for particular methods of treatment. It is common for professionals to discover through this inquiry a set of unrealistic beliefs that support shameful but unrealistic views of the disease: that patients are to blame for the disease, that the infectious disease is contagious, that they are morally or physically weak, or that the disease is a source of stigma. Such an inquiry affords the professional the opportunity to discuss and refute these shameful beliefs and to provide alternative explanatory models.

Use of Support Groups

Certain patients and families of patients with potentially humiliating conditions make good use of therapeutic or support groups made up of people with similar disorders. The obese, alcoholics, families of alcoholics, families of brain-injured patients, women who have undergone radical mastectomies, families whose infants died of sudden infant death syndrome, infertile couples, and families of the mentally ill have all organized self-help groups.

Response to Patients Who Fail to Accept Advice

With patients who are obese, who smoke, or engage in other behaviors that obviously impair health, the professional runs the risk of humiliating these patients with lectures or confrontations during each visit. One solution to this problem is to educate such patients about their illness during the first visit and then assure them that this will be the last such "lecture" until and unless the patient initiates the discussion. Another method of responding to such diseases is to encourage the patient to define the problem: "Are there any other problems that you would like me to help you work on?" Patients who acknowledge their own problems are more apt to maintain their dignity than those who are confronted by others with their weaknesses.

Professionals' Management of Their
Own Shame and Humiliation

One of the most difficult but important tasks for physicians and nurses in the clinical encounter is the recognition and management of their own shame and humiliation. A clue to this situation is one's anger at the patient, one's inadvert humiliation of the patient, or one's wish not to see the patient again. By attending to any of these signals, the professional can explore whether he or she feels shamed or humiliated by the patient. The professional can then analyze the dynamics of the relationship and plan a therapeutic response. For example, a frustrated and embarrassed physician whose patient is not responding to treatment asks the patient: "Are you sure you are taking the medications I have prescribed?" The patient, feeling insulted that his integrity has been questioned, says "I do not think we are getting anywhere. Perhaps I should consult with another doctor." The physician, further humiliated by the patient's request, can continue the downhill spiral of counterhumiliation by encouraging the patient to leave. Alternatively, the physician can return to the critical juncture and address the insult: "I did not mean to offend you by my question about your taking the medicine. I apologize. I was just attempting to be as thorough as possible." In another example, a 55-year-old woman consults a physician for her "high blood pressure." He performs the proper examinations, confirms the diagnosis, and recommends that the patient lose weight, lower her salt intake, take antihypertensive medications, and return in three weeks. The patient returns in five weeks and informs the physician that she is a religious woman and that God has told her that she does not need to lose weight, lower her salt intake, or take pills. The physician, feeling humiliated that his carefully thought-out recommendations were not heeded, humiliates the woman and her religious beliefs by saying: "Did your God tell you who your next doctor will be?" Had this physician been aware of his feelings and response, he could have made one of many nonhumiliating responses, such as: "Is there some way in which you would like me to help?" After all, the patient did return.

Physicians and nurses can also gain some mastery over their humiliation by creating an atmosphere among their peers where these feelings can be openly discussed instead of being avoided for fear they would be perceived as weak or unprofessional. Such discussions and labeling of emotions diminish the psychologic need for counterhumiliation on the part of physicians and provide profound insights into the suffering of patients.

NEGLECT OF THE SIGNIFICANCE OF SHAME AND HUMILIATION IN HEALTH CARE

It is curious that experiences of shame and humiliation are generally ignored in the medical and nursing literature. I shall offer three possible explanations. First, even as physicians and nurses treat patients with the greatest sensitivity, respect, and decorum, it has not been part of the medical tradition to inquire as to the subjective experience of the patient. Second, in our concerns as physicians and nurses to do no harm, it is difficult for us to contemplate how we inevitably contribute to the suffering of shame and humiliation in patients. Finally, neither patients, nurses, or physicians like to acknowledge or discuss their own shame and humiliation. It is shameful and humiliating to admit that one has been shamed and humiliated.

REFERENCES

Goffman, E. (1963). *Notes on the management of spoiled identity*. New York: Simon & Schuster, Inc.

Groves, J. (1986–87). Physician, sketch thyself. Harvard Med. *Alumni Magazine, 60,* 36–38.

Levin, S. (1967). Some metaphysical considerations on the differentiation between shame and guilt. *Int. Jour. Psychoanal., 48,* 267–276.

Lewis, H.B. (1971). *Shame and guilt in neurosis*. New York: International Universities Press, Inc.

Lindsay-Hartz, J. (1984). Contrasting experience of shame and guilt. *Am. Behav. Sci.,* 27, 689–704.

Lynd, H.M. (1958). *On shame and the search of identity.* New York: Harcourt Brace & World, Inc.

Miller, S. (1985). *The shame experience.* Hillsdale, NJ: The Analytic Press.

Noll, P. (1989). *In the face of death.* New York: Viking.

Rosenberg, M. (1979). *Conceiving the self.* New York: Basic Books.

Updike, J. (1989). *Self-consciousness.* New York: A. Knopf.

Wurmser, L. (1981). *The mask of shame.* Baltimore: Johns Hopkins University Press.

14

The Suffering of Suicide: The Victim and Family Considered

James A. Knight

In Albert Camus's *The Fall*, we meet a character whose mission in life has grown out of an experience with a suicidal young woman. Camus has his hero, Jean-Baptiste Clamence, carry the message that a life that is not transcended in the service of another is a lie. In the story, Jean-Baptiste has devoted the last years of his life to the pursuit of a strange calling, to be a judge-penitent. He captures his listeners through a confession of the lies of his own life and thus forces them to confess in their turn and to be judged as miserable liars as Jean-Baptiste himself. In his own account, Jean-Baptiste describes as the turning point in his life the following incident. One night, while walking home after midnight in a contented mood and crossing a bridge, he vaguely notices the form of a young woman bent over the railing, seeming to contemplate the river—a picture of loneliness, of suffering. He stops, but does not turn around. Shortly thereafter, he hears a woman's cry, several times repeated, floating down the river, then an interminable silence. He learns something from this experience that radically changes his entire life: refusal to act as your sister's or your brother's keeper sometimes leaves you strangely crippled.

The book ends with Jean-Baptiste delirious and dying, avowing his fervent hope that the young woman might throw herself in the river again and give him a second chance to save her, and himself.

This is a poignant picture of the suffering of suicide. The young woman's contemplation of the river and her repeated cries on jumping into the river, the response or lack of response to her cries, the broken connection to the human community, and the wounding of the survivor all reveal a picture of the multifaceted phenomenon of suicide and where we as health care providers fit into this picture.

Our understanding of suicide is limited and our attitude toward it is frequently ambiguous. At times, we romanticize suicide and at other times, we condemn suicide. To say that one has not considered suicide as a course of action is probably to deny the truth, as implied in philosopher John McDermott's statement: "I would not trust a person who has not at some point in his or her life considered suicide as an option" (1977). Thus, our interest in this topic has both an objective and subjective dimension.

Many have testified to the sense of autonomy and control that comes with the realization or acceptance of the option of suicide. F.W. Nietzsche has expressed well that feeling: "The thought of suicide is a great consolation. By means of it, one gets successfully through many a bad night" (1967, p. 99). Likewise are the words of 17th-century physician Sir Thomas Browne, in his book of self-revelation, *Religio Medici*: "We are in the power of no calamity while death is in our own" (1963, p. 54). Such testimonies as these make the phenomenon of suicide a part of the human condition and bring it into the purview of all.

The importance of Sigmund Freud's theorizing about a death instinct lies not in the fact of death alone but in the possibility of self-inflicted death as fundamental to human psychological experience. Psychiatrist Kurt Eissler (1955) has elaborated on that ubiquitous human suicidal possibility:

> *Relatively rare as suicide actually is, it must have a deep meaning, since of no one can it be said with certainty that he would never commit it. . . .That man can commit suicide and that the potentiality of such an action rests on every person . . . that every human being possesses during most of his lifetime the capacity of committing suicide should be made the center of investigation. [p. 64]*

The literature on suicide is vast in quantity and approaches the subject from many directions. The individual meaning of suicide, however, holds the greatest attraction for study. Although several dimensions of the suicide problem will be discussed, one must turn to the *inside* of the psyche to find the real meaning for each individual and, to some extent, for the broader human community. As James Hillman states, "Because suicide is a way of entering death and because the problem of entering death releases the most profound fantasies of the human soul, to understand a suicide we need to know what mythic fantasy is being enacted" (1976, pp. 51–52).

MEANING AND MOTIVATION

The dynamics leading to the act of suicide are diverse. It is likely that more than one motive is operating in most individuals who desire to bring closure to their lives. Yet, there are some common denominators regarding meaning that most suicides share.

Of special interest are those who are preoccupied with suicide almost as their way of life. They derive comfort from the knowledge that they will control the time and the circumstances of their death. A sense of controlling how and when they will die appeals to the autonomous strivings of certain suicidal persons. An unwillingness to accept life on any terms but their own characterizes others who succumb to suicide. They set many conditions for their living. These persons often seem conditionally attached to life and willing to continue with life only if it meets their conditions. Shortly before he committed suicide, Ernest Hemingway told his friend and biographer, A.E. Hotchner, that if he could not exist on his own terms, then existence would be impossible, that he had lived that way and that was how he must live (Hotchner, 1966). Was not Hemingway saying that he could not tolerate any threat to how he perceived himself, any loss of control over what happened to him?

Others refuse to accept a diminished quality of life. They assess their situation in an apparently rational manner and then take steps to end their lives. This group will be discussed later in this chapter in the section on rational suicide.

Another category of motivation in suicide is expressed best as a question: "Does the human being have values that transcend one's own survival, and are there situations when a person, in order to fulfill one's existence, needs to bring one's life to a close?" Possibly this question is similar to what James Hillman is saying in *Suicide and the Soul*, that the existential decision to kill oneself might be a necessary decision in terms of affirming the soul. This question brought some comfort to the parents of an 18-year-old who committed suicide one summer when everything seemed to be going well for him and when his future looked bright, at least to those around him.

The act of suicide is often described as Janus-faced, with one face looking toward life and the other toward death. Clinically, it appears that the suicidal person wants both to die and to live. The crucial question is, however, what the act of killing oneself seeks to assert. In killing oneself, one is taking action to do something about one's life, is doing something about one's life. Thus, in trying to understand motivation in suicide, we see the act of suicide as a "cry for help" or as a communication to others of an effort to improve one's life. Bringing closure to one's life may appear to be the only reasonable way to break out of "encirclement" or "entrapment" and assert whatever one wants to or must assert about one's life. On another level, the suicidal act becomes a way to transcending the state of severe distress associated with the circumstances that threaten the intactness of the person.

The "cry for help" of the suicide, according to William F. May, is more likely a "cry for change" (1983). As May points out, the suicide is crying out for a particular kind of help—help that will radically change his or her life. There is no interest in or intent to return to the former existence only divested of the wish to die. As Hillman sees it, the suicide wishes for the experience of death, namely, the death of his or her old life (1976). Thus, the suicide wants and seeks to die out of the former life and to come into a new life. The suicidal person reaches out for the death experience as a radical self-transformation, a restoration of vitality and wholeness through the decisive act of suicide. The revolutionary dramatist Antonin Artaud's thoughts amplify this view: "If I commit suicide, it will not be to destroy myself but to put myself back together again. Suicide will be for me only one means of violently reconquering myself" (Alvarez, 1972). Maybe Gabriel Marcel is expressing essentially the same idea when he speaks of suicide as a radical rejection of being, that is at the same time "a demonic affirmation of self" (Marcel, 1960).

In working with a suicidal patient, our concern should be less with the suicidal choice and more with helping the person understand the meaning behind this choice, for that person's choice is asking directly for the death experience. Carl Jung, in his writings, emphasizes that death has many guises and does not usually appear in the psyche as death *per se*, as extinction, negation, and finality. Even when physical life is coming to a close, the psyche of the individual often produces images and experiences that show continuity.

Jung views the "experience of death" as separable from physical death and not dependent on it, as an experience that appears in order to make way for transformation. Without dying to what now exists, there is no place for renewal. The psyche favors the "death experience" to usher in change. In this context, the suicide impulse is seen as a transformation drive, as an attempt to move from one realm to another by force through the "experience of death" (Jung, 1960). Suicide then becomes the urge for "hasty transformation," as Hillman describes it (1976)—the urge to die all at once because the psyche missed its death crisis before and did not transform as it went along. This would be true usually not for the elderly but for younger persons where this impatience reflects a psyche that has not kept pace with its life. In the elderly, it reflects a life that no longer nourishes with experiences a still-hungering soul. All the same, transformation is sought.

Suicide is only one of the modes of the "death experience." Some of the others are depression, failure, exaltation, amnesia, psychosis, to name only a few. The mode to the experience is not as important as the experience itself. Unfortunately for some, organic death through actual suicide may be the only mode through which the "death experience" is possible.

Two major components appear to be part of most suicides. One relates to inner disturbance of powerlessness, despair, and a sense of being trapped. The other is what Robert Jay Lifton describes as the universal logic of suicide and its relationship to meaning and immortality (1979). Even when one component seems to predominate, there are likely to be quiet manifestations of the other. No matter how despairing the suicidal patient, he or she sees suicide as a means of transcending inner death, of transformation, of a reconnection in the sense of immortality or the continuity of life.

The varied imagery of suicide compels us to look at what is psychologically specific about suicide, and at the same time, to try to classify its different forms. There are fundamental differences in the suicides of the deeply depressed, the fragmented schizophrenic, the terminal patient who wants to be spared further suffering or to save the family further trauma, and the person who quietly in Socratic fashion adds up life's assets and liabilities and declares bankruptcy. While different, each performs an act of self-destruction and speaks to us in language that is loud, and often clear. As Lifton points out, however diverse the meanings of induced death in various cultural and historical situations, one should not be blinded to the essential feature of any suicide—its violent statement about human connection, broken and maintained (1979, p. 239).

Depression is a substantial part of the picture of at least 50 percent of suicides. People who feel depressed and also feel hopeless are the ones who are at risk for suicide. Depression by itself usually does not carry the risk. When, however, it is coupled with feelings of hopelessness about the future, the person enters a high risk category for suicide. This is true regardless of the age of such persons. These people are aware of their own disintegration or of the threat of such disintegration.

William Styron, in writing of the devastating dimension of his own depression and depression's potential for leading to suicide, called for a greater understanding of the suicide's suffering. Prevention will be hindered and the age-old stigma against suicide will remain, according to Styron, unless we can realize that the vast majority of those who do away with themselves—and those who attempt to do so—do not do it because of any frailty, and rarely out of impulse, "but because they are in the grip of an illness (depression) that causes almost unimaginable pain. It is important to try to grasp the nature of this pain" (1988).

Similar to the group suffering from feelings of depression and hopelessness is another group whose depression may be less significant but who is affected by despair. In this group, despair is the significant factor—a sense of profound absence of meaning and purpose, of the impossibility of human connection, of pervasive hopelessness. The person feels blocked or hemmed in, and feels that there is no possibility of changing this or achieving meaning. The person frequently senses, especially in the case of the suicidal adolescent, that this is a permanent and unalterable condition. If a future can be imagined, it is imagined to be worse than the present, particularly if the person's perception of the future is colored by despair and hopelessness. In broader dimension, the suicide can create a future only in killing himself or herself. In planning and carrying through the suicide, the person for that period of time lives with an imagined future. As Ludwig Binswanger writes in his famous case study of his patient, Ellen West, only in deciding to kill herself was she able to find herself and choose herself (1958). We see in suicides such as that of West the articulation of the theme of self-completion, of locating oneself in the design of things—in other words, a transformation.

In the context of motivation, it is important to mention what Lifton describes as "the suicide image-construct" (1979, p. 254). When a family member has committed suicide, especially a parent, one is likely to form a strong image of that act. Later, in tough situations, an image of suicide as an option is evoked, an image that is often intensified by each life-threatening encounter. This image-construct will be discussed again in the section on the family of the suicide victim.

The following examples of patients and their suicidal behavior will focus on meaning and motivation in suicide.

Sylvia Plath's Depression and Rage

Depression haunted Sylvia Plath, poet and novelist, who killed herself at age 30, shortly after the publication of her autobiographical novel, *The Bell Jar* (1971). She had made a serious suicide attempt ten years before her successful one. Her life was a long struggle of battling fierce rages and depression. In one of her poems, she described her 30 years of life as a black shoe in which she had lived as a foot. Not long after writing a number of poems with similar themes, she broke out of that black shoe by bringing closure to her life, with the help of a gas oven. Many have studied her life in an effort to explain her self-destruction. One thing is certain. Her tormented life knew the meaning of suffering, and her autobiographical novel and more than 252 published poems attest to that. She raged against the monster within and tried to purge it from her soul through her writings. She finally took direct action against the darkness within and in ending her suffering also ended her life. While her writing may have given considerable meaning to her suffering, and it may well have been her intention for it to do so, she finally decided that rest from the conflicting passions of her soul could be found only in sleep—undisturbed sleep (Stevenson, 1989). Although it is not clear precisely what transformation she sought in her suicide act, we know she demanded change and brought it about.

The Dream of a Plane Crash

A 30-year-old woman who saw her life as bankrupt, made a serious suicide attempt with a sedative-hypnotic drug. She had failed to sustain a number of important relationships, was depressed, alienated from self and others, and troubled about a future that seemed dark and without hope. At the same time, she was an attractive person, had good occupational skills, and was not without physical resources. Just the same, "bad luck" seemed to follow her, and life lost all joy. There was "coldness" everywhere and no "warmth." She sought "release" in an overdose of pills, and heroic medical interventions were necessary to rescue her from death. After awakening from three or four days of unconsciousness, she reported a dream so real to her that she wondered if it were not actually true. She recalled that she was in an airplane, flying over mountains. The plane encountered difficulties and crashed in a narrow valley between two mountain ranges. She and the pilot walked away together unharmed from the crash. As she told her dream, she appeared radiant and joyous. Life took on new meaning. She had survived a big crash and had done so with the pilot. Thus, she was not alone. The "near death experience" was for her truly a transformation in which she felt a cosmic unity and found a new sense of personal worth and meaning. Her life in the months and years that followed validated her transformation. Although life continued to offer her a share of tribulation and sometimes genuine suffering, her transpersonal perspective became an effective suicide preventive. In confronting death, and actually experiencing a near death, though as a dream, she became able to engage life, to find renewal.

Hating Mother and Never Seeing God

One Sunday morning, in making rounds on a psychiatric service, I came face to face with a young woman, crying her heart out and constantly repeating: "I'll never see God. I hated my mother, and she died while I still hated her." In her state of depression and despair, she had made a suicide attempt and had been brought to the hospital. What did she seek through this death experience? Was it a form of atonement? A way of finding mother and healing the broken connection? A transformation from the way of hate to a new life in love? Maybe all of these. One thing is certain, her pain was out of control. Healing came to her through being helped to look and search within. Fortunately, her mother continued to exist for her as a psychological reality with whom she learned to communicate; and therein came the continuing opportunity for a different kind of relationship. Even the prohibition against her seeing God became a thing of the past and no longer valid. This person could have described her situation with words from D.H. Lawrence's poem *Healing* (1964), about being ill from wounds inflicted on the soul and on the emotional self. Lawrence goes on to say that only time and patience and a difficult repentance can free oneself from the endless repetition of the wheel of suffering. Freedom and change came for this patient in embracing the death experience through a frontal assault upon herself. At some level and in some realm, it appears that she sought wholeness, renewal through a decisive act of suicide.

The Mentally Retarded 18-Year-Old's Search for Father

"I am afraid I am not who I wish I was, and I am sad about that. I am lonely and homesick for my father. I want to find him. . . .Maybe he is also looking for me and sad because he has not been able to find me. . . .Maybe I decided to go to God for God to help me find him." These are the words of an 18-year-old mentally retarded man whose family did not know or refused to tell him who his father was. I saw him first after a suicide attempt, and at that time, he was preoccupied with finding his father. (His mother had never been married, and there was no male ever around that he could identify as his father.)

In listening to this young man, one is reminded of the words of Thomas Wolfe in Of *Time and the River*: "When shall the lonely of heart come home? What doors are open to the wanderer? And which of us shall find his father, know his face, and in what place and in what time and in what land?" (p. 2).

He reported that during the suicide experience he had had a dream-like recollection of himself and an older man clinging together as they were lifted toward the skies above. Thus, one can assume that in his longing for closeness to and knowledge of his father, he had decided he would have to die and go to heaven where he and his father would find one another. In his conscious thinking, however, he spoke as if his father was alive but that unfortunate circumstances were keeping them apart. At a deeper level, he had decided that finding one another in heaven would be easier to accomplish than doing so on earth.

RATIONAL SUICIDE

In recent years there has emerged a more open discussion of suicide as an acceptable option in certain of life's circumstances. One factor underlying changing attitudes toward suicide has been the development of life-support technologies that enable health care personnel to extend the survival of critically ill patients far beyond the point where the conditions for meaningful life exist. The use of these medical technologies can transform the process of dying into a seemingly unending nightmare or void. In reaction to the abuse of these medical technologies, many have become supporters of the concept of the right-to-die, and, by extension, to the right-to-suicide. Organizations have been developed to promote a wider acceptance of the practice of rational suicide—suicide not only in response to terminal illness but to other forms of disability when the quality of life or the ability to affirm oneself as a human being is greatly compromised.

The defining characteristics of a rational suicide relate to the person's ability to make an autonomous choice, uncoerced and informed. These defining characteristics usually include three important dimensions: (1) individuals possess a realistic assessment of their situation, (2) the mental processes leading to their decision to commit suicide are unimpaired by psychological illness or severe emotional distress, and (3) the motivational basis of their decision would be understandable to the majority of uninvolved observers from their community or social group (Siegel, 1986). While not wanting to discount the validity of motivation in rational suicide, one can say that there are blemishes on all three of these defining characteristics—maybe not enough to question strongly the rationality of the act, but enough to question the possibility of complete clarity of thinking.

While the intent or goal of rational suicide may be a worthy one, it may inadvertently increase the suffering of those faced with the choice, especially certain terminally ill patients. One must remember that not all terminally ill patients want to hasten their death, but may want to prolong their lives for as long a period as possible. Siegel and Tuckel point out a critical dilemma in rational suicide. If suicide were to become an accepted norm, this might intensify pressure on certain individuals to end their lives so they would not be a burden to their families or society. The option to commit suicide then could be converted into an obligation to take one's own life (Siegel & Tuckel, 1984–1985). Patients confronted with this kind of choice may experience profound anxiety, particularly if their own values conflict with something society is sanctioning.

Some brief stories of patients whose actions fit the category of rational suicide will show something of the reasonableness of their thinking.

Betty Rollin's Mother

A good example of rational suicide is the case of Betty Rollin's mother, as described in the book, *Last Wish* (1985). Her mother was terminally ill with ovarian cancer, in chronic pain, and with available therapies all already tried. Because of intestinal obstruction, she was unable to keep food down or control her bowels, and this condition had existed for a long time. In reasonable command of her mental faculties, she asked her daughter to assist her in committing suicide, and her daughter complied.

The Call to Say Good-Bye

One morning an 84-year-old man called this author to say that he had decided to bring closure to his life and was calling to thank me for the 'faithful psychiatric care that I had given him over many years as his doctor and his friend. He was not calling for me to intervene; he was of clear mind, with nobody dependent on him physically or emotionally. He said that he knew I would prefer that a person should leave the time of death to God, but that the time now was right for him.

Before relating further developments in his suicide, a statement about his life is indicated. This man was reared by a widowed mother, had graduated from law school, and had worked mostly as a writer. All of his life he had been plagued by depression that periodically rendered him unable to function, but he continued to write. Now, aside from his depression, he had become increasingly disabled from heart and kidney disease, but he managed to live alone and care for himself. At this point, however, he was faced with going to a nursing home, for he could no longer care adequately for himself even in the supportive apartment building in which he lived. Although he had the promise of continued care from his doctors, he could not and would not tolerate his loss of freedom and independence. "I am ravaged by disease," he said to me on the phone, "I am no longer me. Today is empty. Tomorrow will be emptier." That type of life was unacceptable, especially when he had the option of leaving a broken body.

Because of the nature of his call, I did take a few moments to suggest other alternatives, which he rejected. Then, not wanting him to receive from me even a hint of condemnation for what he was about to do, I searched carefully for a word of caring and affirmation. I remembered that he had told me several times that if there was a heaven and if he arrived there, the first thing he would do would be to find his mother and sing her a song of gratitude for having been such a good mother. Taking my cue from that, I said to him: "When you arrive there and see your mother, tell her that your doctor friend said that she reared a marvelous son."

Intervention in this patient's situation did not seem right, although I have often asked if his telephone call, at some level, may not have been a cry for help. Definitely, it was a cry for change. Life in this world was no longer nourishing for him, and he sought in the act of death the transformation he desired.

Grant Us Thy Peace

Another example of a suicide that fits into the category of rational is that of Elizabeth and Henry Pitney Van Dusen. Van Dusen, age 77, was the retired president of New York's Union Theological Seminary and a distinguished Presbyterian minister. He and his wife, Elizabeth, age 80, discussed suicide with their family and friends. They prepared a statement before taking an overdose of sleeping pills in their Princeton, New Jersey, home. The statement or suicide note was signed by the wife and contained a description of their physical conditions and how they arrived at their decision, which they considered responsible and appropriate. The note acknowledged that they both had had full and satisfying lives. The husband had had a stroke five years ago that had left the speech of this highly articulate man essentially incomprehensible. The wife's arthritis had grown worse, and she and her husband were becoming increasingly weak and unwell. They did not want to die in a nursing home. The suicide note was closed with these words: "O Lamb of God that takest away the sins of the world, grant us thy peace" (Phipps, 1985 and "Good Death," 1975). After the Van Dusen's suicide, a committee of the Presbytery of New York City, reflecting on the serious and rational decision of these persons of deep religious faith, concluded that "for some Christians, as a last resort in the gravest of situations, suicide may be an act of their Christian conscience" (Phipps, 1985).

No Patience with Disability

The brilliant psychoanalyst Bruno Bettelheim, 86, alone and ailing in a Maryland retirement home, committed suicide by placing a plastic bag over his head. He grew up and was educated in Sigmund Freud's Vienna, spent a year in the Dachau and Buchenwald concentration camps, and after gaining his release, came to the United States in 1939. At the University of Chicago, he embarked on his life's work with severely disturbed children. In 1984, Gertrude, his wife of 43 years, died. The loss was devastating, and he began to succumb to a despair within himself. Three years later, in 1987, he suffered a stroke, and after that, he began to complain that he could not think anymore. For a person accustomed to vigorous thought, that loss became an insurmountable threat to his integrity of self. He also was not prepared for the loss of independence he experienced in the retirement home and soon regretted the move to that kind of institution. The right course of action was as clear to him as it was in the fairy tales he discussed in his best-known book, *The Uses of Enchantment.* Those who knew him well see his suicide not as a surrender, but as a final act of mastery over life. As Hans Steiner, chief of psychiatry at Stanford's Children's Hospital emphasized, Bettelheim saw what was in store for him and did not want it (Plummer, Wilhelm, & Matsumoto, 1990).

ADOLESCENTS AND SUICIDE

Although essentially anything that is said about the suffering caused by suicide or thoughts of suicide has relevance to adolescents, this age group deserves recognition because of the greatly increased incidence of teenage suicide during the past three decades.

Suicidal behavior is a multidetermined symptom, and this is especially true in the adolescent. Factors that enhance risk can be grouped into categories involving the current state of ego functioning, current status of affect and behavioral expression, current interpersonal relations, and past developmental history (Pfeffer, 1990). Extensive assessment of these risk categories is critical in the work both of prevention and intervention. A cognitive approach is often needed with respect to adolescents' perceptions of their circumstances (Beck et al., 1985). Their perceptions are usually dark and pessimistic and must be dealt with in an encouraging and optimistic manner.

It is generally believed that adolescents are more likely to respond to a difficult situation with suicidal behavior if they have previously encountered losses, family problems, abuse, neglect, or suicidal behavior by family members or friends. Adolescents' limited perspectives on life can lead them to feel that a failure or the loss of a relationship is permanent and that there will be no second chance. In the face of feelings of hopelessness, they are vulnerable to self-destructive behavior. Are there further sociologic factors that may have a special impact on adolescents and contribute to their self-destructive behavior? Among the factors often cited are the fragmentation of the nuclear family, the loss of a sense of community, the threat of nuclear holocaust, the diminishing influence of organized religion, easy access to guns and drugs, excessive violence in society and the media, and possibly the diminishing social taboo against suicide. Closely related to sociologic factors may be economic ones in that job opportunities and rewarding employment are not always available. Of course, many of these factors are *outside* of the person, but they can tie themselves to what is going on *inside* the person.

During the past three decades, there has been an over 300 percent increase in the suicide rate in the age 15-to-24 group. The increased use and availability of alcohol and drugs are usually given as major factors in this increased rate. Yet, we know that alcohol and drug use may result from as well as cause depression, isolation, physical and mental debility, losses of all kinds, and the feeling that there is no future.

In studying the potentially suicidal adolescent as well as reviewing available information on adolescents who have actually committed suicide, one is impressed with how the attitudes of these adolescents involve extreme discounting of the existence, and significance, of solutions and change possibilities of their problem, as well as any personal ability to create a solution. Jacobs (1978) has highlighted the five conditions that seem to characterize the potentially suicidal adolescent—conditions that form something of a composite picture:

1. Potentially suicidal adolescents view the problem in the final stage as not of their own making.
2. They feel that they did all they could to resolve their problem.
3. The problem is not just of the moment, but in the broader context of a long-standing history of problems that escalated of late to a point exceeding human endurance.
4. Death must be viewed as necessary, as the only way out.
5. The suicidal adolescents are sorry and beg from others indulgence, believing that they have the right solution, although others may not understand their logic.

The insolvable problem looms as a significant factor in the suicidal behavior of certain adolescents, as well as in children. Often this insolvable problem is tied causally to a depressive attitude, especially when the person is pressured constantly to resolve the problem and threatened by sanctions if the problem is not resolved. The depressive attitude can be made worse by a sense of intangible responsibility for the welfare of others and by the frustrating inability to satisfy significant others. Israel Orbach delineates the steps in the self-destructive process in the family context where there is isolation and lack of support systems (1986). Self-esteem deteriorates when the family does not act as a protective shield against frustrations and other menacing experiences in the environment. In the absence of an outlet for inner tensions through being listened to and in sharing, the young person turns the anger and tensions against self. The accumulation of failures to satisfy family and the seemingly unending flow of new problems leave the person with feelings of frustration, worthlessness, helplessness, and hopelessness. The person's self-image becomes one of failure when basically destructive coping patterns of the family persist. The person may grow more helpless and hopeless and decide that only a drastic action of escape can bring relief. Sometimes the young person, in admitting that a so-called insolvable problem may have a resolution, becomes fearful that in turn the resolution would create a new and equally insolvable problem.

A boy's preparatory school student, in the movie *Dead Poet's Society*, illustrates major dynamic factors at play in adolescent suicide. Neal, a teenager, gets caught between wanting to live his own life, as his English teacher advises, and not being able to disobey his tyrannical father, who wants him to go to medical school. Unable to deal with the pressure, he kills himself. He felt trapped and in an untenable situation with no resolution or future. In suicide, he no longer had to deal with either of the two alternatives facing him: his choice of an acting career or his father's choice for him of a medical career. In this struggle, of course, he received no support or understanding from his somewhat dysfunctional family.

Suicidal adolescents in the end perceive their problems as insolvable— no genuine solution now or ever. There is loss of hope and with the loss of hope comes great suffering. In those final moments, they sometimes give away their prized possessions. One cannot help asking if these gifts are not symbolic of their affirming or seeking a bond to others even in death.

FAMILY OF THE SUICIDE VICTIM

Suicide is one of the most difficult types of death with which a bereaved person must deal. Mourning is made more difficult because usually there was no time to anticipate the separation or to say good-bye. As Victoria Alexander points out, to a great extent, the process of mourning after suicide is the struggle to find a way to say good-bye after the door has been closed (1990). The literature is abundant on the sequelae of bereavement resulting from suicide (Ness & Pfeffer, 1990).

Suicide can leave for the family a legacy of shame, social stigma, reproach, and damaged self-image. The family members may seek a scapegoat to blame, and they often end up blaming themselves or a particular family member. They discover that others may not want to discuss their loss with them in a meaningful manner, and they find themselves gradually withdrawing from interactions with others. At times, family members avoid discussing the death with others who may be willing and open to discussion, thereby slowing recovery.

Survivors need but rarely have an outlet for a not uncommon undercurrent of anger against the deceased who chose, intentionally or unintentionally, to inflict trauma and pain. Support groups, when available, as well as individual counselors, can furnish a forum where the strong feelings of anger, guilt, shame, and disappointment can be expressed and understood. Significant and invariably asked questions can also be more easily raised in that kind of therapeutic setting. Did I cause the suicide or fail to hear or heed the cry for help? Will our other children now see suicide as a viable option in problem solving and subject the family to another suicide? How could a member of our family ever want to punish us so or express such anger or hate, or lack of concern? Did he really mean to inflict this kind of scar on us? Could I myself ever commit suicide? The question may be more general and center on "why the deceased committed suicide." This question usually leads to an honest search for causes or meaning and what part the survivor played in the death. The role of the family may be significant indeed in the suicide act.

It has been said that only individuals who are wished dead by someone kill themselves. Studies have been done of certain successful suicides whose families had wished them dead. These victims also were in circumstances where they did not have the ability to retaliate or free themselves from being a seeming burden on family or significant others. As Richman and Rosenbaum have written, suicidal behavior is likely to occur when there is increased stress accompanied by hostility and perceived death wishes from the family and other significant others, when the suicidal person is unable to retaliate, and when external support is unavailable or withdrawn (1970). After the suicide takes place, such families may or may not have a genuine awareness of the part they played in the suicide act.

Even in rational suicide related to terminally ill patients, families may contribute to the broken connection leading to the suicide. Any death, whether natural or by suicide, is an interpersonal crisis. Terminally ill patients often see their loved ones withdraw from them. The resulting social isolation of the patient can create a psychosocial void and contribute to a greater sense of hopelessness and despair in the terminally ill. The abandonment by family then becomes a major factor in the choice of this kind of death. In retrospect, family members may realize what they have done, and their guilt and grief are made more distressing.

Two questions deserve special attention. In consultation with family members after a parent, child, or close relative has committed suicide, the question generally arises as to whether the inclination toward suicide can be inherited. Along with that question is a similar one. Are not people more likely to attempt suicide when other family members have done so? As for genetic transmission, there is no evidence to support that, but one cannot rule out genetic vulnerability that might be associated with suicide. In counseling family victims of a suicidal member, what is important, according to Lifton, is the recognition of a family transmission of what he calls the "suicide image-construct" (1979, p. 254). Lifton describes "the suicide image-construct" by saying that if a family member, especially a parent, has committed suicide, one is likely to form a strong image of that act, an image that can take on great relevance for one's own struggles. Whenever one feels abandoned, experiences loss or separation, or feels immobilized, an image of suicide may be evoked. In a situation where a family suicide has loomed large, a family member can come almost to equate death with suicide. That experience would create, from the beginning, an encompassing suicide construct that would be called forth and possibly intensified by each threatening life encounter. Of course, those in whom this construct has developed can deal with it in a variety of ways. For some, like the imagery of death, it can be a source of creative energy. In others, it can become a kind of repository of unacknowledged despair. Between these two responses to this construct are many others, including threats told to oneself or to others that if something does not happen or if my situation does not improve, I will kill myself.

While the comments above have focused on the family, the broader human community must not be overlooked in how it responds to the suicide of one of its members. Suicide is a reminder that we have failed to embody as a family and community the commitment not to abandon one another, that we have failed to offer the trust necessary to sustain our lives in health and illness. Thus suicide, no matter what the circumstances that brought it about, may remain a judgment upon the supporting fabric of those around the suicide victim. Motivation is never completely clear in suicide and, to some extent, remains an enigma or shrouded in mystery. Even when explanatory notes are left behind, they invite interpretation.

Because suicide can quickly project a negative condemnation of life, this condemnation extends to the relationships with those who live on after—the family and the community.

We often hear of cases such as that of a mother afflicted with an incurable disease who, in lingering on, can exhaust the family, financially and emotionally. That mother may be justified in taking her own life for the sake of the family, when all the circumstances are considered. Although there may be positive aspects of this reasoning, and great relief may come to some homes, in other homes we see problems. In these other homes, the mother's taking of her own life may become an indictment upon the family's loyalty and love. The family may ask why the bonds of human trust were not strong enough to withstand hardship. Thus, the mother's suicide, so carefully chosen for its good, may leave a negative impact on the family, cause them to question their love and loyalty, and open the way for the family's chronic mourning. The family's suffering, expected to end with that of the mother's, may now become interminable, or at least so until intervention is sought.

ETHICAL AND VALUE ISSUES IN SUICIDE

Ethical and values issues in suicide are complex and many in number. The influence of our Judeo-Christian tradition remains strong. This influence relates to the Biblical message of God's sovereignty over human life, found throughout the Bible. The Koran's message is similar: "It is not given to any soul to die, save by the leave of God, at an appointed time." Yet, religiously speaking, the notion of suicide as an unforgivable sin has few, if any, defenders in contemporary moral philosophy.

One can go a step further and say that it is difficult to muster compelling arguments against suicide in the competent individual. At the same time, in arguing that psychologically competent individuals have a *prima facie* right to take their own lives, the duties they have to others may override their right to do so.

Further, while suggesting that there is no moral proscription against the terminally ill taking their own lives, procedural safeguards must be developed to protect vulnerable persons from coercion. Many subtle forms of coercion could push a terminally ill patient toward moving ahead and getting out of the way to save health care resources or to spare family a variety of distresses. Persons who do not want to should never feel even a hint of coercion that they should take their own lives.

The dimension of coercion needs further emphasis. As has been mentioned, there may be no sound reasons to think that suicide cannot in principle be a rational choice in situations such as those of certain terminally ill patients. Yet, as Battin points out, if suicide can be rational, then an additional and difficult problem faces us. The principle of paternalism, now used to justify suicide prevention activities, could require encouragement of suicide when it is a rational act (1982, p. 192). Although this could be a disturbing result, perhaps its impact could be blunted by considering suicide as a right, something that the person is ultimately entitled to choose or reject.

The Bible does not say much about the morality of suicide, but the values inherent in the Biblical tradition center around the question of whether or not suicide violates one or more of three obligations: to oneself, to others, and to God.

The Bible tells of six self-killings. The three best known of these are Judas, Saul, and Samson. The Biblical writers neither condemn nor commend these persons who have taken their own lives. As Phipps has said, perhaps the Biblical narrators thought it was fitting for Samson, Saul, and Judas to respond to their varied situations by committing suicide. Later, St. Augustine added another dimension by commenting that Samson had received special divine permission. Augustine concluded: "He who knows it is unlawful to kill himself may nevertheless do so if he is ordered by God" (*City of God*, Book 1, Sections 18–26).

The famous Anglican preacher John Donne in his 1608 treatise, *Biathanatos*, while agreeing with many of his theological predecessors in declaring suicide generally a forbidden act, felt that it is nevertheless permissible if commanded by God. It could be a summons from God. Donne believed that the voice or will of God was transmitted in conscientious reasoning, especially on matters about which the Bible gives no clear direction or definite judgment (Clemons, 1985). This idea is not far removed from Hillman's question: ". . . .may not God speak through the soul or urge an action through our own hand" (1976, p. 32).

In general, however, the position of Christianity until recent times has been one of prohibition. A central figure in that development was the fourth century theologian, Augustine, whose viewpoint over the centuries has strongly influenced both Roman Catholics and Protestants. It must be emphasized, however, that Augustine's prohibition was developed largely to combat self-killing in particular situations, such as religious zealotry and martyrdom. The Augustinan prohibition, however, was not really designed to regulate suicides due to physical or mental suffering, old age, altruism toward others, personal or societal honor, and disabling illness.

Thus, as Battin states (1982, p. 194), the result is that Western society has evolved without developing a reasonable, equitable, and humane set of laws and practices regarding the ending of one's life. Battin goes on to say that we should attempt to codify a set of rules to regulate self-killing in spite of the fact that there would be dissent from particular portions of laws, conventions, customs, or practices to the making up of any such code. At the heart of any attempt to codify a set of moral rules concerning suicide might be the strategy of construing *suicide as a right*. This does not necessarily mean that suicide is a right, but that progress in our treatment of suicide might be made by encouraging ourselves to consider suicide in that way (Battin, 1982, pp. 195–196). In this type of consideration, we are then forced to acknowledge what other factors can override this right to commit suicide and what claims for noninterference or assistance this right might impose upon other persons.

A major ethical principle in medical practice is respect for the autonomy of the psychologically competent individual. It seems then appropriate and right to view many suicides as potentially rational and dignity-promoting. At the same time, we should not lessen our efforts to prevent suicide that is irrationally or pathologically chosen or that defaults in an obligation to others. Out of this grow another question already mentioned that has frightening implications and that may partly account for the strength of the suicide taboo operative in Western culture. Do genuinely paternalist considerations properly employed in the prevention of suicide also favor the promoting of suicide when it seems to be the rational thing to do (Battin, 1982, p. 195)?

PREVENTION AND INTERVENTION

There is important work to be done in primary, secondary, and tertiary prevention of suicide. In primary prevention, we have the task of strengthening social supports, enhancing communication especially in the family, and educating communities as to the causes and extent of suicide in the different age groups. The most important aspect of secondary prevention is the identification of suicide potential before an attempt and mobilizing effective interventions. Tertiary prevention entails the prevention of debilitation or complications after an attempt and the development of strategies to avoid recurrence, while addressing the needs of the suffering victim.

One aspect of suicide prevention is frequently a superficial enterprise in that we interpret the "cry for help" in a narrow sense and not as William

F. May does in his concept of a "cry for change." Thus, we try only to block the suicide act. This is a worthy step, but if our preventive actions stop there, they do not go deep enough. Possibly this focus on interrupting the plan for suicide has led psychiatrist Thomas Szasz to describe much of the work of suicide prevention centers as fraudulent. Szasz speaks of the suicide prevention center worker answering the telephone call of a suicidal person, pleading with the person to cling to life, and at the same time, motioning to another worker to trace the call and dispatch the police to take the person into custody and to bring the person to a hospital. Szasz sees this action as devious, coercive, and fraudulent (1986). Often the prevention stops there, but our efforts could assure authenticity if they did more than resist suicide or temporarily relieve the person of the impulse to break out of his or her entrapment. The suicide's cry is for a radical change in his or her life. Until we address in depth this wish for change, we have done little on behalf of prevention.

Many besides Szasz raise questions about intervening to prevent a suicide by stressing that this is interfering with the autonomy of another person. Although objections to intervention may have merit, there are some situations where intervention is indicated, possibly obligatory. There is a right to intervene when another intends suicide (a) if that person is *not* able to choose freely and rationally because of insanity or impairment of rational choice, and (b) if that person is defaulting on an obligation to others. In all efforts at intervention, persuasion is a much better approach than coercion. Coercive techniques used by health professionals and others are at the heart of many criticisms of suicide prevention and intervention. Our efforts should have more in mind than just the physical protection of the suicidal person. Stanley Hauerwas puts in eloquent language what is really involved in prevention:

> *The refusal to let an attempted suicide die is only our feeble, but real, attempt to remain a community of trust and care through the agency of medicine. Our prohibition and subsequent care of a suicide draws on our profoundest assumptions that each individual's life has a purpose beyond simply being autonomous. [1986, p. 107]*

A good starting place in suicide prevention and intervention is with psychiatrist Viktor Frankl's question addressed to the person ruminating about or contemplating suicide: "What is it that has kept you from doing it?" Whatever reason individuals give, and they usually give some reason, Frankl seizes upon it and uses it as a lifeline, as something around which to build meaning and a future. Such a question must be asked lovingly and with great concern so that its intent will not be misinterpreted.

Suicide prevention is not a narrow enterprise. When we think in terms of the brokenness of community, injustices inflicted upon many in our society, unrelieved suffering, alienation, and despair as factors in the suicide of our brothers and sisters, then our task is to work for conditions that make the inclination toward suicide less frequent. Even in those cases in which the suicide addresses not a social or interpersonal situation, but physical distress and pain, we have the ability to respond effectively as caregivers.

In our efforts at intervention with suicidal persons, rational evaluation and human understanding are sometimes replaced by either an unsympathetic attitude or an overly paternalistic one. Neither of these attitudes is helpful. What is needed is genuine empathy as a first step. Empathic immersion into the suicidal person's inner life will help that person appreciate that another can accept and understand his or her hopelessness and desperation. Further, empathy is necessary in helping the suicidal person discriminate between the forces that are behind the suicidal person's wish to die. A look at those forces or motives, and an understanding of them, is a more urgent task than focusing on preventing the suicide.

Intervention in suicide involves walking down that "dark road" and immersing oneself into that world in which the suicidal person is living. One soon discovers that most suicidal persons have a predisposition to overestimate the magnitude and insolubility of their problems. Coupled with this, as has been emphasized by those "who have been there," is an exaggerated negative view of the outside world, of themselves, and of the future. An awareness of what and how a suicidal person is thinking and feeling may lead those intervening to see quickly that the suicidal person's plight has a way out, and soon hope begins to dawn.

CONCLUSION

Gabriel Marcel has written ". . . the fact that suicide is always possible is the essential starting point of any genuine metaphysical thought" (1961, p. 26). Thus, any true awareness of ourselves is an acknowledgment that the possibility of suicide belongs to the human condition. As goodness and evil are not strangers to our nature, neither is suicide. Whether we ever embrace it, and under what circumstance, is another matter. Yet, for the person caught up in the "life of suicide," as Farber describes it, or carrying within the "suicide-construct," to use Lifton's term, the possibility of being the author of one's own death exercises a demonic and seductive fascination (Farber, 1966). That type of person we encounter less frequently than the person in despair with suicidal pre-occupations and longing to die—a despair that Sören Kierkegaard (1954) describes as sickness unto death, a despair that carries the threat of disintegration, of loss of control over what is happening to one's self.

For most of us, suicide holds no demonic or seductive fascination. Nor is despair a part of our lives. Yet, each of us knows that suicide is an option that could be exercised in the right circumstance, that the option is a part of the human condition. In the broader context, our interest in and concern with suicide include but extend beyond being our brother's or sister's keeper to involvement in a dialogue that is actually a working through of our feelings about death and in turn an acceptance of our finitude, thereby finding renewed vitality.

REFERENCES

Alvarez, A. (1972). *The savage God*. New York: Random House.

Alexander, V. (1990, May). Family's grief response after suicide is complex and painful. *The Psychiatric Times*, pp. 15–17.

Battin, M.P. (1982). *Ethical issues in suicide*. Englewood Cliffs, NJ: Prentice-Hall.

Beck, A.T., Steer, R.A., & Kovacs, M., et al. (1985). Hopelessness and eventual suicide: A 10-year prospective study of patients hospitalized with suicidal ideation. *American Journal of Psychiatry, 142*, 559–563.

Binswanger, L. (1958). The case of Ellen West. In R. May, E. Angel, & H. Ellenberger (Eds.), *Existence: A new dimension in psychiatry*. New York: Basic Books.

Brown, T. (1963). *Religio medici*. Cambridge, Eng.: Cambridge University Press.

Camus, A. (1956). *The fall*. New York: Knopf Publishers.

Clemons, J.T. (1985, May 8). Suicide and Christian moral judgment. *The Christian Century*, pp. 466–469.

Eissler, K.R. (1955). *The psychiatrist and the dying patient*. New York: International Universities Press.

Farber, L.H. (1966). *The ways and the will*. New York: Basic Books.

Good death? (1975, March 10). *Time*, pp. 83–84.

Hauerwas, S. (1986). *Suffering presence*. Notre Dame. South Bend, IN: University of Notre Dame Press.

Hillman, J. (1976). *Suicide and the soul*. New York: Spring Publications.

Hotchner, A.E. (1966). *Papa Hemingway*. New York: Random House.

Jacobs, J. (1978). *Adolescent suicide*. Irvington, NY: Irvington Publications.

Jung, C. (1960). *The structure and dynamics of the psyche*. Collected Works (Vol. 8). New York: Pantheon Books.

Kierkegaard, S. (1954). *Fear and trembling and sickness unto death*. Princeton, NJ: Princeton University Press.

Lawrence, D.H. (1964). *The complete poems of D.H. Lawrence*. Collected and edited by V. de sola Pinto and W. Roberts. London: William Heinemann, Ltd.

Lebacqz, K., & Engelhardt, H.T. (1979). Suicide. In D.J. Horan & D. Mall (Eds.). *Death, dying, and euthanasia*. Washington, DC: University Publications of America.

Lifton, R.J. (1979). *The broken connection*. New York: Simon & Schuster.

Marcel, G. (1960). *The mystery of being*. Chicago: Henry Regnery.

Marcel, G. (1961). *The philosophy of existentialism*. New York: Citadel Press.

May, W.F. (1983). *The physician's covenant*. Philadelphia: The Westminster Press.

McDermitt, J. (1977). Personal communication. Texas A&M University, College Station, Texas.

Ness, D.E., & Pfeffer, C.R. (1990). Sequelae of bereavement resulting from suicide. *American Journal of Psychiatry, 147*(3), 279–285.

Nietzsche, F.W. (1967). *Beyond good and evil*. London: Geo. Allen & Unwin, Ltd.

Orbach, I. (1986). The insolvable problem as a determinant in the dynamics of suicidal behavior in children. *American Journal of Psychotherapy, 40*(4), 511–520.

Pfeffer, C.R. (1990). Clinical perspectives on treatment of suicidal behavior among children and adolescents. *Psychiatric Annals, 20*(3), 143–150.

Phipps, W.E. (1985, October 30). Christian perspectives on suicide. *The Christian Century*, pp. 970–973.

Plath, S. (1971). *The bell jar*. New York: Harper's.

Plummer, W., Wilhelm, M., & Matsumoto, M. (1990, April 2). Bruno Bettelheim had infinite patience with children, but not with the ravages of old age. *People Weekly*, pp. 51–52.

Richman, J., & Rosenbaum, M. (1970). Suicide: The role of hostility and death wishes from the family and significant others. *American Journal of Psychiatry, 126*(11), 1652–1655.

Rollin, B. (1985). *Last wish*. New York: Simon & Schuster.

Siegel, K. (1986). Psychosocial aspects of rational suicide. *American Journal of Psychotherapy, 40*(3), 405–418.

Siegel, K., & Tuckel, P. (1984–1985). Rational suicide and the terminally ill patient. *Omega, 15*(3), 263–269.

Stevenson, A. (1989). *Bitter fame: A life of Sylvia Plath*. New York: Houghton Mifflin.

Styron, W. (1988, December 19). Why Primo Levi need not have died. *The New York Times*, p. 23.

Szasz, T. (1986). The case against suicide prevention. *American Psychologist, 41*(7), 806–812.

Wolfe, T. (1935). *Of time and the river*. New York: Scribner & Sons.

15

Suffering in Silence and the Fear of Social Stigma: Survivors of Violence

Blair Justice

Suffering in silence is often rooted in damage to the human capacity to feel joy and love, to care and to be caring. This capacity is identified with soul in recent psychological and psychiatric studies (Bradshaw, 1988a; Shengold, 1988) as well as earlier writings (Schreber, 1903; Freud, 1911).

A "hole in the soul" (Bradshaw, 1989), and the more profound "soul murder" (Shengold, 1988; Bradshaw, 1988b), are both terms currently being used to explain the developmental origins of crippling shame or flawed self found in survivors of a wide range of violence. This violence may take the form of physical or sexual abuse in childhood or may occur later as seen in victims of rape, spouse battering, and elder abuse. More subtly, and perhaps more widely, the "soul violence" may be incurred from emotional indifference or other affective maltreatment on the part of parents toward children.

Only recently have researchers begun to demonstrate some of the biological correlates to soul damage and to the shame, suppression, insecurity, or low self-esteem that often characterizes such injury. Emerging evidence suggests that psychological or emotional trauma is accompanied by measurable physiological disturbance (Pennebaker & Beall, 1986).

Pennebaker, among others, has shown that the suffering in silence that victims often experience has physical correlates which appear to increase their risk of illness (Pennebaker, 1989). Chronic activation of the sympathetic nervous system, with effects on immunocompetence, seems to be associated with the lack of support (Bovard, 1985) felt by many victims as well as with the profound reluctance to reveal their soul damage.

As we will see, the silence of such sufferers is often not due so much to a fear of social stigma as it is to a branding within the family of being bad or wrong at the core of one's self. The shame that characterizes much suffering in silence may not originate with sexual or physical abuse or with any other violence condemned by society. It may stem from developmental treatment that leaves children with the conviction that they are flawed, that their very inner selves are defective and shameful (Bradshaw, 1989).

The soul damage represented by a diminished self is a starting point for understanding the phenomenon of suffering in silence. After elaborating on what soul injury constitutes and looking at the emergence of "soul" as a clinical concern, this chapter will consider why the family is the source of much of the violence suffered as well as the silence that permits it. Next, some of the psychological and biological dynamics of those who suffer in silence and some of the physical, emotional, and behavioral consequences will be reviewed. Last, a few interventions that seem useful for treating and preventing the problem and promoting recovery will be considered.

SOUL DAMAGE AS A PSYCHOBIOLOGICAL REALITY

Although the history of both science and philosophy continues to remind us of the futile attempts to locate the soul in the body—as if it were a tangible, dissectible organ—"soul" has survived in both psychology and medicine as a useful term for referring to certain core human capacities. The capacities have to do with loving, caring, experiencing joy, and having a sense of identity and direction (Schreber, 1903; Rosen, 1989;

Raffin, Shurkin, & Sinkler, 1989). Because each of these is—like consciousness—experienced in the human nervous system, all have psychobiological correlates (Noonan, 1989). The most graphic demonstration of
the connection between soul capacities and neurobiology can be seen in
the effects that radical frontal lobotomy or leucotomy may have on a
person's values, strivings, ability to care or be caring, and sense of self
(Nathan, 1987).

The capacities that the soul stands for have their origins in embryonic
development (Grobstein, 1988; Verny & Kelly, 1981) and grow in the
learning process and from environmental influences throughout life
(Ornstein & Sobel, 1987). They are necessary for adaptation and the
meeting of basic human needs. Among the most primary and powerful of
these are the need for attachment and the need for autonomy. As Erikson
(1950) has noted, much of the later developmental success of a human
depends on satisfactory completion of the first two stages of life. It is in
these initial stages that we begin to learn trust and self-confidence from
having our needs met for love and separateness, for dependence and
independence, for attachment and autonomy. When the quality of attachment and autonomy is impaired, we can expect a reduced capacity for
feeling and giving love, for experiencing joy, for reaching out into the
world, for developing a separate identity that goes with a sense of self and
soul (Erikson, 1988).

A "hole in the soul," as Bradshaw has called it, often results in shame
(Bradshaw, 1988a). At the core of the hole, he has found, is "toxic
shame." This sense of shame seems to begin in the second developmental
stage in which young children are needing to explore the world beyond
mother or primary caretaker and to experiment with their own coping
behaviors. If children are given to believe that there is something in them
that is wrong or bad—as opposed to being corrected for specific behaviors—then toxic shame can result.

Although Bradshaw identifies soul damage and shame with unsatis-
factory Stage 2 development in particular, traumatic events that occur
later may be equally powerful in leading to suffering in silence. This is
especially true for trauma that carries a social stigma, including incest,
sexual abuse outside the home, and rape. Abuse of the elderly by adult
children is another example, as will be noted later in this chapter.

Because the soul is associated with capacities distributed in the brain
from the limbic system to the frontal lobe (Raffin, Shurkin, & Sinkler,
1989), diminishing one's soul not only blunts emotions but also impairs
the "instinctual energy" that fuels feelings and animates behavior.

Shengold (1988) notes the lack of anger or indignation that can be found among victims of soul murder. "Soul murder," described by Shengold as a dramatic term and not a clinical diagnosis, dates back to the 19th century and was considered by Freud in some of his early case studies (Freud, 1911). Soul murder may not only deplete the energy necessary for anger or love but may also produce the paradox of victims identifying with those who inflicted the violence. As Shengold (1988) points out, such victims are deprived of their own identity as they become possessed by another and lose their souls in the bondage.

The use of the term "soul" in the early history of medicine, science, and psychology is well documented (Cohen, 1961; Veith, 1969; Hillman, 1975). As modern science distanced itself from philosophy and theology, the term fell into disfavor when better knowledge of the body established that the soul was nowhere to be found in any of the many locations early writers assigned to it—head (Plato), heart (Aristotle), pineal gland (Descartes), brain ventricles and cerebrospinal fluid (others). But as Noonan (1989) has pointed out, the idea of a seat of a soul—a central core—is so powerful that even modern anatomists cannot ignore it. As recently as 1988, it was noted in an anatomical textbook, The Human Brain (Nolte, 1988), that the pineal gland, which is a small organ deep within the brain, is not likely to be the seat of the soul because pineal tumors fail to cause changes that would be expected with distortion of the soul.

In any event, "soul" continues to be found in the writings of clinicians and scientists who recognize the need for such a concept to capture what it means to be alive and to be human. The term is derived from the Latin anima and, across the centuries, has referred to the principle of life that animates existence (Veith, 1969; Raffin, Shurkin, & Sinkler, 1989). "Soul" not only separates living from nonliving matter but also bestows individuality or identity (Barnes, 1987). The soul is seen as having certain kinship with the internal core of self, with one's essence and with properties attributed to consciousness. When it is diminished, some damage can be expected to one's sense of identity or separateness and to the inner life that characterizes human consciousness.

Kass, trained in both medicine and biochemistry, views the soul as representing some integrating and organizing power of the body and mind that is lost at death (Moyers, 1988). The technical and ethical problems emerging from the new advances of life-support systems have complicated the very definition of death (Veatch, 1989). In reviewing definitions of death, Veatch includes irreversible loss of the soul as one of the considerations related to the capacity for consciousness or social interaction. Whether loss of the soul can be measured in such a way as to be among valid criteria of death is problematic. Others in medicine and psychotherapy are suggesting that the soul can be diminished, even "murdered," while a person remains alive. The effects may be such that the person feels dead inside and shows little vitality or interest in life. Life remains, however, and suffering in silence is one of the traumas of such a life. The next section of this chapter will examine how the family may be both the source of the violence causing the suffering and the reason for the silence.

THE FAMILY AS A PARADOX

Since the signing of the Magna Charta, the idea that a "man's home is his castle" has been inviolate in Western society (Justice & Justice, 1990). Many have historically interpreted this principle as meaning that what goes on inside one's home is nobody else's business. The family is seen as a unit in society entitled to privacy and freedom from intrusion. It is idealized as the place where people can find love and understanding, where they can return each day from the hard knocks of the outside world and receive warmth and succor. The paradox is that the family is also the place where, statistically, a person stands the greatest chance of being a victim of violence (Steele, 1976).

This paradox leaves survivors of physical abuse, sexual abuse, or any other shaming treatment with the unreality of the family inflicting violence while simultaneously being held up as a sanctuary of love. Both the family and society reinforce the idea that what happens within the home is not something to disclose to others and that parents and caretakers always have the child's best interest at heart.

The idealized image of a loving family and good parents places a heavy burden on those who have few resources to meet the demands of daily life much less live up to the high expectations of society. The coping deficiencies in a family often do not reflect a lack of just material resources. Family violence occurs across the economic spectrum (Justice, 1983). Personality and character disorders play a major role in the shaming treatment of children, wives, and the elderly in the homes of the affluent as well as the low-income (Bradshaw, 1988a).

In *Soul Murder*, the first case study discussed by Shengold (1988) is of a desperately unhappy and depressed man whose parents were extremely wealthy. They were also heavy drinkers who battled each other and treated their two sons with a total lack of loving care and empathy. As a child, Mr. A was the frequent subject of the parents' sarcasm and ridicule. There was no loving attachment stage and little development of self and identity from freedom to explore and become competent. By the time Mr. A entered therapy as a married adult and father, he hated himself. He could never laugh except when drunk and had an inability to respond lovingly to his wife and children. He never spoke out against his childhood hell because he saw himself as defective and wrong, deserving what he got.

HOW MANY VICTIMS ARE THERE?

Although the kind of abuse Mr. A experienced can cause as much soul damage and suffering in silence as the more overt trauma of physical and sexual abuse, no one knows the true incidence or prevalence of emotional maltreatment that occurs in the absence of physical or sexual abuse. In Texas, as well as other states, the law clearly proscribes emotional abuse in the Family Code (*Texas Penal Code*, 1984). How much there is remains unknown. The problem of defining emotional abuse is one barrier to determining magnitude. Thus much of what is known about such trauma comes after the fact from the casualties, whose despair, depression, addiction, or general dysfunction finally brings them to someone's attention.

The most reliable data on the extent of physical abuse come from two large-scale surveys done ten years apart, using nationally representative samples. Household interviews were conducted in which parents were asked about how much pushing, grabbing, shoving, slapping, kicking, hitting with an object, using a knife or gun had gone on in their families in the preceding 12 months (Strauss, 1980). Both studies found an extremely high incidence of severe physical violence against children and a high incidence of abuse of spouses (Strauss & Gelles, 1986). In 1975, the severe child abuse rate was computed at 14 out of every 100 families, based on what parents acknowledged in the interviews (Strauss & Gelles, 1986). In 1985, the figure was 10.7. For severe violence against spouses, the rates were 6.1 for 1975 and 5.8 for 1985. "Severe violence" included kicking, biting, punching, hitting with an object, beating up, or using a knife or gun.

For both physical and sexual abuse, reported cases vastly under-represent the magnitude of the problem. Although solid data for sexual abuse in the family are not available, various surveys have estimated that the incidence of incest in the American population is from 5 to 15 percent (Justice & Justice, 1979). While sexual abuse outside the family is also prevalent and the cause of much trauma and suffering in silence, this chapter will focus on violence within the family, which remains the place where abuse is most likely to occur. Elder abuse is another type of violence occurring in families, and its victims share some of the same dynamics and stigma that characterize the suffering in silence of abused children and battered wives. Understanding the cultural and societal influences in this silence is important for gaining a perspective on why the family and individual keep violence a secret.

THE SILENCE OF SOCIETY

Since the very dawn of humankind, certain violence has carried a stigma of abomination. The mark of Cain branded anyone who killed a brother. Although incest also carried an early taboo, a number of cases involving royalty and religious figures were a matter of historical record long before any serious attempts were made to assess just how extensive this practice was. Physical abuse of children and wives never carried such a taboo. Uniform legislation designed to protect children against such violence did not exist in the United States before the 1960s (Justice & Justice, 1990). Laws against wife battering are even more recent.

Society, then, has shown a certain ambivalence about the subject of both sexual and physical abuse. In the case of incest, longstanding taboos imply that it is unspeakable. Its prevalence suggests that most people would rather just not talk about it more than they want to try to understand how society may contribute to its occurring. The featuring of children as sexual objects in the media, commercials, and advertisements has continued since the heyday of sexual permissiveness in the 1970s. Both sexual and physical abuse still carry a societal burden of denial. A reluctance to "interfere," to find out what is going on in families, characterizes societal denial.

The life of Shelly Sessions is a case in point (Sessions & Meyer, 1989). From the eighth grade on, Shelley was used for the sexual gratification of her stepfather. According to *Dark Obsession: A True Story of Incest and Justice*, Bobby Sessions testified in court that he had had as many as 500 "turns," sexual encounters, with the daughter of his second wife. Bobby is described as a "classic narcissist" who saw himself as exempt from all rules but freely lectured other parents on the need to keep their daughters off the streets and protected. Because he was rich and powerful, people listened—and refused to believe the worse about what Sessions was doing in his own family. Even after Shelley broke away and charges were filed against her stepfather, what Sessions had done was treated lightly. He was allowed to plead guilty to a single count of having sex with an underage girl and "sentenced" to spend a year in a private psychiatric residential facility in Dallas. Within six months, he talked his way out and returned home.

Another example is Shirley Turcotte (WGBH, 1988). She was sexually abused by her father from the time she was a toddler until she ran away from home at age 14. To her neighbors she had no sparkle and looked gray and drab—the kind of signs seen in soul damage. Her brother, Wilfrid, would regularly be beat up by their father, who made a living as a nightclub comedian. On one occasion, after going to school with black eyes and a swollen lip, he told a teacher what had happened. The school nurse and a children's aide went to talk to the father, but left without any further questions after Turcotte told them that Wilfrid and his brother had got into a fight.

Neither neighbors nor school officials wanted to believe the signs of what was going on in the Turcotte family. Their silence and inaction contributed to wrecking the lives of two children. It was only years later, after much therapy, courage, and determination, that Shirley was able to face what had happened and reconstruct he life for a public documentary entitled *To A Safer Place* (WGBH, 1988). Her brother Wilfrid, three years younger, was left with no self-confidence, a jail record for assault, and drug charges against him.

SUFFERING AND SILENCE IN THE FAMILY

While people outside the family prefer to look the other way rather than to see the trauma of a Shelley, Shirley, or Wilfrid, those inside the abusive system have their own reasons for suffering in silence. Both conscious and unconscious factors perpetuate the secret of family violence. The list of such factors is long, and the interplay between what is conscious and what is not involves when the violence started, what form it took, how long it went on, who did it, why nothing was done to stop it, and other considerations. The factors include fear, shame, guilt, mistrust, and acceptability.

Fear

On the conscious level, fear is the most often cited reason for keeping silent (Justice & Justice, 1979). Parents who have sex with their children may threaten them with greater harm if the secret is disclosed. Fathers may tell daughters that "it would kill your mother if she found out." Or, the men may say that they will be taken away to jail and the family will be split up if the incest becomes known. Similar threats may be made to both children and wives who are being physically abused. The specter of abandonment is used to keep the victims silent.

Shame

Suffering in silence is also reinforced by a sense of shame on the part of the abused. Like Mr. A as a child, many survivors have such soul damage that they become convinced that they deserve maltreatment. They conclude that something must be terribly wrong with them in the very core of their being to have such violence inflicted upon them. Those who later get therapy often insist they had to be beaten to be made to do the right thing (Erickson, Egeland, & Pianta, 1989).

Shame takes other forms too. Because of the idealized societal image of a family as always being loving and protective, many victims of violence feel there is a shame and stigma attached to revealing what went on in their homes. There is the shame of admitting that one's own parents dispensed more violence than love. There is the shame and embarrassment, for the abused elderly, of acknowledging that the very children one raised turn out to assault or exploit their own parents (Prevention of elder abuse, 1990). There is the shame of a battered wife in confessing she was "such a fool" in having so grossly misjudged the man she married who now beats her.

Many children are inculcated early with the idea that they and their family must always look good to others. Although they may have "toxic" parents who are alcoholic or abusive, it often takes years before such children can acknowledge that the family which looked so perfect from the outside was sick inside. Children who are constantly reminded that they "have everything"—good clothes, nice cars, big house, plenty of money—may start questioning their own experience of what they know the truth to be, what their reality actually is. To defend against the pain of violence, they may cling to an illusion and false image of reality rather than confront their trauma and shame of pretense. Maintaining such an illusion requires victims to keep silent about the pretense.

A number of sexually abused children feel shame over the feelings of arousal they had in some of the encounters with those who violated them. As they grow older and learn more of society's condemnation of incest and other forbidden sexual activities, they fear the stigma attached to such experience. The victim's shame and silence may be reinforced by a parent or stepparent in the family who learns of the incest but refuses to inter-vene on behalf of the child. An abused daughter may be told that her own provocative behavior is what caused her father or stepfather to molest her ("Ann," 1990). In some cases, a child at times may welcome the fondling or sexual contact he or she receives (Justice, 1990). Such encounters may be the only attention the child gets from the parent. If he or she feels sexually aroused by the experience, his or her shame is compounded. The child feels wrong and dirty about both wanting the contact and being responsive to it. Even if the incest becomes known, the suffering in silence still continues from the deep-rooted fear that someone will find out about the feelings of arousal.

Guilt

While shame is rooted in a sense that something is defective at the very core of one's self, guilt comes more from the feeling that one's behavior is wrong (Forward, 1989). Many children who are emotionally abused may feel guilty about never learning to be the kind of son or daughter they think their parents need or want (Miller, 1981). Although such children may never incur physical or sexual mistreatment, they suffer a more insidious kind of abuse. Their mothers and fathers may play the parent role perfectly and even give excessive attention to the child. What the child reads in their eyes, however, is the message that "you have no desires or needs separate from mine, so I will be in charge of your life and tell you what you want." When the child tries to individuate and develop as a person with separate needs and desires, the parent shows great displeasure. Such children become convinced that their natural wishes and needs must be wrong, and their guilt drives them to make lifelong efforts to please the parent and comply with what the parent wants. Their suffering can be as profound as the pain from more overt abuse.

Another form of this kind of emotional maltreatment occurs in homes where the child learns very early that though the parents are attentive, they are too full of their own anxieties and fears to be truly nurturing. The parents may be so threatened by everyday problems that occur in the course of daily life that the child learns quickly to behave in such a way that no additional burden is put on the parent. The message that the parent gives to the child is "I am more needy than you, so your job is to take care of me emotionally rather than my taking care of you." Such a child may spend a lifetime trying to make the parent happy and feel deeply guilty for having failed to do so. The consequence for such a child is a lifetime of quiet despair.

Mistrust

If there is any one lesson that practically all survivors of family violence say they learn early on, it is that people cannot be trusted. If children cannot depend on their parents to meet their needs, whom can they trust? When children turn to their parents for love and nurturing and instead receive betrayal and abuse, mistrust is learned (Helfer, 1974). If a battered wife cannot depend on her husband to provide warmth and closeness, then what relationship can she trust for emotional strokes?

When victims of abuse override their mistrust of people and disclose to someone what is happening to them, they are often met with disbelief. The tendency by school authorities, neighbors, relatives, doctors, and others not to believe an incest story or other account of abuse is diminishing as public and professional awareness increases. As was noted earlier, however, most people prefer to believe that families provide love not violence, and, therefore, what an abused child or battered spouse reports meets with doubt and disbelief.

Shirley Turcotte's beat-up brother, Wilfrid, was not believed. People could not believe what was happening to Shelley Sessions, although all the signs of incest were blatant. Other survivors of incest have repeatedly reported that they attempted to tell a teacher or nurse or neighbor but got nowhere. When disbelief is encountered, the mistrust already present in the abused is simply confirmed. The survivor too often has no choice but to live in silence.

Acceptability

An often overlooked reason for silence about family violence is that some victims were taught that what went on in their home was the same as within any family—it was the norm and therefore to be expected. They learned that whatever a parent might want to do to a child was acceptable, since the child was "owned" by the parent. Or they were told some lie by the father that having sex with his daughter was what fathers do so that they can teach them "the right way" ("Ann," 1990). Yeager tells of having been beaten regularly by his father but not having any idea such abuse was out of the ordinary (Yeager, 1990). As a child Mr. A, in *Soul Murder*, was not allowed to visit in the homes of schoolmates because his parents wanted him to believe that their maltreatment of him and his brother was the standard behavior in all families.

Only in the last decade have police departments been mandated in many states to arrest the husband at the scene of domestic violence where there is good reason to believe he is beating his wife (Sherman & Berk, 1984). Previously, police officers made no intervention, accepting that a man has a right to hit his wife. A number of cultures and subcultures still sanction second-class status for wives as well as children. Violence is accepted, and the victims believe they have no recourse but to suffer in silence.

CONSEQUENCES OF SUFFERING AND SILENCE

The damage from living in an abusive family is physical, emotional, and behavioral. Although neurological injury or similar damage of a lasting nature is a possible consequence of family violence, the more common physiological effect of abuse is the influence on the body of the emotional aspects of the trauma and deprivation.

Within the last decade, findings from the fields of psychoneuroimmunology and behavioral medicine have identified mechanisms by which lack of love, nurturing, and emotional support can affect growth hormones, metabolism, bone healing, as well as the immune system (Bovard, 1985). Already well documented are cases of psychodwarfism, which reflect the results of emotional deprivation in young children (Ferholt, Rotnem, Genel, Leonard, Carey, & Hunter, 1985). More common, yet less recognized, is the effect on T cells and B cells of the immune system from high levels of stress chemicals associated with abuse and deficient emotional support (Kiecolt-Glaser, 1986). Epinephrine, norepinephrine, and cortisol become excessive from chronic stimulation of the posterior hypothalamus, and these neurotransmitters and hormones are associated with immune suppression (Justice, 1988). Prolonged activation of the posterior hypothalamus and sympathetic nervous system is found in environments offering little support. On the other hand, stimulation of the anterior hypothalamus and parasympathetic nervous system accompanies acceptance, affirmation, and affection.

The pioneering work of Pennebaker (1989) has indicated that when trauma is suppressed in memory, physiological effort is required to keep it buried. This effort is reflected in higher levels of galvanic skin response, respiration, heart rate, and other physiological measures (Pennebaker, 1990). It also seems to result in lower immune competence and more frequent visits to physicians for illness (Pennebaker & Hoover, 1985).

Deflecting the Pain and Trauma

Suffering has been defined as a response to pain (Feuerstein, Labbé, & Kuczmierczyk, 1986). Survivors of violence use a variety of responses to divert themselves from the pain, including such psychological defense mechanisms as repression, suppression, and dissociation. Each is designed to keep the pain out of one's awareness or at least to minimize conscious suffering. Repression is an unconscious defense, which holds the trauma out of conscious memory but does nothing to keep the effects on the body and physiological systems from occurring. Suppression serves a similar function but is more conscious. Dissociation is a "distancing" defense, which is usually learned early. A number of children who incur violence adopt the defense of "splitting off" or removing themselves psychologically from what is happening to them physically (Briere & Runtz, 1988; Lindberg, & Distad, 1985). While being subjected to various sexual acts, they learn to image they are somewhere else—such as in the wall and not on the bed (*Incest: The Victim Nobody Believes*, 1976). Because dissociation proves helpful for separating one's self from the trauma, victims often automatically continue to use the technique as an adult, with unhappy results. In its most extreme form, dissociation is a basic dynamic in multiple personality disorder (Redeker, 1989).

Other common attempts to deflect pain include denial, discounting, and rationalization. Although all ego defenses are necessary survival tactics for a child, each carries a cost when it continues to be used in adulthood. In addition to these physiological costs, consequences include failure in relationships, depression or joylessness, substance abuse, other addictions, and promiscuity.

Failure in Relationships.   Despite the defenses, old feelings of shame, fear, and mistrust "bleed through" to awareness and work against the survivors' attempts to establish close, satisfying relationships with others. Every relationship, particularly with a member of the opposite sex, often turns out to be a struggle. Survivors of abuse struggle with meeting their needs for love while being afraid and suspicious of intimacy. Women who were sexually abused as children may be unable to get close to any man. They may start a relationship but then abruptly terminate any physical contact as they hear from their lovers the words used by their abusers as the men coax them into sex (Justice, 1990). They may carry such shame that they do not feel worthy of any kind, loving man and unconsciously seek out men who end up exploiting or abusing them. They may be so fearful about not pleasing or being abandoned that they cling desperately to a man, even one they distrust or who is abusive.

Depression or joylessness.   The soul damage that abuse victims received may leave them with so little capacity to care about themselves that they are chronically depressed. Like Mr. A, they have no sense of joy in life. They may consider suicide and even attempt it (*Incest: The Victim Nobody Believes*, 1976). Because they may have no one they truly trust or feel free to turn to for support, they have few friends and are isolated.

Substance abuse.   Alcohol and other chemicals become a means by which survivors of violence can further "numb" awareness. Such chemicals may be used in an attempt to feel the joy or spontaneity they long for but seldom experience without drugs.

Other addictions.   Any number of compulsive behaviors may be used to alter mood or deflect pain or unhappiness. Even if a survivor of incest or physical abuse stops drinking or using other drugs, other compulsions may be turned to as a diversionary defense. These may include compulsive smoking, eating, spending, gambling, exercise, coffee drinking, co-dependency, or sex.

Promiscuity. Sex may be used in a hopeless attempt to divert the mind and spirit from feelings of pain. Because sex may have been the only form of attention the child received, the adult survivor may also use promiscuity as a futile way to satisfy needs for warmth and closeness. For others, undiscriminating sex is a means of confirming a deep sense of shame and worthlessness.

TREATMENT AND RECOVERY

Studies of resilient children have added to our knowledge of what it takes for survivors of abuse to recover from family violence. Some children, even those in the most chaotic and abusive families, manage on their own to grow up relatively unscathed. One factor that distinguishes them from the many more who suffer long-term damage is the recognition that they were not responsible for what happened to them (Mrazek & Mrazek, 1987). Despite having been told that they were beaten for their "own good" or sexually abused because they "asked for it," they realized that the blame lay elsewhere—with their parents' alcoholism or other dysfunctional behavior. The resilient children also maintained some sense of "lovableness" by finding an adult in their lives who showed caring feelings for them. They kept before them an image or memory of love and kindness through belief in some good person or God.

In a cohort study of 700 children In Hawaii, one in 10 were found to have withstood the adversity of having alcoholic or mentally ill parents (Werner & Smith, 1977). Again, one distinguishing factor was the ability of the child to find at least one person—a teacher, neighbor, grandmother—who gave them some sense of being loved. For those who did not find such a person in childhood, a 12-step support group or effective psychotherapist may provide the experience of affirmation and acceptance that was missed.

Studies of women who have come from abusive backgrounds but do not in turn mistreat their own children also have been helpful in understanding recovery and survival (Recklin & Lavett, 1987). One common characteristic they shared was the recollection of early abuse and the memory that they rejected violent behavior as a means of expression. The ability or willingness to remember the pain of the past is often the first step in therapy for survivors who recover best. The reclaiming of the experience is followed by a reliving of it emotionally. Mechanical recitation of past abuse is not enough. The deep thoughts and feelings attached to the experience must be released (Pennebaker, Kiecolt-Glaser, & Glaser, 1988). Then release of it can come, and relief is experienced.

The relief is both physical and emotional. Recent research has demonstrated the physiological changes that occur when deep thoughts and feelings of trauma are disclosed over time, either in writing or orally (Pennebaker, Hughes, & O'Heeron, 1987). Controlled studies have shown that those who systematically release such thoughts and feelings have fewer illness episodes and visits to physicians than people who do not (Pennebaker & Susman, 1988).

As has been noted in this chapter, the reason that disclosure or confiding carries the power to heal seems to be related to the fact that inhibition—the holding in of pain or distress—requires work (Pennebaker, 1990). The "work" consists of the physiological effort represented by inhibition, and it is stressful. Like any other stress, it raises the levels of catecholamines and other stress chemicals such as cortisol. It is the circulation of such chemicals at high levels over time that is believed responsible for contributing to immune suppression, as well as arterial damage, and to increasing the risk of illness and disease.

A state or community suffering a common disaster is as subject to serious physical and emotional consequences as are individuals who experience personal trauma. An example is Armenia in the Soviet Union, where 70,000 were killed and 240,000 were left homeless as a result of an earthquake in December 1988. Medical teams from the United States were struck by the inability of many of the survivors to express grief (Merrill, 1989). There were no shared rituals—provided by many cultures by religious litany or sacred services—for giving people a voice to their pain. Religion had been stamped out under Communism for many decades. Churches were empty and people has "no vocabulary" for expressing and "processing" their trauma, observed Ronald Merrill, one of the surgical consultants from the United States. As a result, he said, there were high rates of hypertension, gastrointestinal disturbances, headaches, posttraumatic stress disorders, and dissociation.

HOW TALKING AND WRITING HELP

When people talk or write about their deepest thoughts and feelings regarding their pain or distress, they free themselves from the work of inhibition and seem to experience physiological relief from reduced stress. Research suggests, however, that it is not simply a matter of ventilating feelings that is responsible for the relief. The benefit seems to come from gaining a better understanding of the problems behind the pain and distress, of breaking through confusion and bringing some sense of coherence to one's cognitions and emotions on the issues. Because such ordering and coherence are apparently essential elements to success in confiding, writing seems to have some advantage over talking about pain and trauma (Pennebaker, in press).

Writing, when done for a prescribed 15 minutes on four consecutive days, requires people to organize their thinking and feelings in such a way that at the end of the period, they emerge with more clarity about themselves and their problems. The relief, both psychological and physiological, seems dependent on gaining this greater clarity in both thought and feeling. The better perspective that emerges leads to a decline in circulating levels of stress chemicals (Justice, 1988).

The newest research shows that health professionals—therapists, counselors, nurses, physicians—and other caregivers who listen day in and day out to stories of pain and distress are equally vulnerable to physiological and psychological effects from such experience (Pennebaker, Barger, & Tiebout, 1989). People who provide social support for those in trauma may be affected physiologically as well as emotionally. Pennebaker's interviews of Holocaust survivors showed signs of disturbance (Pennebaker & Susman, 1988). The disturbance is associated with being confronted by trauma—one's own or someone else's—as opposed to confronting pain directly. When one takes the initiative and confronts trauma, such as in confiding, then relief is gained. Caregivers of all kinds, including people giving social support and those serving as therapists, nurses, and "listeners," are strongly urged to systematically practice confiding—either on paper or by talking into a tape recorder or to willing listeners. Through such exercises, they can help protect themselves against illness.

For protection, then, from pain and for recovery from the suffering rooted in violence to the mind, body, and soul, opening up and breaking the silence are critically important. Because the survivor of such violence has usually tried in the past to confide in someone, only to be disbelieved or held responsible for what happened, breaking the silence "goes against the grain" (Yeager, 1990). Relief from the pain of both past and present, however, can come only from the release and reordering of the thoughts and feelings about the distress. To open up and confide so that such a release and reordering are possible often requires evoking that part of the soul Tillich (1952) has called courage.

REFERENCES

"Ann" (Speaker). (1990). *Sexual abuse, incest: Cause, effect, recovery*. Co-dependency Education and Discussion Series at St. John the Divine Episcopal Church, Houston.

Barnes, J. (1987). Psyche. In R.L. Gregory (Ed.), *The Oxford companion to the mind* (pp. 48–49). Oxford: Oxford University Press.

Bovard, E.W. (1985). Brain mechanisms in effects of social support on viability. *Perspectives on Behavioral Medicine, 2*, 103–129.

Briere, J., & Runtz, M. (1988). Symptomatology associated with childhood sexual victimization in a nonclinical adult sample. *Child Abuse & Neglect, 12*, 51–59.

Bradshaw, J. (1988a). *Healing the shame that binds you*. Deerfield Beach, FL: Health Communications.

Bradshaw, J. (1988b). *Bradshaw on the family*. Deerfield Beach, FL: Health Communications.

Bradshaw, J. (1989, February). *Dysfunctional family systems: A public health perspective*. Presentation at the University of Texas School of Public Health, Houston.

Cohen, H. (1961). The evolution of the concept of disease. In B. Lush (Ed.), *Concepts of medicine* (pp. 159–169). Oxford: Pergamon Press.

Erikson, E. (1950). Growth and crises of the healthy personality. In M.J.E. Senn (Ed.), *Symposium on the healthy personality* (pp. 91–146). New York: Josiah Macy, Jr. Foundation.

Erikson, J.M. (1988). *Wisdom of the senses*. New York: W.W. Norton.

Erickson, M.F., Egeland, B., & Pianta. (1989). The effects of maltreatment on the development of young children. In D. Cicchetti & V. Carlson (Eds.), *Child maltreatment* (pp. 647–648). Cambridge: Cambridge University Press.

Ferholt, J.B., Rotnem, D.L., Genel, M., Leonard, M., Carey, M., & Hunter, D.E.K. (1985). A psychodynamic study of psychosocial dwarfism: A syndrome of depression, personality disorder and impaired growth. *Journal of the American Academy of Child Psychiatry, 24*(1), 49–57.

Feuerstein, M., Labbé, E.E., & Kuczmierczyk, A.R. (1986). *Health psychology: A psychobiological perspective*. New York: Plenum Press.

Freud, S. (1911). Psycho-analytic notes on an autobiolgraphical account of a case of paranoia (dementia paranoides). In J.W. Strachey (Ed.), *The complete psychological works of Sigmund Freud* (vol. 12). New York: W.W. Norton, 1976.

Forward, S. (1989). *Toxic parents*. New York: Bantam Books.

Grobstein, C. (1988). *Science and the unborn*. New York: Basic Books.

Helfer, R.E. (1974). *A self-instructional program on child abuse and neglect*. Chicago: Committee on Infant and Preschool Children of the American Academy of Pediatrics, and Denver: National Center for the Prevention and Treatment of Child Abuse and Neglect.

Hillman, J. (1975). *Re-visioning psychology*. New York: Harper & Row.

Incest: The victim nobody believes. (1976). Sausalito, CA: Gary Mitchell Film Company.

Justice, B. (1983). Determinants of family violence. *Texas Medicine, 79,* 43–47.

Justice, B. (1988). *Who gets sick: How beliefs, moods, and thoughts affect health.* Los Angeles: Tarcher.

Justice, B. (1990, February). *Emotional maltreatment of children.* Presentation at Governor's Conference on Prevention of Child Abuse, Texas Coalition for the Prevention of Child Abuse, Austin.

Justice, B., & Justice, R. (1979). *The broken taboo: Sex in the family.* New York: Human Sciences Press.

Justice, B., & Justice, R. (1990). *The abusing family,* Revised edition. New York: Plenum Press.

Kiecolt-Glaser, J. (1986, March). *Clinical psychoneuroimmunology in health and disease: Effects of marital quality and disruption.* Paper presented at the annual meeting of the Society of Behavioral Medicine, San Francisco.

Lindberg, R.H., & Distad, L.J. (1985). Survival responses to incest: Adolescents in crisis. *Child Abuse & Neglect, 9,* 521–526.

Merrill, R.C. (1989, September). *Armenia, SSR: Grief in a godless state.* Presentation at The Institute Forum, Texas Medical Center, Houston.

Miller, A. (1981). *The drama of the gifted child: The search for the true self* (R. Ward, Trans.). New York: Basic Books.

Moyers, B. (1988, October). [Interview with Leon Kass, author of *Toward a more natural science: Biology and human affairs*]. *World of Ideas.* New York: Journal Graphics, p. 2.

Mrazek, P.J., & Mrazek, D.A. (1987). Resilience in child maltreatment victims: A conceptual exploration. *Child Abuse & Neglect, 11,* 357–366.

Nathan, P.W. (1987). Nervous system. In R.L. Gregory (Ed.), *The Oxford companion to the mind* (pp. 514–534). Oxford: Oxford University Press.

Nolte, J. (1988). *The human brain: An introduction to its functional anatomy.* St. Louis: C.V. Mosby.

Noonan, D. (1989). *Neuro-: Life on the frontlines of brain surgery and neurological medicine.* New York: Simon and Schuster.

Ornstein, R., & Sobel, D. (1987). *The healing brain.* New York: W.W. Norton.

Pennebaker, J.W. (1989). Confession, inhibition, and disease. *Advances in Experimental Social Psychology, 22,* 211–244.

Pennebaker, J.W. (1990, March). *Writing is healing.* Presentation at Hawthorne Training Conference, Houston.

Pennebaker, J.W. (in press). *Opening up: The healing powers of confiding.* New York: W.W. Morrow.

Pennebaker, J.W., Barger, S.D., & Tiebout, J. (1989). Disclosure of traumas and health among Holocaust survivors. *Psychosomatic Medicine, 51,* 577–589.

Pennebaker, J.W., & Beall, S.K. (1986). Confronting a traumatic event: Toward an understanding of inhibition and disease. *Journal of Abnormal Psychology, 95,* 274–281.

Pennebaker, J.W., & Hoover, C.W. (1985). Inhibition and disease. In R.J. Davidson, G.E. Schwartz, & D. Shapiro (Eds.), *Consciousness and self-regulation* (Vol. 4, pp. 107–136). New York: Plenum.

Pennebaker, J.W., Hughes, C., & O'Heeron, R.C. (1987). The psychophysiology of confession: Linking inhibitory and psychosomatic processes. *Journal of Personality and Social Psychology, 52,* 781–793.

Pennebaker, J.W., Kiecolt-Glaser, J.K., & Glaser, R. (1988). Disclosure of traumas and immune function: Health implications for psychotherapy. *Journal of Consulting and Clinical Psychology, 93,* 473–476.

Pennebaker, J.W., & Susman, J.R. (1988). Disclosure of traumas and psychosomatic processes. *Social Science and Medicine, 26,* 327–332.

Prevention of elder abuse. (1990, February). *Houston Town Meeting on Aging.*

Raffin, T.A., Shurkin, J.N., & Sinkler, W. (1989). *Intensive care: Facing the critical choices.* New York: W.H. Freeman.

Recklin, R., & Lavett, D.K. (1987). Those who broke the cycle: Therapy with non-abusive adults who were physically abused as children. *Psychotherapy, 24,* 790–798.

Redeker, M.A. (Fall, 1989). Mending shattered minds. *The Magazine.* Chicago: Rush-Presbyterian-St. Luke's Medical Center.

Rosen, D.H. (1989). Modern medicine and the healing process. *Humane Medicine, 5,* 18–23.

Schreber, D.P. (1903). In J. McAlpine & R. Hunger (Eds.), *Memoirs of my nervous illness.* London: Dawron (1955 ed.).

Sessions, S., & Meyer, P. (1989). *Dark obsession: A true story of incest and justice.* New York: G.P. Putnam's Sons.

Shengold, L. (1988). *Soul murder: The effects of childhood abuse and deprivation.* New Haven: Yale University Press.

Sherman, L., & Berk, R.A. (1984). The specific deterrent effects of arrest for domestic assault. *American Sociological Review, 49,* 261–272.

Steele, B. (1976). Violence in the family. In R.E. Helfer & C.H. Kempe (Eds.), *Child abuse and neglect.* Cambridge, MA: Ballinger.

Straus, M.A. (1980). Stress and child abuse. In C.H. Kempe & R.E. Helfer (Eds.), *The battered child* (3rd. ed., pp. 86–103). Chicago: University of Chicago Press.

Straus, M.A., & Gelles, R.J. (1986). Societal change and change in family violence from 1975 to 1985 as revealed by two national surveys. *Journal of Marriage and the Family, 48,* 465–479.

Texas Penal Code (7th ed.). (1984). St. Paul, MN: West Publishing.

Tillich, P. (1952). *The courage to be.* New Haven: Yale University Press.

Veatch, R.M. (1989). *Death, dying, and the biological revolution.* New Haven: Yale University Press.

Veith, I. (1969). Historical reflections on the changing concepts of disease. *California Medicine, 110*, 501–506.

Verny, T., & Kelly, J. (1981). *The secret life of the unborn child*. New York: Summit Books.

Werner, E.E., & Smith, R.S. (1977). *Kauai's children come of age*. Honolulu: University of Hawaii Press.

WGBH Educational Foundation (Producer). (1988). *To a safer place* [Documentary film]. Boston: WGBH Transcripts.

Yeager, M. (Speaker). (1990). Sexual abuse, incest: Cause, effect, recovery. (Co-dependency Education and Discussion Series). Houston: St. John the Divine Episcopal Church.

THEORY-RESEARCH-PRACTICE RELATIONSHIPS

Science, both a process and a product, is a coherent organization of theoretical formulations and research findings related to a specific field of knowledge. The ultimate goal of science is to explain empirical reality and, thus, to increase control over it (Burns & Grove, 1987). The basic building blocks of science are theory and research. Theories help to satisfy human beings' need for imposing order on naturally unorganized experiences by providing systematic structures for interpreting individual behaviors, events, and circumstances. Research is the vehicle for developing theory. It is a systematic method used to gather the data needed for the theory. Its purpose is twofold: to develop or to test theory. In theory generation, the phenomenon of concern suggests things to study. In theory testing, the theory dictates the data to be collected (Fawcett & Downs, 1986). Theory and research both help to identify the focus, means, and goals of a discipline's practice (Meleis, 1985).

Research, particularly quantitative research, has been the predominant process for obtaining scientific knowledge, the produce of science. Researchers adhering to this school of thought have roots in the logical positivist tradition. They have adopted the natural science model of research, which seeks causes of social phenomena while controlling for contextual variables that may confound the relationship between the phenomena of concern. It was this positivist view that led to the wide acceptance of the so-called "hard science" perspective that the quantitative, scientific approach is the only way to discover and verify new knowledge (Duffy, 1986).

During the past decade, however, there has been a pendulum shift away from the quantitative paradigm and toward more qualitative-phenomenologic approaches for producing scientific knowledge. This shift has been due, for the most part, to researchers' frustration and disenchantment with trying to use quantitative methods to gain understanding of human beings and their behavior. Researchers are increasingly giving respect to qualitative methods, the sole purpose of which is to gain knowledge and understanding of people, events, conditions, historical factors, and other phenomena of concern to human beings (Duffy, 1986). Qualitative researchers study phenomena inductively from the frame of reference of the subjects involved. They seek to document and interpret subjects' world views, values, and meanings. At no time are subjects manipulated or controlled. They are studied in their natural habitat (Taylor & Bogdan, 1984).

THEORETICAL FORMULATIONS ON SUFFERING

No one disputes the notion that suffering is a universal human experience. Despite this fact, there has been little discussion outside of theology and philosophy about the nature of suffering. Copp (1974) and Cassell (1982) both note this lack in medical, nursing, and other health-related literature. Copp believes that suffering, like death, is often not studied because it is inextricably linked to personal existence which, when acknowledged, becomes a personal threat. In a less personalized vein, Cassell believes that lack of discussion in medical journals springs from medicine's adoption in the 17th century of the Cartesian dualism of the mind-body split. Medicine's focus is only on the body. Since suffering involves the whole human being, it does not belong within medicine's purview.

Frankl (1963), the founder of Logotherapy, was an early writer on the topic of suffering. A survivor of the German concentration camps, Frankl views suffering as a unique and inevitable human experience. He believes that no suffering can defeat us if we are prepared to search for its meaning in our lives. Frankl and his protégé Lukas (1986) wrote a great deal about suffering without ever precisely defining it. Instead, both authors accept the fact of suffering in human lives and focus mainly on psychotherapeutic strategies to help suffering individuals find meaning in their experiences and take charge of their lives.

Several authors have found it helpful to deal with the concept of suffering by differentiating it from related phenomena. By contrasting it with grief, Das (1971) concludes that suffering is a reaction to a present and painful reality, whereas grief relates to an external loss that no longer exists. Kubler-Ross (1969), and later Bake and Keller (1978), describe the dynamics of suffering through their loss and grief models. Copp (1974) attempts to define suffering in relation to pain and addresses its physical aspects. Her conclusions are based on interviews with 148 patients about their experiences of pain related to surgery. Initially, Copp assumed that this pain was a form of suffering. She later changed her mind when she observed that some patients suffered in anticipation of their pain rather than in response to it. Copp also identifies common descriptors of suffering: challenge, punishment, weakness, relief, strategy, loss, enemy, and value.

Benoliel and Crowley (1977), in discussing suffering and pain, recognize suffering's association with guilt. In crises, as people search for meaning, they have remorse for past events and often feel guilty about wishing ill toward others. Davitz and Davitz (1981) and Davis (1981) define suffering in connection with physical and mental pain or psychological distress. Each of these phenomena can occur alone or together.

More recently, Foley (1987) has presented a paper on 11 attitudes of personal suffering. These attitudinal components were gathered from the author's listening to patients' reports about their suffering, from reading his reflections and clarifications about his clients' suffering, and from analyzing the literature on the topic. Foley then categorized each component into 11 attitudes toward personal suffering:

1. *The Punitive Attitude,* which is the personal realization that God punishes people for the sins they commit in life.
2. *The Testing Attitude,* where persons are inclined to exclaim that God is testing their loyalty by sending suffering into their lives.
3. *The Bad-Luck Attitude,* where persons believe that their suffering is due to chance or bad luck.
4. *The Submission-to-the-Laws-of-Nature Attitude,* where the person passively submits to the laws of nature, since suffering is the automatic result of nature taking its course.
5. *The Resignation-to-the-Will-of-God Attitude,* where persons believe that suffering in their lives is the will of God for them.
6. *The Acceptance-of-the-Human-Condition Attitude,* wherein persons believe they should keep working despite the limitations suffering imposes on what they can accomplish.
7. *The Personal-Growth Attitude,* where people believe they will grow into better persons through the suffering in their lives because some good can be drawn out of evil, no matter what amount or type of suffering is involved.
8. *The Defensive Attitude,* where persons banish the appearance of suffering from conscious awareness so as not to experience its full impact.
9. *The Minimizing Attitude,* where people adopt the attitude that their suffering could be much worse.
10. *The Divine-Perspective Attitude,* where persons find meaning in suffering only when they turn it over to God and when they view it from God's perspective.
11. *The Redemptive Attitude,* where people believe their suffering is contributing to the work of redemption by their offering of it to Christ.

Foley is currently studying whether, and what, constellations of attitudes exist in the minds of suffering persons. He is attempting to determine whether the constellation of attitudes changes with age, religiosity, or membership in special groups such as hospice residents, hospital patients, or permanently handicapped.

All of the above literature is consistent with most writing on suffering: it relates suffering with pain, distress, and loss. With the exception of Copp (1974), who defines suffering as a human state of anguish due to bearing pain, injury, or loss, no writer has offered a precise definition of suffering. Foley however, has added a new dimension with his 11 attitudes toward suffering which encompass cognitive, affective, and action-tendential components.

During the past decade, several authors have discussed the concept of suffering more comprehensively. Cassell (1982) discusses the nature and causes of suffering in patients undergoing medical treatment. Refuting the Cartesian duality of mind-body split, he holds that suffering is experienced by persons, not merely by their physical bodies. Its source is in the challenges that threaten an individual's intactness as a complex psychosocial entity. Suffering is a highly personal matter that can be differentiated from physical pain. It can include physical pain but is not limited to it. Cassell notes that people in pain frequently report suffering from the pain when they feel out of control, when the pain is overwhelming, when its source is unknown, when the meaning of the pain is ominous, or when pain is chronic. Cassell concludes that when injuries to the integrity of the person are sufficient, the person suffers. The only way to learn whether, and to what extent, suffering is present is to ask the person directly. Only through an understanding of the nature of suffering within the context of a person's life can relief of suffering begin.

Battenfield (1984), after an extensive review of the literature on suffering, concluded that writers on the topic seemed unable to weigh, challenge, or confine the concept of suffering within linguistic parameters.

> When dissected, its stature and function divulge little of the whole-to-part meaning and, once segmented, collated and filed into new categories, it tends to move from dynamic to static, and fit only the convenience of the investigator, rather than the sufferer. [p. 36]

She then developed a schema of attitudes held by sufferers toward their suffering. This schema built on Frankl's assumption that the highest level of suffering was to find meaning in life. Using a panel of six experts, Battenfield achieved consensus on the proposed schema, entitled "Qualitative Responses Observable in Situations of Suffering."

Her schema includes three major phases, three categories within the recovery phase, and a number of factors characterizing each phase:

Phase I.	*Initial Impact:*	Immobility, shock, dulled senses; Hurt, agony; Disbelief, denial, evasion.
Phase II.	*Turmoil Without Resolution:*	Fear; Anger, striking-out, revolt; Depression; Shame; Guilt; Hopelessness, helplessness, despair; Feelings of abandonment, separation.
Phase III.	*Recovery*	
	A. *Coping:*	Changing attitude; Altering course; Finding courage through others.
	B. *Accepting/ Understanding:*	Nonresistive acknowledgment; Facing limitations; Resignation, stoicism.
	C. *Finding Meaning:*	Expanding self-awareness, growth; Developing unity of existence with nature; Developing and strengthening interpersonal relationships; Reappraising and strengthening values; Developing creative activities; Finding joy despite suffering.

Battenfield then field-tested the schema in informal, open-ended, individual interviews with nine subjects in a variety of settings to determine whether the components delineated were distinguishable as levels of suffering. She concluded that the field trial achieved its goal: the dimensions of suffering were detected, and the schema was judged to be an objective guide usable in observing suffering responses and in assessing specific attitudes of suffering along schema dimensions.

In a more comprehensive and theoretical approach, Kahn and Steeves (1986) focused on the experience of suffering and attempted to justify and begin theoretical development of the phenomenon. They critically examined relevant literature in order to conceptualize and clarify the concept and then developed a comprehensive definition of suffering:

> . . . *suffering is experienced when some crucial aspect of one's own self, being, or existence is threatened. The meaningfulness of such threat is to the integrity of one's own experience of personal identity. Pain, for example, may or may not invoke suffering. Whether suffering is invoked by pain depends more on the meaning the individual gives to the pain in relation to the integrity of personal identity than it does to the amount, degree or type of pain. Any threat to personal integrity, whether painful or not, can invoke suffering.* [p. 626]

Kahn and Steeves close their paper with a discussion of how this theoretical definition of the suffering experience gives rise to relational statements that form the base for empirical testing. They state that their definition of suffering has been carefully crafted to avoid reliance on a mind-body duality. They caution that in order to gain full understanding of the concept, research into suffering should not reduce the unit of analysis beyond that of the living, embodied person. They do not believe that suffering can be studied in terms of molecular or neurological parameters. It is a lived experience; as such, suffering is more than just a collection of behaviors. Kahn and Steeves argue that an expedient approach for developing a theory of suffering is to undertake phenomenological examination of the lived experience of suffering.

RESEARCH ON THE CONCEPT OF SUFFERING

Early research on suffering, defined as degree of pain and/or psychological distress, has been well summarized by Kahn and Steeves (1986). Nurses' inferences of patient suffering were found to be significantly related to their own socioeconomic and cultural backgrounds, patient ethnicity, and patient diagnoses (Davitz & Davitz, 1981; Davitz & Pendleton, 1969a, 1969b, 1969c, 1969d; Davitz, Sameshima, & Davitz, 1976), but not to nurse age, marital status, education, experience, specialty practice, or patient gender (Davitz & Davitz, 1981; Davitz & Pendleton, 1969b). Oberst (1978) found an association between patient's age and nurses' inferences of suffering, but this finding was not confirmed in three later studies (Davitz & Davitz, 1981; Mason, 1984; Dudley & Holm, 1984).

Starck (1983) developed the Meaning in Suffering Test (MIST), a 20-item instrument that measures patients' perceptions of the meaning they ascribe to their suffering on a seven-point Likert scale. The instrument is based on Frankl's conceptualizations of the meaning of human suffering. Content validity, internal consistency, reliability, and construct validity evidence were empirically demonstrated (Starck, 1983, 1984; Starck, Ulrich, & Duffy, 1987). The MIST was then used to investigate patients' perceptions of the meaning of suffering. Starck (1983) found that patients' perceptions of suffering (n=101) differed according to their ethnic background, gender, marital status, degree of chronicity of health problems, and number of hospitalizations, The majority of subjects believed that suffering was more indicative of the human condition than a punishment for sin; unavoidable suffering was beneficial, helping them to understand life better; individuals varied in the amount of suffering that they could tolerate; suffering had meaning; and some good things came from suffering. In a similar study, (n=83) Starck, Ulrich, & Duffy (1987) found, using stepwise regression analysis, that patients whose diagnoses were of a nonpsychiatric nature, who rated their suffering as high, and who had the most education, were more likely to find greater meaning in their suffering. When a 10-point, unidimensional scale, rating the subject's amount of suffering was used as the dependent variable, psychiatric patients who viewed their illnesses as permanent and who found the most meaning in their suffering were more likely to rate themselves higher on the amount of suffering they experienced. The researchers concluded that differences based mainly on diagnostic group and level of education contributed most to explaining variance in the meaning patients find in their suffering and in the amount of suffering they experience.

THEORETICAL AND RESEARCH CONSIDERATIONS

As the above review of the suffering literature indicates, some work has been done, but more work is needed. Suffering, whether physical, psychological, or existential, is universal in its scope. All human beings suffer. Taylor and Watson (1989) believe the level of suffering, tragically, determines the quality of human existence.

From a theoretical perspective, the majority of definitions of suffering are too narrow and simplistic, conceptualizing suffering only as a degree of physical and/or psychological pain. Clinical observations demonstrate that suffering encompasses far more than just pain or distress. It is an experience of the total self. As such, it includes and is influenced by personal experiences and meanings, cultural values and norms, and specific levels and types of suffering. Because human beings are unique and holistic, their suffering is ultimately a personal matter (Cassell, 1982).

Kahn and Steeves (1986) offer an excellent beginning-to-be-precise definition of the concept: suffering is experienced when some crucial aspect of one's own self, being, or existence is threatened. They believe that potentially testable theoretical statements can be built upon this definition. Such theoretical development benefits the client's experience of suffering and the health care provider's experience of the client's suffering. A number of research questions can thus be formulated.

The Client Perspective

1. When does pain, loss, or other type of distress threaten the self and thus become suffering?
2. How does one reduce the threat to self, which will then decrease the suffering?
3. Do particular attitudes, values, and beliefs influence the types and amount of suffering that persons experience?
4. Can personality changes bring about changes in the degree of suffering human beings experience?
5. Do specific coping patterns and styles influence the suffering experience?
6. Does social identity influence suffering?
7. Do persons of different demographic characteristics suffer differently? In what ways? To what extent?

The Provider Perspective

1. How does the health care provider infer suffering in a client?
2. What types of suffering give rise to what types of interventions?

3. Does the helper-client relationship influence the suffering experience?
4. Do certain provider characteristics influence the client's suffering?
5. What therapeutic contexts are conducive to mitigating suffering?
6. Does intervention into suffering make a difference in recovery from illness and alleviation of actual or potential stressors?

The Theoretical Perspective

1. Is suffering a unidimensional concept or a multidimensional construct?
2. If suffering is a multidimensional construct, are the dimensions related or independent of one another?
3. If suffering is a focal concept, what are its antecedents and consequents?
4. What are the philosophic and epistemologic aspects of suffering?
5. Can extant theories be identified and refined to contribute to an understanding of human suffering?
6. Do new theories of suffering need to be developed?
7. What concepts are embedded in the suffering experience?
8. What are the linguistic, social, and professional uses of the term "suffering" in Western and non-Western cultures?
9. What taxonomies and/or schema might be needed to understand the various facets of the suffering experience?

METHODOLOGICAL ISSUES

As conceptual clarification of suffering occurs, models and propositions for hypothesis testing will be developed. This will give rise to questions about which research paradigm to choose as the basis for testing these hypotheses. The tendency will be toward using the more traditional quantitative research paradigm which is based on logical positivism. This author, however, echoes Kahn and Steeves' (1986) caveat that human suffering is a lived experience of the total person, not an isolated behavior. It is, in Schrag's (1980) view, dependent upon and inseparable from a configuration of context, event, meaning, and expedience. Thus, at this point, a phenomenologic approach is warranted. The goal of this qualitative approach would be to arrive at theory, not to test theory.

Deeper understanding of the human experience of suffering is needed. Suffering is difficult to study even under the best of conditions. To dissect it into parts and measure it in a purely mechanistic way, as quantitative research does, will result in missing the forest because of a focus on the trees.

Qualitative research methods are needed first because they accommodate these important conditions to know and to understand fully the nature of human suffering—its essence, expressions, and interpretations. This research will permit the establishment of a phenomenological baseline of human suffering. This thorough description of the "world of the sufferer" will provide researchers and theorists with fully developed concepts within and/or related to the suffering experience. With these clarified concepts, resulting theory and empirical studies will have more relevance to the concept of suffering since they will adhere more closely to empirical reality. The reality of persons who suffer is a relatively unexamined world. Establishing a phenomenological baseline on human suffering would elevate this relatively unexamined aspect of life to a new level of understanding and appreciation.

All health-related disciplines are at the point where their leaders and practitioners share knowledge that can guide thoughts, decisions, and actions. No longer can each discipline expect to use only its own knowledge base. Knowledge must be made known and shared for the benefit of society. How we can best pursue, explicate, and verify the meaning and nature of human suffering across disciplines and across cultures is a major challenge facing theoreticians, researchers, and practitioners. Only through the generation, testing, dissemination, and use of such knowledge can interventions be developed to promote healthy lifestyles on a worldwide basis.

REFERENCES

Baker, J.M., & Keller, L.K. (1978). Loss: Some origins and implications. In D.C. Longe and R.A. Williams (Eds.), *Clinical practice in psychosocial nursing: Assessment and intervention*. New York: Appleton-Century-Crofts.

Battenfield, B.L. (1984). Suffering—A conceptual description and content analysis of an operational schema. *Image: The Journal of Nursing Scholarship*, XVI, 36–41.

Banoliel, J., & Crowley, D. (1977). The patient in pain: New concepts. *Nursing Digest*, Summer, 41–48.

Burns, N., & Grove, S.K. (1987). *The practice of nursing research: Conduct, critique and utilization*. Philadelphia: W.B. Saunders.

Cassell, E.J. (1982). The nature of suffering and the goals of medicine. *New England Journal of Medicine, 306*, 639–645.

Copp, L.A. (1974). The spectrum of suffering. *American Journal of Nursing, 74*, 491–494.

Das, S. (1971). Grief and suffering. *Psychotherapy: Theory, Research and Practice, 8*, 8–9.

Davis, A.J. (1981). Compassion, suffering, morality: Ethical dilemmas in caring. *Nursing Law and Ethics, 2*, 1–2, 6.

Davitz, L.J., & Davitz, S.H. (1981). *Inferences of patients' pain and psychological distress*. New York: Springer.

Davitz, L.J., & Pendleton, S.H. (1969a). Nurses' inferences of suffering: Cultural differences. *Nursing Research, 18*, 100–103.

Davitz, L.J., & Pendleton, S.H. (1969b). Nurses' inferences of suffering: Clinical specialties. *Nursing Research, 18*, 103–104.

Davitz, L.J., & Pendleton, S.H. (1969c). Nurses' inferences of suffering: Patient diagnosis. *Nursing Research, 18*, 104–105.

Davitz, L.J., & Pendleton, S.H. (1969d). Nurses' inferences of suffering: Patient characteristics. *Nursing Research, 18*, 105–107.

Davitz, L.J., Sameshima, Y., & Davitz, J.R. (1976). Sufferings as viewed in six different cultures. *American Journal of Nursing, 76*, 1296–1297.

Davitz, L.J., & Pendleton, S.H. (1969). Nurses' inferences of suffering. *Nursing Research, 18*, 2, 100–107.

Dudley, S.R., & Holm, K. (1984). Assessment of the pain experience in relation to selected nurse characteristics. *Pain, 18*, 179–186.

Duffy, M.E. (1986). Qualitative research: An approach whose time has come. *Nursing & Health Care, 7*, 237–239.

Fawcett, J., & Downs, E.S. (1986). *The relationship of theory and research*. Norwalk, CT: Appleton-Century-Crofts.

Foley, D.P. (1987). Eleven interpretations of personal suffering. Paper presented at the Annual Convention of the American Psychological Association, August 29, 1987. New York City.

Frankl, V.E. (1963). *Man's search for meaning: An introduction to Logotherapy*. New York: Holt Rinehart & Winston.

Kahn, D.L., & Steeves, R.H. (1986). The experience of suffering: Conceptual clarification and theoretical definition. *Journal of Advanced Nursing, 11*, 623–631.

Kubler-Ross, E. (1969). *On death and dying*. New York: Macmillan.

Lukas, E. (1986). *Meaning in suffering: Comfort in crisis through Logotherapy*. Berkeley, CA: Institute of Logotherapy Press.

Mason, D.J. (1984). An investigation of the influences of selected factors on nurses' inferences of patient suffering. *Journal of Nursing Studies, 18*, 251–259.

Meleis, A. (1985). *Theoretical nursing: Developments and progress.* Philadelphia: J.B. Lippincott.

Oberst, M. (1978). Nurses' inferences of suffering: The effects of nurse-patient similarity and verbalizations of distress. In M.J. Nelson (Ed.), *Clinical perspectives in nursing research*, pp. 38–60. New York: Teachers College Press.

Schrag, C.O. (1980). *Radical reflection and the origin of the human sciences.* West Lafayette, IN: Purdue University Press.

Starck, P.L. (1983). *The meaning of suffering experiences as perceived by hospitalized clients.* Unpublished final report. Troy State University School of Nursing, Troy, Alabama.

Starck, P.L. (1984). Patients' perceptions of the meaning of suffering. *International Journal of Logotherapy, 7*, 137–142.

Starck, P.L., Ulrich, E., & Duffy, M.E. (1987). *The suffering experience of hospitalized patients.* Unpublished final report. The University of Texas Health Science Center at Houston School of Nursing, Houston, Texas.

Taylor, S.J., & Bogdan, R. (1984). *Introduction to qualitative research methods: The search for meanings* (2nd ed.). New York: John Wiley & Sons.

Taylor, R.L., & Watson, J. (1989). *They shall not hurt: Human suffering and human caring.* Boulder, CO: Colorado Associated University Press.